Women In Love (1969) is the most well-known film of a D.H. Lawrence novel. It was included in the British Film Institute's Top 100 British movies. People always cited *Women In Love* as their favourite Ken Russell film. Russell complained that he has made better films than *Women In Love*, his third feature as director, but recognized that it seemed to chime with the public. Russell is right there: *The Devils, Savage Messiah,* and *The Music Lovers* are better movies cinematically, but it's *Women In Love* that people remember more than those three pictures.

MEDIA, FEMINISM, CULTURAL STUDIES

The Sacred Cinema of Andrei Tarkovsky
by Jeremy Mark Robinson

Jean-Luc Godard: The Passion of Cinema/ Le Passion de Cinéma
by Jeremy Mark Robinson

Mel Brooks: Genius and Loving It!
by Thomas A. Christie

Liv Tyler: Star In Ascendance
by Thomas A. Christie

John Hughes and Eighties Cinema
by Thomas A. Christie

Stepping Forward: Essays, Lectures and Interviews
by Wolfgang Iser

Wild Zones: Pornography, Art and Feminism
by Kelly Ives

'Cosmo Woman': The World of Women's Magazines
by Oliver Whitehorne

Andrea Dworkin
by Jeremy Mark Robinson

Cixous, Irigaray, Kristeva: The Jouissance of French Feminism
by Kelly Ives

Sex in Art: Pornography and Pleasure in the History of Art
by Cassidy Hughes

The Cinema of Richard Linklater
by Thomas A. Christie

The Christmas Movie Book
by Thomas A. Christie

The Erotic Object: Sexuality in Sculpture From Prehistory to the Present Day
by Susan Quinnell

Women in Pop Music
by Helen Challis

Detonation Britain: Nuclear War in the UK
by Jeremy Mark Robinson

Luce Irigaray: Lips, Kissing, and the Politics of Sexual Difference
by Kelly Ives

Helene Cixous I Love You: The Jouissance *of Writing*
by Kelly Ives

Julia Kristeva: Art, Love, Melancholy, Philosophy, Semiotics
by Kelly Ives

Feminism and Shakespeare
by B.D. Barnacle

FORTHCOMING CINEMA BOOKS

Akira: The Movie and the Manga
Ghost In the Shell
Legend of the Overfiend
Fullmetal Alchemist
Tim Burton
George Lucas
Francis Coppola
Orson Welles
Pier Paolo Pasolini
Ingmar Bergman
Contempt
Pierrot le Fou
The Pirates of the Caribbean Movies
The Twilight Saga
The Harry Potter Movies

WOMEN IN LOVE
KEN RUSSELL
D.H. LAWRENCE

POCKET MOVIE GUIDE

Jeremy Mark Robinson

Crescent Moon

First published 2015. © Jeremy Mark Robinson 2015.

Printed and bound in the U.S.A.
Set in Optima, 9 on 12pt.
Designed by Radiance Graphics.

The right of Jeremy Robinson to be identified as the author of this book has been asserted generally in accordance with sections 77 and 78 of the Copyright, Designs and Patents Act 1988.

All rights reserved. No part of this book may be reprinted or reproduced, stored in a retrieval system, or transmitted, in any form or by any means, electronic, mechanical, photocopying, recording or otherwise, without permission from the publisher.

British Library Cataloguing in Publication data available for this title.

ISBN-13 9781861715075

*Crescent Moon Publishing
P.O. Box 1312
Maidstone, Kent
ME14 5XU, Great Britain
www.crmoon.com*

CONTENTS

Acknowledgements 7
Picture Credits 7
Abbreviations 7

PART ONE: D.H. LAWRENCE AND
WOMEN IN LOVE
1   D.H. Lawrence 11
2   *Women In Love,* the Novel 20
3   *Women In Love,* the Movie 32

PART TWO: KEN RUSSELL
4   Introduction To Ken Russell 106
5   Ken Russell: England's Great Visionary Filmmaker 116

APPENDICES
1   *The Rainbow* 205
2   *Lady Chatterley* 217
3   Video and DVD: Availability 237
4   Fans on *Women In Love* 238

Filmographies 239
Bibliography 244

ACKNOWLEDGEMENTS

Thanks to Ken Russell.
Thanks to Sammi Davis.
Thanks to John Baxter.

To the copyright holders of the illustrations.
To authors quoted and their publishers.

PICTURE CREDITS

Ken Russell. MGM. United Artists. Warner Bros. Vestron. Virgin Vision. Trimark Pictures. Major Motion Pictures. New World Pictures. Goodtimes Enterprises. BBC. Columbia. Associated British Picture Corporation. Channel 4 Films. London Films. RM Associates. HBO. RBT Stigwood Productions. Hemdale. British Film Institute.

British pounds have been converted to US dollars at a rate of 1:1.6.

ABBREVIATIONS

- BP   *A British Picture* by Ken Russell
- DL   *Directing Film* by Ken Russell
- Bax   *An Appalling Talent* by John Baxter
- G   *Ken Russell* by Joseph Gomez
- PF   *Phallic Frenzy* by Joseph Lanza
- RC   *Reel Conversations* edited by G. Hickenlooper

1

D.H. LAWRENCE

D.H. Lawrence (September 11, 1885 - March 2, 1930) spawned more versions of himself than many other writers. There are the Lawrences in the works: the poet, playwright, correspondent, novelist, painter, travel writer, historian, critic and psychologist. In his output, and in criticism since, Lawrence plays a number of roles: sociologist, Marxist, traveller, prophet, literary critic, feminist, mystic, martyr, politician, folklorist, theologian, agony aunt, hippy, genius, liar, fascist, Midlander, poet, pantheist and chronicler.

It's not unusual for a writer to tackle many formats: Lawrence Durrell wrote plays, poems, travel books, novels, letters and also painted (D.H. Lawrence also used those forms, including painting). But Lawrence has received more critical attention than most modern British authors. He is in the William Shakespeare, Thomas Hardy and Charles Dickens league. Aside from Shakespeare and Samuel Beckett, there seem to be more books and articles and conferences on Lawrence than anyone else. Keith Sagar's *A D.H. Lawrence Handbook* lists 500 items in its bibliography, up to 1979. Since then the number has grown even more massively: we've had BBC TV versions of *Sons and Lovers* (1981), *Lady Chatterley's Lover* (1993), and *The Rainbow* (BBC, 1988), a Ken Russell *The Rainbow* (1989), an Australian *Kangaroo* (1986), *The Priest of Love* on Lawrence's life (1981), the centenary celebrations in 1985, the dreadful ITV *Sons and Lovers,* soft porn films of *Lady Chatterley's Lover* (1981) and *The Young Lady Chatterley* (1989), *Women In Love* (2011), and the 50 and 60 year after-death celebrations (1980, 1990), etc.

D.H. Lawrence's popularity in the cinema was really launched by United Artists' *Women In Love* adaption of 1969, directed by Ken Russell; other films of the time included the American versions of *The Fox* (1968), and *The Virgin and the Gipsy* (1970).

Like Thomas Hardy and William Shakespeare (among British authors), D.H. Lawrence is an industry, a cultural icon, the subject of TV, radio, magazines, films, vacations, tours, lectures, courses, festivals, shops, cafés, walks, etc. The tourist industry exalts the rural Lawrence, the homeboy who made good but never forgot his roots. The general public exalts the social geographer, politely ignoring his violent rants, his sometimes bizarre philosophies (such as of blood and race), his flirtations with fascist ideology, and his attacks on institutions such as marriage, the Church, religion, education and Britain. Thomas Hardy is much easier to market in some respects: 'Hardy's Wessex' – how lovely and rustic and homely it is, re-affirming bourgeois attitudes. Not so Lawrence, born into the grim and grimy East Midlands. Beauty is harder to find there – or at least the easily packaged, inoffensive, marketable kind of beauty beloved of the media since Victorian times.

One of the main attractions of D.H. Lawrence – it's the same with Thomas Hardy, Jane Austen and Emily Brontë – is love/ romance/ relationships (his stories are essentially relationship stories). It's his central subject. When he writes of love and relationships he can weave in just about anything he likes. Love – or the better terms 'romance' or 'relationships' – makes Lawrence popular (including the movie of *Women In Love*; as Ken Russell noted, it's romantic, and that's what people like).

His fiction stands at the centre of his work, not his travel books, his letters, his plays or poems. It's D.H.L.'s fiction that gets talked about more than anything else. Because he tells stories, and people are so hungry for stories (stories continue to dominate global media – secular versions of ancient myths. All commercial movies are story-based).

D.H. Lawrence is not as simple as this, however. He did not write, as Thomas Hardy did, for a domestic (romantic) fiction magazine market. Lawrence wrote his books in the archetypal modernist fashion: in exile, abroad, uprooted, restlessly travelling. Each book is a stand-alone product, not part of a franchise or a series.[1] Each book is meant to be literary fiction (rather than populist or pulp fiction). Though he constructs most of his art around a story, Lawrence's fiction is always psychological, polemical, religious. His target is states of being, primarily, as well as social institutions, religions, materialism, marriage, the Church, education, etc.[2] Like Samuel Beckett, Lawrence is dynamic, taking ages to explore the ontological states of his characters (he prefers a lot of space, like James Joyce or John Cowper Powys, in which to spread his wings – and taking so long makes his work tricker to condense in a movie). Reading Lawrence can be difficult. With his simple, rhythmic language he takes you deeper and deeper into the modern soul. You don't know where you are, it's a big space full of conflicts, feelings, ideas, views of all kinds, and always an emphasis on the body and its pulsations, its feelings, its reactions. You have to be in the mood for Lawrence, as with James Joyce, Virginia Woolf and Samuel Beckett. It's not 'light reading': like the movies of Ingmar Bergman or Jean-Luc Godard, it demands quite a lot more from the consumer than many novels (Godard noted that movies usually demand only a small percentage of your attention, but his movies asked for 90% or more). 'Stream of consciousness' is the usual term, but in Lawrence's work streams of being, of feelings, of presences, or of unconscious, is more accurate.

D.H. Lawrence polarizes readers and writers as few other writers do. People either love or hate him. Few are indifferent. In the opinion of many he is the key writer in English of the 20th century. Many writers have been

---

[1] A 'D.H. Lawrence' franchise of movies, in the manner of the many superhero franchises like *The Avengers*, *Superman* or *X-Men*, is a bizarre idea!
[2] Beckett is the true postmodernist; he does away with story and plot, with just about everything. His characters hobble through dim forests, but the motion is not for story, it parallels the writer at the typewriter.

influenced by Lawrence: Anaïs Nin, Henry Miller, Lawrence Durrell, Norman Mailer, Margaret Drabble, Raymond Carver, Richard Aldington, George Orwell, Ted Hughes, W.H. Auden, Charles Bukowski, Anthony Burgess, Robert Creeley, William Carlos Williams, etc. Many people championed Lawrence: F.R. Leavis, Keith Sagar, Aldington, Nin, Miller, Harry Moore. Henry Miller typifies those who love Lawrence: he is a Christ, a hero, a passionate soul, a heroic genius, a visionary, etc. This view – of Lawrence as a heroic genius of love and life – is still held by many today.

▼

D.H. Lawrence's chief concern is life – more and more of life. But the struggle for a vital, vivid kind of living occurs in love, in relationships, and in particular in erotic relationships. Love is one of Lawrence's characters' main means of transcendence. His characters struggle to come into being, as he said of Thomas Hardy's protagonists (a rather generalized notion, but it does describe Lawrence's characters, more than Hardy's). From Cyril in the early novel *The White Peacock* (1911) to Connie in his last novel, *Lady Chatterley's Lover* (1928), all Lawrence's characters grapple with love and lovers.

D.H. Lawrence's ideas of love were not new – they are traditional Western, Judæo-Christian notions. He turned love, as Westerners have done since Plato, into a religion, a cult, a dogma, a mysticism. Like (Christian) mystics such as John of the Cross or Jan Ruysbroeck or Dionysius the Areopagite, Lawrence speaks of love as a becoming, a travelling, a means to transcendence and being. Love for him is relative, joyous, difficult, multiplitic, two-in-one (*Selected Essays*, 24-28). His real theme is the drawing-together of men and women (which's what *Women In Love* is all about. It is one of the obsessions of the West since earliest times. Jean-Luc Godard noted that love is probably the primary theme of cinema).

Where D.H. Lawrence differs from many modern authors is in his exaltation of the body. One must love 'in entire nakedness of body and spirit', he asserts.[3] Lawrence

---
[3] *The Letters of D.H. Lawrence*, 1934, 203.

hated sex in the head (ib., 557), promiscuity (ib., 773), sentimental love (*A Selection From Phoenix*, 335), and masturbation (ib., 316f). One must have 'a proper reverence for sex', he claimed (ib., 331). Sex is holy for Lawrence. Sex begins with the real hungers and needs and joys of the body (ib., 334); it is the 'supreme desire' (*A Study of Thomas Hardy*, 56); it flows to 'the very furtherest edge of known feeling' (ib., 52). In the sex act the rivers of blood of the man and woman merge.[4]

Love and sex are not everything for D.H. Lawrence. There is a beyond-love state. Sometimes it is solitude, sometimes it is a blood-oath sworn with one's brother, as in *Women In Love*. Lawrence wanted to go beyond ordinary love, beyond the passion-and-death scenario.[5] But Lorenzo is very ambivalent about love and sexuality. Sometimes he believes wholly in the mystical union of two people, that two people can become one (*A Study of Thomas Hardy*, 75). This is Lawrence of *The Rainbow* days (the mid-1910s). He modified his position on this Neoplatonic two-in-oneness later, saying the two rivers still commingle, but retain their separateness (*A Selection From Phoenix*, 349). In the late Lawrence (1920s), sex is a vulnerable, delicate, tender thing that is so easily smashed, it must be cultivated. This is Lawrence's view in *Lady Chatterley's Lover.* But he is a Puritan. Too much sex is bad, he says (yet Connie Chatterley and Oliver Mellors are obsessed with sex). Like André Gide and Rainer Maria Rilke (writers of the same era), Lawrence is not an advocate of promiscuous sex. His concept of sex is highly ascetic, despising people who have been 'crucified into sex'.[6] In the 'Tortoise' poems, he wrote of sex as a crucifixion, a primal scream torn from pained reptiles (ib., 365-6). In 'He-Goat', Lawrence writes of orgasm-addicts that might be out of William Burroughs' fiction who stink from 'orgasm after orgasm after orgasm' (ib., 382).

In D.H. Lawrence's works, sex is sometimes painful, as in the Marquis de Sade-Georges Bataille tradition. In the "Excurse" chapter in *Women In Love*, Ursula and Birkin

---
4 *Fantasia of the Unconscious*, 104; *A Selection From Phoenix*, 350.
5 *Fantasia of the Unconscious*, 191.
6 *Poems*, 1972 361.

make love in that highly emotional manner, familiar now because of Lawrence's way of describing it. Unable or unwilling to be specific, to write about genitals, Lawrence paints bodies clothed in darkness and mystery. It is a form of writing about sex that has been parodied endlessly since *Women and Love* and *Lady Chatterley's Lover*.[7] Here, Lawrence gives sex a religious treatment:

> They threw off their clothes, and he gathered, lambent reality of her forever invisible flesh. Quenched, inhuman, his fingers upon her unrevealed nudity were the fingers of silence upon silence, the body of mysterious night upon the body of mysterious night, the night masculine and feminine, never to be seen with the eye, or known with the mind, only known as a palpable revelation of mystic otherness.
> She had her desire of him, she touched, she received the maximum of unspeakable communication in touch, dark, subtle, positively silent, a magnificent gift and give again, a perfect acceptance and yielding, a mystery, the reality of that which can never be known, mystic, sensual reality that can never be transmuted into mind content, but remains outside, living body of darkness and silence and subtlety, the mystic body of reality. (*Women In Love*, 403)

Too much sex and too much dwelling on sex is bad, D.H. Lawrence claims. Yet he fills most of his novels with sex: *Sons and Lovers, The Rainbow, Women In Love, Aaron's Rod, Lady Chatterley's Lover* – these are all books which examine sexual relations in detail. In his essays too Lawrence discusses sexuality at great length: the psychology of it, how it works in nature, in symbolism, in emotion, and so on.

Many of D.H. Lawrence's notions of sexuality are simply rubbish. He is wrong about masturbation, homosexuality, abstinence, and promiscuity. His idea that clitoral orgasm (such as Kate's in *The Plumed Serpent*) is bad and that vaginal orgasm is good (or better) is also junk. He projects his fears idiosyncratically onto the world. He makes generalizations out of individual cases. He can be puritanical, old-fashioned, misogynist, and often hysterical (but he can also be tremendously insightful, perceptive and illuminating).

---
[7] Spike Milligan's send-up of *Lady C* is priceless!

There are moments of bliss in D.H. Lawrence's characters' love-relations, but they are rare. Fighting seems to be more common (or if there is a bliss, it is freighted with ambiguities). The battles, from *The Rainbow* to *The Plumed Serpent*, are intense. In *Women In Love* the Lawrencean male starts to want something more than love – this forms the final scene of the 1969 movie, where Rupert Birkin insists, to Ursula's pained bewilderment, that there is something more, for him, than a relationship with a woman, than man-woman relations.

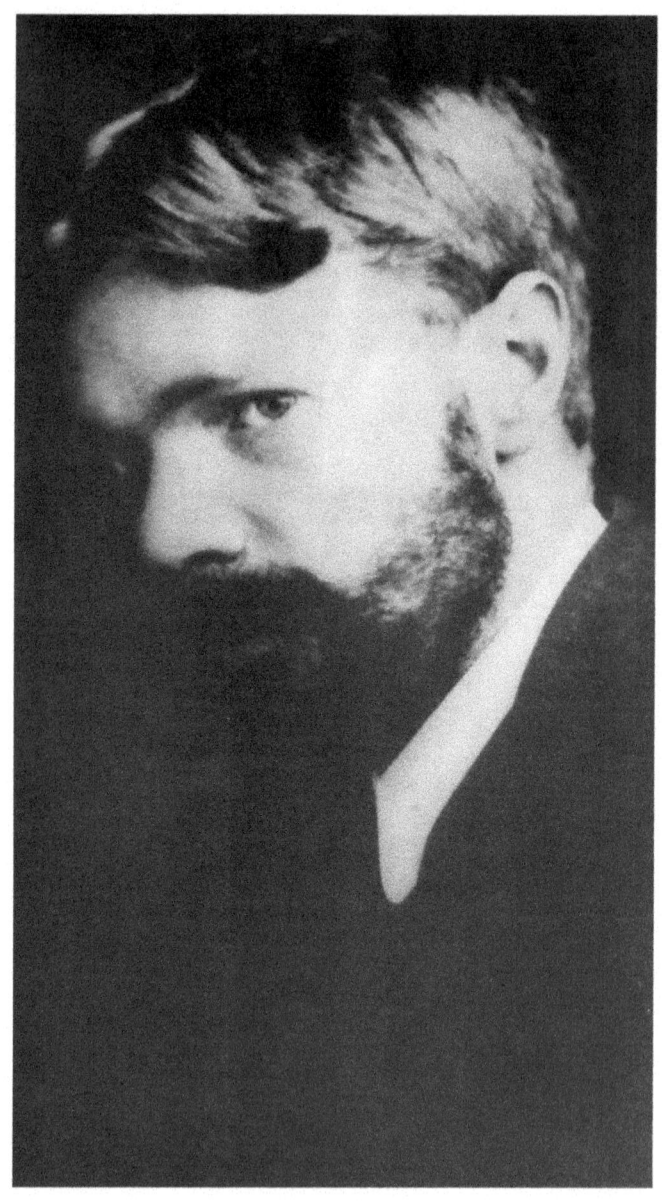

D.H. Lawrence

D.H. Lawrence in Italy (Tuscany, late 1920s).

2

WOMEN IN LOVE, THE NOVEL

Ash in the mouth throughout this classic book (completed in 1916, *Women In Love* was published in 1920, when the 1969 movie was set) – ash in the characters' mouths, after every scene, every meeting. Such a disgust, an antagonism, in this book. The characters bicker viciously. Such self-torture here. The characters squirm and convulse even at the most trivial of things. Rupert Birkin says something and Hermione Roddice writhes in agony. It's ridiculous. Everything is over-strained, on the point of collapse. The people seem to be in their death-throes. Many of the characters are pathetic – Hermione, and that stupid crowd at the Café Royal – Possum, Halliday and co. (dropped from the 1969 movie). How tiresome they all are, and how tiresome much of the novel is. It's such a let-down, in some respects, after the ecstasies of *The Rainbow*. The blackness that lay in the hearts of the characters in *The Rainbow* has now become fore-grounded, and the whole world is blackened, and tastes of ash.

Gudrun Brangwen is her sister Ursula's wilder side. She takes over Ursula's fierce questioning characters in *The Rainbow*. For me this is a weakening of power, and makes *Women In Love* less effective than *The Rainbow*. Gudrun wants to know where to go (56); Ursula has already jumped, and Rupert Birkin acknowledges that Ursula has already 'burst into blossom' (186). Indeed, Ursula burst into blossom at the end of *The Rainbow*, but her troubles are not over yet. She fights violently with Birkin – he going for freedom, she for love (193). 'Birkin is consistently associated in the novel with images of death,' writes Daniel O'Hara in "The Power of Nothing in *Women In Love*":

> Lawrence has shown Ursula in transition from an idolisation of the ultimate vacancy of death to the radical critique of such idolisation when it is embodied for her in the person of Birkin. (156)

As the 1920 English novel progresses, Rupert Birkin comes out with pure Lawrencean polemic – going beyond, lapsing out, becoming unconscious, etc (92-94). But he is all flux. To Gerald Crich, Birkin says he wants the 'finality of love' with one woman (109-110). This is a death-of-God society. Without the woman there is nothing, 'seeing there's no God' (110). But later, to Ursula, Birkin talks of singleness and freedom, of going beyond love. Birkin is all flux, and he is described visually as a lambent, quivering figure.[1]

The men are associated with machinery, with death and despair (Gerald Crich and the train, the mines, etc). D.H. Lawrence spoke of a sense of despair as you approach London (113). He meant the mechanized, industrialized, gigantic modern city. Yes, that is part of any urban centre. But London is also the most exhilaratingly wonderful city on Earth.

The Goddess has been ousted from the man's world. The men go about naked in an unspoken but heavily homoerotic way, while the Goddess is reduced to an ugly, primitive statue of a woman in labour (133). Rupert Birkin likes the finality of its sensuality, but Gerald Crich is repelled by the statue. It's beyond him, something he cannot control.

As in *The Rainbow,* there are moments of intensity, of magic and ritual in *Women In Love* – when Gudrun watches Gerald dive into the lake, or when Hermione tries to kill Birkin, or when Gerald punishes the mare. Ursula and Birkin continue to have their debates on love and life. She asks, like Arthur Rimbaud, 'What am I doing here?' (208). Birkin brings in his concept of the star-equilibrium.

---

[1] How are you going to visualize that? As a colourful, soaring angel out of Japanese animation? No, not in a quasi-realist movie financed in 1969 by an American studio!

Two five-pointed stars in contact, face-to-face.[2] But men have an extra point, the phallus. And this is the cause of much of the conflict between the sexes.

All these tensions, between each couple, culminate in the chapter "Water-Party" in *Women In Love*. Water is associated here with death.[3] Gerald Crich dives into the water in one of the first times Gudrun sees him – later he will walk into the frozen water of ice and snow in the mountains, to die; the Breadalby crowd go swimming; Gerald drops Gudrun's book in the water; Ursula and Birkin punt out to an island; then there is the long, excellent boat party chapter, which became one of the extraordinary sequences in the 1969 film adaption.

In bliss, the girls go off together, and the men come to find them. Gudrun Brangwen dances, in another of D.H. Lawrence's great set-pieces, when he turns the energy up and writes brilliantly.[4] Her dancing is wonderful – it is how Ursula should have reacted to the horses at the end of *The Rainbow*. Gudrun's dancing raises her above Gerald, while Rupert Birkin's strange shuffle perplexes Ursula (235). In this sequence, Lawrence brings together his four beings, and pushes them into focus. Each character is revealed in their attitude to love. Birkin is typically Lawrencean with his notion of the 'dark river of dissolution' (238), a different form of death to Gerald's, but to Ursula it's still death.

Gerald Crich is born again, in a deathly sleep, lapsing out for the first time ever (245), while Gudrun Brangwen realizes her power over him. Then the death, the drowning, in the midst of life, and love, and pleasure, and only a few inches away. This is a terrific scene, one of those which D.H. Lawrence excels at. For he is still naturalistic, still within the bounds of the believable, and he is also psychologically true and heavily symbolic. Death *is* that close – there's the party-goers gossiping and

---

[2] Such a visual motif might have made into the movie adaption.
[3] There is a real strangeness in D.H. Lawrence's use of water – in the drowning sequence in *Women In Love*, for instance, so powerfully filmed by Ken Russell & co. (the lovers entwined in the mud of the drained lake).
[4] And Ken Russell and company responded with one of the finest sections of the 1969 movie.

laughing on the surface of the water, and it's all warmth and glowing light. Yet underneath is utter cold and blackness, another world altogether. This is a Beyond of Birkin's that is uninhabitable by humans. Even the King of Death, the Lord of the Underworld, Gerald, comes back from it exhausted and pale. This is a really wonderful scene, and it would be great with a single drowning. But Lawrence goes one better, and has a couple down there. It's crucial, and shows what could happen to the two couples of the novel if they venture into the waters of the unknown. For Gerald and Gudrun it would mean death, for Ursula and Birkin it means uncertainty. Because Birkin hasn't yet fully worked out his new cult of life-beyond-love.

But the best thing about this sequence comes at the end of the "Water-Party" chapter. It is Gerald who notices it: 'She killed him' (258). This image, of the entwined lovers at the bottom of the lake, focuses many of the symbols and themes of the novel: the couple, man and woman, death, water, darkness, and feminine soul-murder. *She* killed *him* – this could be more of D.H. Lawrence's misogyny. But surely he's trying to say that you must love and take into account the whole of the woman, not just the material or sexual aspects. Gerald only sees the body and presence of Gudrun, the things he desires, and her power over him (something he greatly fears and resents),[5] while Birkin only sees the beyond-self of Ursula, and denies her other sides. The point of the book is (partly) to show that much of love is projection, that the male projects onto the female what he desires, and that the female is eternally disappointed. The woman sees the whole man, from his body to his soul and all points in between. The man is partially blind, and only sees the parts he wishes to see.

So much despair in this 1920 book, so much weariness, blackness and violence. But the frustration and despair these characters feel has no solution. Ursula, Birkin, Gerald and Gudrun are sinking down and down. Nothing can save them. Some of them – Gerald and

---
[5] Oliver Reed brought out this fear and desire in the movie.

Gudrun – don't want to be saved (Gerald committs suicide).

This is very much a modern novel. It is open. There is no linear thrust forward. The book wallows. The characters swerve from scene to scene, but they go in circles (the film only had time for one repetition). The book could be 20 or 2,000 pages long. Each scene could be compressed, or expanded. Scenes could be added or taken away, with no great loss to the book. Because the point of the novel – the evocation of weariness and despair – is there in every part of it, all the way through. The whole book is so tired, so weary. It is loose, and uneven. Uneven because sometimes D.H. Lawrence is coasting, then suddenly he works up his energy, and races forwards.

The trajectory of the 1920 text is towards death. Death in the midst of life. Death for characters who are just beginning to really live. They are in their 20s and 30s, at the height of their powers, yet they feel death all around them, all inside them. Not just in Gerald Crich, but also in Ursula Brangwen. She is dying, she thinks (260f). The despair of the age deeply affects her, this girl that was so full of life, so yearning for life and more life, in *The Rainbow*. Now she seems a shadow of her former self, just a foil for Rupert Birkin. Death and darkness everywhere, then. Even when Ursula and Birkin make up after their bitter argument in "Excurse", you can't believe they're happy. The despair is too deep. Their happiness is ephemeral. Joy in *Women In Love* is rare. *The Rainbow* is characterized by yearning – it is full of yearning. Everything is on the up. *Women In Love* is the opposite – everything is seeping down, sinking away, collapsing, fading, falling apart. The decay is everywhere – in the soul, in the families, in the relationships, in the towns, the work, the life. *Women In Love* is all psychological, with hardly any exterior scene-setting at all. It is so different from the conventional, 19th century novel. The break with the past is complete. Hatred is the norm for much of the novel. How most of the characters *hate* each other! (267). Each character is arrogant, finding new ways and new reasons for hating the others.

The structure of *Women In Love* is psychological – each section is structured around a conflict of minds: the four characters brought together in "Water-Party"; the two men in "Man to Man"; then Gerald and Gudrun in "Rabbit"; Ursula and Birkin in "Moony"; and the two men again in "Gladiatorial"; and the two women in "Woman to Woman" and so on.

So D.H. Lawrence has his characters studying the subject of the book – love, announced in the title – from a variety of angles. Love, or the death of love, stands like a statue at the heart of the book. The lovers walk around it, admiring it from a multitude of viewpoints.[6]

When Ursula and Gudrun Brangwen are together they can transcend men and their yearning for them. But when Rupert Birkin and Gerald Crich are together they are still yearning – Birkin for his star-equilibrium, and Gerald for something to alleviate his burden of boredom. Really all these characters are one. Birkin and Gerald are both death-obsessed, and they both drag their women into their deathly worlds. Ursula and Gudrun are really two sides of the same person. Gudrun merely takes on the rage of Ursula of *The Rainbow* era. The book could have been done using one person – an amalgam of Ursula, Birkin, Gudrun and Gerald. This single character could make love to itself, like a hermaphrodite, because that is what the people do anyway in *Women In Love*. They each make love to themselves. They project like mad, and get all upset when the other person doesn't conform to their mirror-image, their desire, their projection (*Women In Love* is a supremely Freudian text, wholly in tune with Sigmund Freud's form of psychoanalysis). How frustrated these babies get, when the mirror shatters, and real life lies behind it, and they realize that other people are not figments of their arrogant, wishful minds, but beings in their own right, *entirely separate*, with their own desires and needs.

The Goddess is dead – she drowned in the lake. Rupert Birkin hates the Goddess, hates domesticity, and

---
[6] Lawrence Durrell did the same thing in his *The Alexandria Quartet*.

bourgeois sex (269). He wants something beyond all that and is the most unhappy of the four. Gerald Crich seems gloomy, but he is bored. When he gets something to do, he exults. He is much more easily pleased than Birkin. Gudrun Brangwen is the most desperate of the four. Her dissatisfaction seems total. Ursula is the sanest, but she's picked someone very neurotic and unbalanced in Birkin.

The Birkin-Ursula romance pivots around religion and spirituality (the moon-shattering sequence in the chapter "Moony", the star-equilibrium, the marriage debate). The Gerald-Gudrun relationship pivots around death, blood and violence (in "Rabbit" with the violent animal, torturing the mare and so on). Ursula and Birkin act out much of their emotional relationship in heated conversations, exchanges of bitter words rather than sweet kisses. This is from "Moony":

> "How long have you been there?"
> "All the time. You won't throw any more stones, will you?"
> "I wanted to see if I could make it be quite gone off the pond," he said.
> "Yes, it was horrible, really. Why should you hate the moon? It hasn't done you any harm, has it?'
> 'Was it hate?' he said.
> And they were silent for a few minutes.
> 'When did you come back?' she said.
> 'To-day.'
> 'Why did you never write?'
> 'I could find nothing to say.'
> 'Why was there nothing to say?' (325)

And so on and on. Even in seemingly gentle exchanges like these there is much tension and angst.

Rupert Birkin tries to shatter the moon and water by force, tries to overcome it as Anton Skrebensky could not in *The Rainbow*. But his fight is rather pathetic. And when the Goddess (Ursula) appears, his ineffectuality is pointed out, and painfully. Birkin, in fact, reveals a rather brutal misogynism from time to time. For instance, he speaks of the Goddess's desire for 'unspeakable intimaces' (*Women In Love*, 343). Something about women repulses him.

In *Women In Love,* Rupert Birkin describes the will to

being as a dying-to-self, the self-denial that mystics speak of:

> "There's the whole difference in the world," he said, "between the actual sensual being, and the vicious mental-deliberate profligacy our lot goes in for. in our night time, there's always the electricity switched on, we watch ourselves, we get it all in the head, really. You've got to lapse out before you can know what sensual reality is, lapse into unknowingness, and give up your volition. You've got to do it. you've got to learn not-to-be, before you can come into being." (94)

SOME SYMBOLS IN *WOMEN IN LOVE.*

D.H. Lawrence uses many water symbols; he is one of the kings of water symbolism in literature. Generally it depicts the flow of life, or the womb of regeneration. Lakes, rivers, oceans and canals all feature prominently. Like Thomas Hardy and John Cowper Powys, Lawrence often uses quiet pools, secluded streams, slow-moving rivers and deep lakes. The horse-dealer's daughter is reborn in a wintry pool in *The Horse-Dealer's Daughter.* She comes out of a womb. The image is Arthurian, recalling the Grail-cauldron of the Welsh Goddess Cerridwen. She nearly dies, but she has her Lancelot, her modern knight, the doctor, to save her. In *Women In Love* the lake kills the newly-married lovers – again the feminine principle, in the figure of Diana, is present. The moon is also there, sinking in the sky. The White Moon-Goddess presides over the drowning.

In the same 1920 novel is the 'dark river of dissolution' motif (238), associated with white Aphrodite, the foam-born Goddess. In much of D.H. Lawrence's fiction the symbols of the moon, whiteness, water, Aphrodite and death are linked together. In the 1916 prequel, Ursula Brangwen uses moon-power to annihilate Anton. Ursula and Anton Skrebensky meet the family by the canal, and a later important scene takes place beside the dark river in the windy, March night:

> Dark water flowing in silence through the big, restless night made her feel wild. (495)

This is pure D.H. Lawrence, pure, superb Lawrence. As he develops the sequence the darkness dominates. The deeper meanings of Lawrence's use of water occurs: Lawrence describes sex using water imagery. The orgasms in his fiction are full of rippling and flowing motions (most famously in *Lady C*). Here the flood is unleashed – the mythical, Biblical Flood that killed the patriarch of the clan, Tom. In the kisses of Anton and Ursula the Flood returns. Now it gives life, not death. The darkness begins to flow and envelop the lovers. The darkness is in motion. The consummation, as in Lawrence's stories such as *The Princess* or *The Ladybird*, occurs in total darkness, but here the people are filled with darkness. The darkness lives and moves, so Anton seems like 'living darkness' while '[s]he was all dark'. If the people are darkness and exist in darkness, and the space itself is also darkness, where does the darkness begin and the people end? Instead, the scenes become darkness moving into darkness. And Lawrence comes out with phrases such as '[d]arkness cleaving to darkness' and goes on to speak of the

> soft flow of his kiss... the warm, fecund flow of his kiss, that... flowed over her, covered her... they were one stream, one dark fecundity. (497)

Darkness cleaving to darkness – it's meaningless, really,[7] but shows what a great stylist D.H. Lawrence was (one might invoke mediæval mystical texts such as the writings of Jan Ruysbroeck or Meister Eckhart or *The Cloud of Unknowing* here). These simple words – *darkness, kiss, moon* – Lorenzo has reclaimed them and put to work to carry his own concerns. The key is the rhythm and repetition: he takes a concept, expresses it, goes back over it and re-words it, and also performs variations on it. For Lawrence's prose flows, often in torrents. Each novel is a river – *The Rainbow* is his biggest river, flowing from such a rich source (the women of Marsh Farm – the novel opens with a river, the Erewash [41]), gathering momentum, flooding and ending up at the sea. (Hence also the form of Lawrence's poetry, which, like Walt Whitman's,

---
[7] Try photographing it in a movie!

employed very long lines, an overlapping, flowing kind of poesie).

Love-making in total darkness is a frequent occurrence in D.H. Lawrence's work. The soft twilights of *Sons and Lovers* and *The Rainbow* gradually become the total darknesses of *The Plumed Serpent, The Princess* and *The Ladybird*. Lawrence's landscapes become more extreme and the light in his landscapes gets more intense – it is a feature of Italy and Mexico. Lawrence's tendency is to go to extremes[8] – to have full moons, or total darkness, or rushing rivers, or over-fertile peacocks, or savage mountains.

THE ENDING.

In *Women In Love* the Tyrolean snowbound mountainscape is a hostile environment. The book has been full of darkness and nightmares, and D.H. Lawrence goes to the other extreme – all that snowy whiteness, which is deathly. It is not the pure, virginal white of traditional Western culture, but the funereal white of Greece, Rome and the Orient – the colour of burial. White can also symbolize a birth into the new – something Gerald Crich does not manage, as he goes to sleep in a white womb. Gudrun Brangwen presides over Gerald's regression to the womb. She is the Scandinavian/ Teutonic Goddess of death, Freyja or Frigg.

The white mountainscape is the perfect location for the end of *Women In Love*, because it has been full of Northern angst and Gerald is like a Teutonic hero. If only the four had gone South, to Italy, to warmer climes. This is where Ursula and Birkin go, and rightly. But D.H. Lawrence was to go to extremes, and although his soul, and Ursula's, yearns for the Mediterranean, he halts his characters on the journey South in the mountains.

In the Gudrun-Gerald story D.H. Lawrence uses the three basic, symbolic colours of life, red, black and white. Red from the rabbit's blood, which unites Gerald and Gudrun in their deathly passion; black in the bedroom where they make love; and white when Gerald dies.

---
[8] Critics say that of Ken Russell, too!

Previously, D.H. Lawrence had used white for its positive life-affirming allusions – of holiness, purity, moon-power and childhood. Now, at the end of *Women In Love,* he reverses his sense of the poetic. *Women In Love* does mark the end of something important in Lawrence's work. After this the fire goes out of his art for some time.

The novel of *Women In Love* ends unresolved. All of the characters remain as they began – in turmoil. There is something beyond love and marriage – this is the debate of the book. But Birkin and Ursula haven't achieved it, and neither has Gudrun. Birkin's yearning for the extra relation with a man has come to nothing: 'it was intolerable, this possession at the hands of woman' says the narrator in Birkin-mode in the middle of the novel (271).

Rupert Birkin's questionings of heterosexual love race from one pole to the other, for Birkin is as reactionary as D.H. Lawrence. *Women In Love* rewrites heterosexual love, reaching a number of ambiguous conclusions that are not really conclusions. The novel remains 'open' to the end. It problematizes heterosexual love, and finds only a shaky fulfilment in homoerotic brotherhood.[9] The novel is apocalyptical, but not final.

Rupert Birkin's rejection of women's love, or, rather, his desire to transcend it, in favour of the blood brotherhood, is a great change, on one level, in D.H. Lawrence's art, and a change in bourgeois, Western fiction. Maria DiBattista writes in "*Women In Love*: D.H. Lawrence's Judgment Book":

> Because marriage is disposed, by the sheer force of institutional inertia and by the reactionary demands of the "feminine" will to enforce a unity where none should exist, Birkin advocates the complementary, revolutionary relation of *Blutbruderschaft*. The truly subversive content of *Women In Love*, its well-conceived threat to the conventional attitudes toward human relationships propagated by the "bourgeois" novel, is in expanding the idea of spiritual mating to encompass a male-to-male relation, a broader and less interested relation than the "egoisme a deux" or "hunting in couples" (439) that characterizes modern marriages. (83-84)

---

[9] 'Shaky' because the Birkin-Crich relationship is not solid or even fulfilling, and it is also full of projection and daydreaming on Birkin's part, and also Gerald doesn't really reciprocate.

In conventional drama, characters are usually changed at the end of a play or a novel. In *Women In Love* there is no great change. Ursula seems no different: the characters are wearier, more cynical and more bitter. The war between love and solitude is not resolved, partly because D.H. Lawrence always sees things in terms of opposition, rather than two, complementary sides.

There is a beyond, argues Rupert Birkin in *Women In Love*, a separateness (208-9). Birkin yearns for something beyond marriage and the 'horrible privacy of domestic and connubial satisfaction', which he finds repulsive (269). Ursula throws herself in fully, while Birkin always keeps something back (343). The struggle is not resolved – it continues right up until the very last words of the 1920 book.

Look at D.H. Lawrence's so-simple style: 'The women were different.' (42) No messing about there: just a plain statement, the authorial control set at full power. *The women were different.* The whole of the saga of the sisters, the two novels *The Rainbow* and 1920's *Women In Love*, pivots around this statement: *the women were different.* At the end of *The Rainbow*, Ursula is the big yearner. At the end of *Women In Love* the roles are reversed: the man turns out to be the big yearner for Something More Than This:

> "You are all women to me" [Birkin tells Ursula] "But I wanted a man, as eternal as you and I are eternal." (583)

3

WOMEN IN LOVE, THE MOVIE

> People come up to me and say, 'I loved your *Women In Love*.' Well, to me, it was one of the worst films I ever made. But it was romantic, and that's what people like.
>
> Ken Russell

Ken Russell reluctantly admitted that people always mentioned *Women In Love* (1969) as their favourite Ken Russell film. Russell complained that he has made better films than *Women In Love*, his third feature as director, but recognized that it seemed to chime with the public. Russell is right there: *The Devils*, *Savage Messiah*, and *The Music Lovers* are better movies cinematically, but it's *Women In Love* that people remember more than those three pictures. *Women In Love* was included in the British Film Institute's Top 100 British movies (of course, a lot of those top 100 movies in that list aren't 'British' at all, and some of them don't deserve to be in the top 100).[10]

Women In Love was one of the first Ken Russell movies I saw (on TV around 1981, I think).[11] It's a film guaranteed to make an impression. Who can forget Alan Bates talking about figs as vulvas, or the haunting water party shot at magic hour, or Glenda Jackson dancing with the cattle? And the scene everyone remembers, probably the most famous moment in all of Russell's output: Ollie Reed and Alan Bates wrestling nude?

---

[10] For example, *Four Weddings and a Funeral*, *My Name Is Joe*, *Life Is Sweet*, *Secrets and Lies* and *Mona Lisa*. In the top 100?! Gimme a break!

[11] For some reason, *Women In Love* is linked in my memory to love relationships – in particular, Alison Dunworth. *Women In Love* and *Far From the Madding Crowd* (and *Doctor Zhivago*): emotional stuff in the English Midlands *circa* 1981.

It certainly helped Ken Russell's career to have made *Women In Love* – it did good business, first of all, and it won an Oscar for Glenda Jackson[12] and was also nominated for the best director,[13] screenplay[14] and cinematography[15] Oscars (good going for a third feature!).[16] It helped too that *Women In Love* contained scenes which had people talking – primarily, that nude wrestling scene. It wouldn't have the same impact today, probably. Or maybe it would: Mel Gibson and Arnold Schwarzenegger completely nude would be sure to get people talking (yep, there are still numerous actors who wouldn't do that scene. In fact, most of the big stars).

The wrestling scene[17] also provided Ken Russell with oft-told anecdotes for chat shows and interviews – about how Ollie Reed had persuaded Russell to change the setting from a moonlit, riverbank scene[18] – 'all in slow motion like a pouffy commercial', Reed complained to Russell (BP, 59);[19] about how Reed and Alan Bates were very reluctant to do the scene[20] but went out drinking the night before and decided to do it; how Russell had an alternative scene planned in case they chickened out; how Reed retired to the toilets to encourage his dick to grow,[21] and so on.

---

12 Beating Jane Alexander, Ali MacGraw, Sarah Miles and Carrie Snodgrass.
13 Russell was up against Federico Fellini, Robert Altman, Arthur Hiller and Franklin Schaffer. Not bad company.
14 Competing with *Mash*, *Airport*, *I Never Sang For My Father* and *Lovers and Other Strangers*.
15 Against Freddie Young (*Ryan's Daughter* – which won), Fred J. Koenekamp (*Patton*), Ernest Laszlo (*Airport*) and Osami Furuya, Sinsaku Himeda, Masamichi Satoh and Charles F. Wheeler (*Tora! Tora! Tora!*).
16 This was the year that *Patton* cleaned up at the Oscars.
17 The nude wrestling scene was filmed at Evanston Castle near Derby, which had a billiards room done out as an Arthurian hall featuring a huge fireplace (the filmmakers decided to use real fire, which made the room very hot.
18 It was to appear in the film with the scenes of Birkin fishing or bathing in the mill stream. Gerald would've discovered him, and joined him in the stream, and they'd be larking about in the water, leading to a wrestling match. The splashing water would've aided in covering up the bodies, of course (Bax, 177).
19 Oliver Reed showed Ken Russell and his wife Shirley how the scene could be played in a drawing room, in one of Russell's regular anecdotes.
20 'I was scared stiff,' Ollie confessed.
21 On that point, there are tricks that could've been employed: body doubles, for a start, for close-ups; a prosthetic penis, as in 1975's *Salò* or 1997's *Boogie Nights*; or even the good, old elastic band, a trick used in porn flicks.

As Ken Russell explained:

> as the day came closer we looked forward to it less and less. Firstly, I knew it was going to be very difficult to shoot. Secondly, I knew it was going to be a tough lighting job, seemingly lit just by the glow of the log fire. And thirdly, I knew neither actor particularly wanted to do it, and Oliver in particular wished he'd never got so drunk as to come round and suggest the wretched thing. (Bax, 178)

▼

Ken Russell said he had turned down *Women In Love* at first, but then he'd read the 1920 novel and decided to do it. But it wasn't Russell's pet project, it wasn't a film he'd been nurturing for years to make, and it wasn't something he'd come up with himself: he was a hired director, and it was the producer and screenwriter, Larry Kramer (b. 1935), who was one of the key personnel behind the project. Kramer is known today as a gay rights activist (he was the co-founder of ACT-UP and Gay Men's Health Crisis), his work against AIDS, the author of plays such as *The Normal Heart,* and the script for 1973's *Lost Horizon*.

Larry Kramer wanted more involvement in the day-to-day shooting of *Women In Love,* he wanted to be around for the filming, rewriting scenes, etc (Bax, 180). But Ken Russell (like many film directors) didn't work like that. Many directors aren't keen on having the screenwriter(s) on set, for a number of reasons (however, Russell did have Christopher Logue on set for some of his later movies).

So although I'm sure many people regard *Women In Love* as 'a Ken Russell film', it's actually more of 'a Larry Kramer film'. And that's also because the script is absolutely vital on a literary adaption, and D.H. Lawrence's fiction is especially difficult to adapt.

Ken Russell wasn't the first film director associated with *Women In Love:* other directors (including Silvio Nazzizano, Peter Brook, Jack Clayton and Stanley Kubrick), had been approached by the Hollywood studio United Artists to direct *Women In Love* before David Picker at UA tried Ken Russell. American writer Larry

Kramer had written the adaption. Silvio Narrizano had worked with Kramer on a script. Only United Artists among the studios wanted to make the film, apparently, and they didn't like the idea of Narrizano (*Georgy Girl, Blue*) directing it. It was Picker and David Chasman at UA who suggested to Kramer that Russell might be suitable for the project.

Ken Russell's regular producers, Roy Baird and Harry Benn, were vital in the production of *Women In Love,* and liaising between the filmmakers and Martin Rosen and Larry Kramer. According to Russell, though, the first *Women In Love* script was 'a tawdry piece of sensationalism' which missed out some of the best scenes in Lorenzo's novel, including the Switzerland episode, and Kramer and Silvio Narrizano had added scenes, such as Gudrun and Gerald tupping in a mine, and the couple riding off into the sunset on Gerald's white stallion (G, 80). Kramer told Russell, 'don't blame me. I did it for Silvio and just wrote it the way he wanted it' (Bax, 169).

Ken Russell said that he and Larry Kramer worked on the script together, with each putting into it what they thought would work from the novel. Russell would visit Kramer at his place with his notes and ideas for the adaption, and Kramer would type them up (Bax, 169). The second script was revised so much that only two or three scenes survived, remembered Russell. These included:

(1) the market scene at night (which Larry Kramer had expanded from the novel);

(2) the classroom scene;

(3) Hermione Roddice's party (though Ken Russell added the ballet, which's pure Russellania – what other screenwriter would add a ballet in the middle of a dramatic scene?!);

(4) Ursula and Greek mythology;

and (5) the early scenes establishing the town.

Ken Russell said he added some dialogue, to link scenes which he wanted to include from D.H. Lawrence's novel, and that Larry Kramer had written some good dialogue (Russell has acknowledged that dialogue isn't his strongest point – and *Women In Love* does contain some terrific crystallizations of Lorenzo's famous speeches).

So, to emphasize yet again: it was Larry Kramer who conceived the idea of doing *Women In Love* (he had optioned the 1920 novel, for instance), and who had written the first script, and much of the second script (in collaboration with Ken Russell). Or, to put it another way, if Davids Picker and Chasman at United Artists hadn't suggested having Russell direct the film, Russell would not have done *Women In Love* as his next project. And also, he had plenty of other things he wanted to make, including more biopics of classical music composers.

Ken Russell admitted that his film of *Women In Love* had 'failed to do the novel full justice', and wondered whether 'the esteemed author would have been satisfied with my best efforts to bring two of his masterpieces to the screen' (DF, 37). Knowing D.H. Lawrence and his work very well, I would say, no, Lorenzo would probably have loathed 99% of Russell's adaptions of his work! Partly due to time constraints, so much is left out (Larry Kramer and Russell cut the 1920 novel down drastically). And the film comes out episodic, without the sequential flow of Bertie Lawrence's novel.

But even more importantly, the 1969 production of *Women In Love* fails to capture the unique substance of the 1920 book, which means not only what happens and the characters and all that, but D.H. Lawrence's prose, its rhythmic, repetitive and musical evocations of sexual love and loving sex and the struggles between men and women.

However, despite its faults, *Women In Love* has become *the* D.H. Lawrence Film, the one by which all subsequent adaptions will be judged (though there were adaptions prior to that (see the section below), and Lawrence himself was not averse to a film adaption of his book. Lawrence had considered a movie of *Women In Love* in the 1920s, according to Harry T. Moore. Tho' what Lorenzo would've made of the 1969 United Artists picture is anybody's guess! He wasn't a big fan of movies (deriding them in *The Lost Girl*), being a more traditional guy in his some of his cultural tastes).

Women In Love ran to 131 minutes. It was released in September, 1969 (G.B), and May 25, 1970 (U.S.A.). Colour was by Deluxe Laboratory (in Hollywood). It was filmed in 35mm in the regular aspect ratio of 1: 1.85. The budget was estimated at $1.25 million or $1.6 million. Rated: 'R'.

Larry Kramer, Martin Rosen and Roy Baird were producers; United Artists and Brandywine produced;[22] Billy Williams was DP; Michael Bradsell was editor; Kenneth Jones was art director; Luciana Arrighi was set designer; Harry Cordwell was set dresser; Shirley Russell was costume designer; George Ball was prop master; Georges Delerue was composer; Jonathan Benson was AD; Charles E. Parker was makeup artist; A.G. Scott was hairdresser; Neville C. Thompson was unit manager; Lee Bolon was location manager; Brian Simmons was sound recordist; David Harcourt was camera operator; and Terry Gilbert was choreographer.

THE SCRIPT.

After agreeing to direct the film, Ken Russell collaborated with Larry Kramer on producing a new script. Russell added many scenes, including the Crichs' picnic (knowing that would be a pricey sequence), and Gudrun Brangwen and the cattle. Russell also invented some new scenes, such as the fig scene (which Russell said he found in one of Lawrence's poems), and Gudrun and Loerke fooling around to Peter Tchaikovsky's *Pathétique Symphony* in the Swiss chalet.[23]

Ken Russell ditched many of Larry Kramer's scenes, including the invented ones like Gudrun Brangwen and Gerald Crich having sex in a mine (but he kept Gudrun and Ursula at the market). Other scenes dropped from

---

22 Brandywine was involved with *Women In Love* – best known for the *Alien* series.
23 There're some in-jokes or self-advertizing here, as Ken Russell's next movie would be about Peter Tchaikovsky, of course, and it would star Glenda Jackson as Nina. For some critics, including that scene was going too far – a self-conscious advert for the director's next movie (but how many in the general audience woulda noticed?).

D.H. Lawrence's book included the rabbit[24] scene (this was shot but left out of the final cut – Russell thought that the movie had already covered similar themes of violence and animals in the scene with the horse and the train).[25] Russell later remarked (in 1973) that much of *Women In Love* was repetitious[26] and pretentious:

> Lawrence simply repeated his theme about the separate-yet-united philosophy of love 8 times over in different guises. I thought twice would be enough in the film for most people to get it. (Bax, 175-6)

Ken Russell and Larry Kramer argued over the screen credit: Russell wanted a co-credit, because he said he had written much of the script himself. Kramer wanted – and got – sole credit. That would've meant an Oscar nomination for Russell. Russell did not share the same vision of the book as Kramer, or the other producer, Martin Rosen, and he often argued with them about it – during shooting, and through the editing process (which can't have helped).

And when they viewed the finished movie, Martin Rosen and Larry Kramer were not happy with it. It was too long. They didn't like the ending or the beginning. Ken Russell agreed with some of their comments, and re-edited the movie before showing it to United Artists. *Women In Love* had originally opened with a long scene in the classroom, full of exposition, involving Rupert Birkin, Ursula Brangwen and Hermione Roddice. It took a few

---

[24] Sex is a mingling of two rivers of blood; after sex the blood is renewed, changed (*Fantasia of the Unconscious*, 104; *A Selection From Phoenix*, 350). Blood is for D.H. Lawrence the individual's essence, a manifestation of their dark being (*Phoenix II*, 236; *Poems*, 1972, 474). It is usually a positive symbol, though in *Women In Love* the rabbit draws blood from Gudrun and the symbolism is of death-through-love. Gerald is associated with bad blood – as when he tortures the mare. Gudrun and Gerald mix the ritual of blood (wrongly) with death.

[25] However, the rabbit (a big, black-and-white one) does appear, in the scenes where Gudrun visits the Crichs' place (to teach his sister Winifred), and Winifred talks about the rabbit – but the dialogue is not about Winifred or the rabbit at all – instead, it's really evoking the nascent Gerald-Gudrun relationship (it's cleverly laid over images of Gudrun and Gerald staring longingly at each other. A simple editing technique, but very effective).

[26] Reading D.H. Lawrence is not to travel neatly from A to Z, in a cause and effect fashion. His stories are in fact very often static, like Samuel Beckett's, or they spiral wildly around the subject, or they attack the same subject from different angles (like the repeated patterns in *Women In Love*).

weeks for a solution to present itself: to cut the classroom scene with a different scene, involving the two women going to the Crich wedding. The classroom scene would then be sliced up, with the vital parts retained, but inserted into a montage, so it became essentially a flashback. That's one standard method of presenting exposition at the top of a movie, by integrating it into a montage, so the audience doesn't get bored sitting through a single, long-winded scene.

Routinely derided by many critics for his flamboyance and vulgarity, or the simplicity of his narratives, Ken Russell in *Women In Love* delivers a relationships movie and a love 'n' romance movie every bit as nuanced and detailed as many classics of the genre. The script by Larry Kramer and Russell expertly charts the two relationships from courtship to consummation to dissolution. And Russell is particularly good at depicting relationships in trouble, and relationships that are falling apart.

'I don't know Lawrence's work well enough to say how close the film is to its spirit,' Russell admitted in 1973 (Bax, 175). And when shooting began, Russell purposedly didn't read of D.H. Lawrence's novels (apart from a couple of biographies).

ADAPTING D.H. LAWRENCE'S FICTION.

In a way, an adaption of D.H. Lawrence's art is doomed to failure, because so much of his fiction occurs in a psychosexual realm, in characters' minds, which exist beyond the reach of most of cinema. A closer look at the 1920 novel reveals how difficult Lawrence's fiction is to adapt for the screen. (The nature poetry aspect is probably the easiest to portray, and Ken Russell succeeds here, having a similar, Romantic love of the natural world, and being the most accomplished British director at putting that nature mysticism onto celluloid).

Part of the problem of adaption D.H. Lawrence's fiction is that, as Ken Russell put it, his characters are 'metaphysical characters enacting some symbolic drama in his own mind, rather like Wagner's *Ring* in music' (Bax,

176).

The battle between the sexes is at its most fierce in *Women In Love*, in all D.H. Lawrence's fiction. All arguments are extended up to death. Things are not just bad, they're deathly. When something goes wrong, it's not painful, it means death. The men are death – both Birkin and Gerald are obsessed by it.

The 1920 novel plays out the age-old connection of love and death. The thing that connects them is sex. Sex and the body are the locations of the fierce duel between love and death. The book is decadent, in its depictions of sex, death, anality, excrement, war, violence, control – this is very much a novel about male obsessions. It explores the male domain of pornography.

Women In Love is static, while *The Rainbow* is cyclic, in motion. *Women In Love* is full of restlessness, but this movement pivots around a single point, the meeting of men and women. *The Rainbow* moves through three generations, but *Women In Love* stays with one generation. It squashes everything together. And D.H. Lawrence splits up the protagonist, Ursula Brangwen, into two, the two sisters, and does likewise with the man. The result is the classic foursome, the Jungian quaternity. Forward motion is suspended in favour of an intense, spatial dialogue. The novel opens with a dialogue, getting straight down to the metaphysics of sex. The sexes are polarized ('the man makes it impossible', says Glenda Jackson's Gudrun early on in the film, as the sisters watch the wedding).

The women in *Women In Love* are seen together, in a sisterhood, in a female bonding. Later, D.H. Lawrence will note that when the sisters were together, they 'were quite complete in a perfect world of their own' (*Women In Love*, 230). Two sisters and two brothers, the latter are later joined by a blood-oath and rite. Lawrence goes down to the most basic fusion, which for him is not vaginal or of the womb, but anal. The anal connection is alchemical, Faustian, at the foundation of organic matter, beyond and below spirit, where atoms fuse and excrement turns into

Freudian gold. (The 1969 movie, like the 1993 *Lady Chatterley*, avoids the anal mysticism).

Ursula destroys Birkin in the chapter "Excurse" in *Women In Love*, but not sexually, as she did with Anton Skrebensky in "The Bitterness of Ecstasy" chapter in *The Rainbow*, but verbally. She flattens him, calls him perverse and death-eating (389). Then comes the famous scene of bowels and loins being caressed. Dark floods of passion are released. For literary critic Jeffrey Meyers, D.H. Lawrence employed Biblical language here 'in order to disguise and ennoble unacceptable acts'.[27] Some critics have noted that this scene really consists of Ursula sucking Birkin's penis while she puts a finger in his ass.[28] But it's got to be more than fellatio with anal frills surely? Lawrence writes:

> She closed her hands over the full, rounded body of his loins, as he stooped over her, she seemed to touch the quick of the mystery of darkness that was bodily him. (396)

This is not just a blowjob, it's far more than that. D.H. Lawrence could have used the unsubtle style of pornography.[29] It's not simply that Lawrence couldn't write *cock* and *cunt* in a novel published around 1916 and 1920 (he could have written it but would have known it wouldn't be published; he waited until *Lady Chatterley's Lover* a few years later, to do that., But he still published it privately). Rather, the language of *Women In Love* is 'mysterious, ritualistic, and contemplative, and cannot be decoded for the details of actual sexual behaviour', remarked John Worthen in 1991.[30]

D.H. Lawrence's aiming for a transcendence to a state of being beyond sex. Touch is the means, but the end is not orgasm, but transformation of being. Sodomy and death and darkness are tied up together in Lawrence's

---

[27] J. Meyers, *D.H. Lawrence*, Knopf, NY, 1990, 221.
[28] C. Wilson. *The Sexual Misfits: A Study of Sexual Outsiders*, Collins, London, 1989.
[29] Porn is full of blowjob scenes: this one might be written thus: 'she grabbed his balls and licked his cock until he pumped his come down her throat'.
[30] J. Worthen, *D.H. Lawrence*, Arnold, London, 1991, 51.

fiction. He uses anal sex to get to the essence of things. For him the essence is of the *body*, based in the *body*, before and after the spirit. A transformation that excludes the body is for Lawrence invalid. The body is the site of the mystery. So start with the body. Sex is one way of getting in touch with the body, but only one of many ways.

The chief means is *touch* – pure touch. David Herbert Lawrence is a priest of touch, not sex. The body is the site of mystery, religion, spirit. If Lawrence describes his characters at all, it is always as *bodies*, as presences, as flesh and blood. There is always get a great sense of physicality in Lawrence's fiction, of people's physical bodies, their physical surroundings. As Gerald Doherty wrote in 1994: '[i]n an astonishing revision, the anus becomes the dynamic source of transcendence'.[31]

Focussing on the anus rather than the womb or clitoris or phallus[32] revises traditional sexual configurations. Instead of being associated with dirt, death and the Kristevan abject, the anus becomes metaphorized as the site of mysticality and transcendence. From death to 'riches', as Ursula calls it.[33]

The chapter "Excurse" in *Women In Love* presents perhaps D.H. Lawrence's most concentrated description of sex (up to that point). The emotions are fierce, tragic, painfully poignant. The language goes to extremes:

> Then a hot passion of tenderness for her filled his heart. He stood up and looked into her face. It was new and oh, so delicate in its luminous wonder and fear... "My love!" she cried, lifting her face and looking with frightened, gentle wonder of bliss... Kneeling on the hearth-rug before him, she put her arms round his loins, and put her face against his thighs. Riches! Riches! She was overwhelmed with a sense of a heavenful of riches. "We

---

[31] G. Doherty. "Death and the Rhetoric of Representation in D.H. Lawrence's *Women In Love*", *Mosaic*, 27, 1, 1994, 69.
[32] n *Women In Love*, Gudrun debunks the phallus – one of the few moments in D.H. Lawrence's fiction where the phallus is denigrated:

His maleness bores me. Nothing is so boring as the phallus, so inherently stupid and stupidly conceited. Really, the fathomless conceit of these men, it is ridiculous – the little strutters. (563)

[33] In *Women In Love*, Ursula touches a deeper darkness with Birkin. The touch is deeper, and the darkness richer (402-3). Pure night surrounds them as they make love. She touches him purely, lambently, unknowingly, in pure being. It is a mystic, sensual and fulfilling consummation.

love each other," she said in delight... Her face was now one dazzle of released, golden light, as she looked up at him, and laid her hands full on his thighs, behind, as he stood before her. He looked down at her with a rich bright bow like a diadem above his eyes. She was beautiful as a new marvellous flower opened at his knees, a paradisal flower she was, beyond womanhood, such a flower of luminousness... She had established a rich new circuit, a new current of passional electric energy, between the two of them, released from the darkest poles of the body and established in perfect circuit. It was a dark fire of electricity that rushed from him to her, and flooded them both with rich peace, satisfaction. "My love," she cried, lifting her face to him, her eyes, her mouth open in transport... It was a perfect passing away for both of them, and at the same time the most intolerable accession into being, the marvellous fullness of immediate gratification, overwhelming, outflooding from the source of the deepest life-force, the darkest, deepest, strangest life-source of the human body, at the back and base of the loins. (*Women In Love*, 392-6)

The challenge for the filmmaker is: how the hell are you going to film that?!! Larry Kramer and Ken Russell, Martin Rosen, Roy Baird and their team devised a number of correlatives or equivalences in the film of *Women In Love*, but I don't think the movie captured what D.H. Lawrence was evoking here (and certainly not the elements of anal-sexual mysticism).[34] Again, it must be stressed that the 'fault' is not with the direction, which pretty much everyone agrees was superb, but the adaption.

Ken Russell, Larry Kramer and the production team of *Women In Love* have a go at depicting Ursula Brangwen and Rupert Birkin making love in front of the fire for this scene: the blocking of the scene has Jennie Linden kneeling before Alan Bates, then a match cut of Birkin

---

[34] *Last Tango In Paris* (1972) was a film which played around with anal sex, the transgressive aspects of it. The scene where Marlon Brando buggers Maria Schneider on the floor of the apartment, using butter as a lubricant, all the while ranting about the family was 'the most famous sex scene in the history of the cinema', remarked Tom Matthews (211-2). It was the sodomy scene that the British Board of Film Censors objected to (as well as the dialogue); there were arguments between the producers and the BBFC, with the BBFC demanding cuts to the scene and the filmakers standing fast. But *Last Tango in Paris* had already played well in France and the U.S.A., so the scene was kept in – with a compromise, half of what the BBFC asked for. Some 50 local councils in Britain banned *Last Tango in Paris*. Pressure groups such as the Festival of Light and the Union of Catholic Mothers campaigned against the film.

walking, with the camera on its side, so Birkin leaning over to Ursula matches with Birkin walking.

The sideways-filmed love scene is shot in Ken Russell's TV commercial style, deliberately ironic: heavily backlit, with a pinky-gold cast, and in slow motion. The lovers, who're naked (well, topless), walk towards each other, smiling, hands outstretched. It's meant to be clichéd and sickly sweet (and sure as hell ain't meant to be taken seriously!). That works within the context of the film, but all of that ecstatic prose in 1920 Lawrence's 1920 novel is lost. No sense in the 1969 film of *Women In Love* of Birkin's loins and darkness, and Ursula's awareness of establishing 'a rich new circuit, a new current of passional electric energy, between the two of them'. And the scene in the novel *isn't* a satire about love and sex; the film sends up the relationship of Birkin and Brangwen, but the novel is doing something else. Sometimes Lorenzo is being ironic and distanced, commenting upon his characters, but more often he's deadly serious (indeed, for some critics and readers, Lawrence's too serious and too po-faced too much of the time. Yep, he really means it!).

The anal mysticism here relates to 'burning out the deepest shames' in *Lady Chatterley's Lover* (1928), where Connie Chatterley is sodomized by Oliver Mellors in an ecstatic, transformative experience. Of Ursula, for example, the narrator says

> She wanted unspeakable intimacies. She wanted to have him, utterly, finally to have him as her own, oh, so unspeakably, in intimacy. (*Women In Love*, 343)

However, Ken Russell, Larry Kramer, Martin Rosen and the production team were not about to depict a woman receiving a spiritual awakening via buggery (it would be another twenty years before Russell tackled *Lady Chatterley's Lover*, but again anal sex was not portrayed – or suggested).

In the novel of *Women In Love*, the physicality is male. It's 'women in love' one reads of, but men's bodies that are foregrounded. Women are decentred, psychologically. Birkin and Gerald are described fully, but Hermione Roddice's body is hardly described at all, and Ursula's and Gudrun's bodies are only depicted occasionally. Men's bodies are portrayed in detail, often through women's eyes. When Gerald stalks into Gudrun's house like a supernatural being, his body dominates the scene. He moves from the death-bed of his father through darkness to the love-bed of his beloved. He feels transformed – it is ecstasy, a miracle, a marvel (430). But Gudrun lies awake, for hours. This is a superb piece of realization – the woman lying awake, holding her man who is in another world as the hours slide by. The woman dies, inside, while the man replenishes himself in sleep. As American feminist Mary Daly writes of Gudrun's state:

> ...it is the dull aching state of one who has sold her body and soul and will continue to do so. It is a state of perfectly false consciousness.[35]

In the United Artists version, Ken Russell and Larry Kramer spend much time building up Gerald Crich's approach to Gudrun Brangwen's house, and his quiet exploration of it, until he comes to Gudrun's room. However, the film can only indicate the sense of time passing for Gudrun as she lies beneath the sleeping Gerald, with some chiming on the music soundtrack, and some Hollywood montage (lap dissolves). Oliver Reed, superb as Gerald, does convey a sense of weighty, unavoidable physicality (and the detail of putting his hand into the mud of his father's grave, then pressing his soiled hands over Gudrun's breasts is effective).

THE DIALOGUE.

Many of the lines of dialogue[36] in the 1969 film of *Women In Love* are taken from the book – but don't let that fool you that this 'captures' the book or is a 'faithful' adaption of the book. But some of Lorenzo's dialogue is too memorable – or too silly – not to use from time to

---

[35] M. Daly, *Gyn/ Ecology: The Metaethics of Radical Feminism*, Women's Press, London, 1979, 364.
[36] Unfortunately, some of the lines are ropily looped.

time.

Of course, nobody speaks like a D.H. Lawrence character in 'real life', in that pontificating, self-conscious, highly intellectual and desperate-to-be-poetic manner.[37] Sure, but nobody speaks like characters out of the works of Alexandre Dumas, Thomas Hardy or Dante Alighieri, either! (Go to Spike Milligan for his wonderful send-ups of Lawrencean lingo).

But Bertie Lawrence just couldn't stop himself: he *had* to say what he wanted to say! He knew he was being ridiculous some of the time, but he went ahead anyway. Just look at his letters! Page after page of rants and complaints (as well as all the other usual domestic, everyday stuff you find in letters). Lawrence must've been a pain to live with at times, and the 1969 United Artists movie captures that in Alan Bates' performance of the priggish, preachy side of Lorenzo. When you want to say, *oh shut up, you jerk!* As people no doubt did to Lawrence when he went too far.

CHARACTERIZATION.

The filmmakers took a somewhat biographical approach to some of the characters in Women In Love, partly because they knew that some of them were drawn on people that Bertie Lawrence knew (understandable in a movie, because you have to start somewhere with a visualization of a character, but it's critically dubious at best). Lawrence's friends John Middleton Murry and Katherine Mansfield were apparently inspirations for Gerald Crich and Gudrun Brangwen (though some critics have suggested that Gerald's appearance (down to the moustache Gerald sports) drew on Sir Thomas Philip Barber, a Nottinghamshire mine owner, and the owner of Lamb Close House (which was Shortlands in the novel). Quite a few critics reckon that Rupert Birkin shared characteristics with Lawrence, which the movie exploited.)

A famous example of this biographical approach in Women In Love was Hermione Roddice, who's loosely based on Lady Ottoline Morrell. There's plenty of

---

[37] Which makes it tricky for actors.

biographical and literary criticism of the Morrell social scene (where people such as Aldous Huxley, Bertrand Russell, John Middleton Murry, Katherine Mansfield, Mark Gertler, Siegfried Sassoon, Lytton Strachey and others were visitors to Morrell's home at Garsington Manor, Oxfordshire), so there's no need to repeat it here.

What counts, though, is that Ken Russell and the filmmakers took a *satirical* approach to some of these characters. Russell said he'd read biographies of D.H. Lawrence, and reckoned that Lawrence didn't like Lady Morrell much, but found her 'a pretentious, selfish woman'. So although *Women In Love* was a piece of fiction, Russell recalled that he had used some of the people that Lawrence drew on in his depiction of them in the movie (Bax, 169). The fact, for instance, that Rupert Birkin shares some of Lawrence's own views: but the filmmakers took this to a literal extreme, and had Birkin look almost exactly like Lawrence himself, complete with the familiar Lawrencean beard and hair, the pale, crumpled suits, the intense way of speaking, the lyrical flights about figs and catkins, and all the rest.

SOME OF THE DELETIONS AND ALTERATIONS.

Women In Love explored sexual relations intimately, Ken Russell said, 'as few movies had before, but I can take scant credit for that. I was only putting on the screen what D.H. Lawrence had written half a century before' (1993, 72-73). Russell admitted that it was 'impossible to film a 600-page novel and be true to the author's vision' (ibid.).[38] Glenda Jackson said Russell respected the book, and handed out copies of it during discussions about the adaption. Russell was not a dictator, Jackson said, but was quite open to ideas and collaboration.[39]

The London scenes, when the Brangwens join the bohemians at the Café Royale, were left out (and the many

---

[38] Ken Russell admitted that *Women In Love* 'had some very good performances in it and it was very outspoken about relationships', but you couldn't cram a 600-page novel into a 2-hour movie (RC, 250).

[39] However, some aspects of the production Glenda Jackson wasn't so happy with, such as Ken Russell having her below Oliver Reed for the rape scene, hiding the fact that she was pregnant, and contending with some of Reed's bad habits.

characters too, such as Halliday and Possum). This was the kind of imagery that Ken Russell would have greatly enjoyed filming (you can get an idea of what they might have been like from the Vorticist club scenes in *Savage Messiah*). For Glenda Jackson, Ken Russell's talent was in creating detailed backgrounds, the 'minute details that really reveal the interior landscape of a human being' (B. McFarlane, 314).

We could explore in detail the many alterations to the novel, the numerous deletions, and the numerous additions. But if you know the novel, you'll know what was left out, and what was added and altered. A 'faithful' adaption of a novel is impossible for lots of reasons. But even if the 1969 movie of *Women In Love* departed greatly from the 1920 novel, it has come to be accepted as a 'faithful' adaption, as well as being *the* D.H. Lawrence movie. (Compare it with other Lawrence adaptions, and you'll soon see just how good it is).

Besides, the 1969 United Artists production did include some fundamental narrative elements of *Women In Love*, such as Rupert Birkin's relationship with Hermione Roddice, Birkin leaving Hermione for Ursula, but also wanting Gerald. As Ken Russell noted, Lorenzo explored his theme repeatedly, going round in circles, and the movie didn't have time for all of the variations that Lawrence loved to put into his books.

UGLY ENGLAND.

There are other themes and elements in the novel of *Women In Love* that the 1969 interpretation did not feature, such as: the search for identity in the modern world; philosophizing on just what life is, and what constitutes a good or useful life (how to *be*); the importance of work or having something significant to *do*; and the ugliness of modern existence (a recurring theme in D.H. Lawrence's fiction, and surely one of the reasons why he left England and went wandering for much of his life). *Women In Love* isn't only about finding fulfilment in love and sex and relationships, it's also about counteracting boredom with a range of activities.

D.H. Lawrence wrote incisively and unapologetically of the horrible, industrial Midlands (in *The Rainbow, Lady Chatterley's Lover* and *Women In Love*, for example). Lawrence was not afraid of severely criticizing his surroundings. 'The weather's awful and we simply hate it up here', Lawrence griped from the Midlands in 1925.[40] He laid into his homeland of Nottinghamshire in many books – the writing reflects his love and hatred of the place. He wrote of the 'ugly winter-grey of houses [that look] like a vision of hell that is cold and angular' in *Women In Love* (450). Lawrence described the modern world of suburban vapidity. Near the beginning of *Lady Chatterley's Lover*, Lawrence's narrator describes the mining village of Tevershall in unambiguous terms:

> ...a village which began almost at the park gates, and trailed in utter hopeless ugliness for a long and gruesome mile: houses, rows of wretched, small, begrimed, brick houses, with black slate roofs for lids, sharp angles and wilful, blank dreariness. (14)

Of a visit to his homeland of late 1926, which helped with the research for *Lady Chatterley's Lover*, Bertie Lawrence described the miners, strikes and policemen in a letter as depressing: 'they've pushed the spear through the side of *my* England' (1934, 674).

In his 1926 essay about his hometown, Eastwood in Nottinghamshire, "Return to Bestwood", Lawrence described the familiar feelings of nostalgia and revulsion that many a homecoming has initiated in people of all ages and countries: 'I feel at once a devouring nostalgia and an infinite repulsion'.[41] Lawrence felt bitter about it, about the mess into which the homeland's slipped. In his essay "Nottingham and the Mining Countryside", Lawrence wrote: '[t]he real tragedy of England, as I see it, is the tragedy of ugliness. The country is so lovely: the man-made England is so vile'.[42] Many would agree with him. (But if Lawrence descended into the 21st century and

---
40 In H. Moore, 1976, 516.
41 In *A Selection From Phoenix*, 146.
42 *A Selection From Phoenix*, 108.

saw what had happened to his dear, old England between 1930 and today, what would he think?!).

THE PRODUCTION OF *WOMEN IN LOVE*.

Location scouting was 'always the most exciting part of a film to me', Ken Russell remarked, describing scouting for locations on *Women In Love* in England in the late 1960s:

> ...finding the locations, conceiving the action to go with them, linking one colour to another and probably just discovering England which, all things considered, is still the most undiscovered country in the world. You might know bits but you can never know it all. We looked for country mansions, water mills, forests, fields, mines and rivers. We'd pencil around all the stately homes, which are naturally marked on that wonderful work of art, the ordnance survey map, and just whip up the drive in a fast car, zip once around the house and be out again before they could shoot at us. (Bax, 170)

A huge number of locations can be found for a movie within a few miles of any point. I know, I've tried it, on my adaption of D.H. Lawrence's *The Horse-Dealer's Daughter*: pick a town in Britain, and within a radius of ten miles you can find cliffs, rivers, lakes, hills, forests, country houses, roads, castles, caves, quarries, etc.

In the novel of *Women In Love,* the settings included Beldover, perhaps based on Quorn or Eastwood, or a variety of towns in Leicestershire and Nottinghamshire. The famous Garsington Manor (in Oxfordshire) probably inspired the depiction of Breadalby, though D.H. Lawrence may have drawn on Kedleston Hall.[43]

Women In Love was shot in D.H. Lawrence's homeland of Nottinghamshire, and also Cheshire, Derbyshire, Durham, Northumberland, Yorkshire (Denaby, Sheffield, etc), Sherwood Forest in Nottinghamshire, Zermatt in Switzerland and Bray Studios. Kedleston Hall near Derby was Hermione Roddice's house (the Neo-classical Robert Adam interiors are particularly fine and instantly recognizable as the work of Adam – the movie ensures there's a shot of the ceiling. The Russian ballet dance was staged in

---
43 See K. Sagar, 1982, 263f.

the circular saloon, based on a Roman temple). The Swiss inn was the Riffelberg Inn in Zermatt. The church (and Brangwens' house) was in Matlock, Derbyshire. The war memorial was in Derby. The funeral was in Belper, Derbyshire. Durham Gerald's home of Shortlands was shot at Elvaston Castle, near Derby. Newcastle's back streets stood in for the mining environment and the market (in both South and North Shields, with Gateshead used for Gudrun on the streets). Also, a school in Sheffield. (Ordnance Survey maps of Blighty were used, as ever on a Ken Russell picture – or any British movie, and also the Royal Commission of Historic Monuments).

Women In Love began filming on September 25, 1968 (ending in December, 1968). Exteriors were shot first (as is often customary), with the scene with Gudrun and the cattle being among the earliest to be filmed.

CASTING AND ACTING.

Casting was tricky on *Women In Love*, Ken Russell said; not finding Oliver Reed and Alan Bates, but finding the right female leads. In 1973, Russell admitted that Jennie Linden was 'too 'pert'', and played Ursula too young. And the actor chosen to play the Brangwen sisters' father hadn't worked out, and Russell and the producers fired him after a week (which producers are very reluctant to do), and hired the ever-dependable, always-excellent Michael Gough.

Ken Russell set the picture in 1920, seven years b4 he was born (*Women In Love* was published privately in late 1920), although it had been written from 1913 onwards (it was conceived as a giant epic that continued the story of *The Rainbow* – Lawrence's 'Brangenwen saga'). The slight shift in years gave the movie a slightly different historical perspective, making it a post-WW1 piece (with quite a few references to the Great War).

The ensemble acting of the central two couples gave the United Artists film much of its power. Yes there was some sex and nudity in *Women In Love* (though not as much as one might expect from Ken Russell). Fundamentally, no film could translate the exact descriptions that D.H. Lawrence offers of sexual relations. Watching actors entwine and pant, from the outside, no matter how good they are, cannot be a translation (or even an equivalent) for Lawrence's amazing prose. (Maybe Orson Welles was right: there are two things you can't film, for Welles: sex and prayer).

For actors, *Women In Love* offered plenty of challenges – not only sex scenes but also other nude scenes (swimming nude, for instance, or cavorting in nature). And dancing. And plenty of dramatic emoting and confrontation. One thing's for sure, you got to do a lot in a Ken Russell movie if you were an actor!

ALAN BATES.

Top-billing in *Women In Love* went to Alan Bates (1934-2003), who's one of those actors who's always wonderful (Larry Kramer had cast Bates before Ken Russell's involvement, and Russell agreed with Kramer that Bates would be great). Prior to *Women In Love,* Bates had appeared in some British and American classics, such as *A Kind of Loving, Whistle Down the Wind, Far From the Madding Crowd, The Caretaker, Zorba the Greek* and *Georgy Girl.* After *Women In Love,* Bates was in *The Go-Between, The Shout, The Rose, Quartet, Britannia Hospital, An Englishman Abroad, A Prayer For the Dying, Hamlet* and *Nijinsky* (a movie Russell wanted to make). An immensely charismatic actor, I remember him vividly playing the lead role on stage in Peter Schaffer's play *Yonadab* (1985) at the National Theatre.

Alan Bates gave a satisfying Lorenzo impression (complete with Lawrencean beard, hair, hat, tie and crumpled suit). Indeed, it's still *the* definitive Lawrence on screen. The costume designer (Russell's wife, Shirley Kingdon), had clearly studied archive photos of Lawrence to emulate the whole look. It made sense, although it was a little obvious, to base Birkin's appearance on Lawrence himself. Looking at *Women In Love* again, three of the four leads are really excellent, their performances include all sorts of nuances.

Alan Bates' Rupert Birkin had most of speeches in the 1969 picture (along with Glenda Jackson's feisty, independent Gudrun), though the endless debates on male-female relations became tiresome (as the tendency in D.H. Lawrence's fiction to produce lengthy diatribes and soap-box lectures can be. There is a *lot* more talk-talk-talk in the novel!). Even so, Bates' Birkin is sent up by the film itself, as well as some of the characters. And Bates was terrific at delivering some of that complex dialogue.

And plenty of the dialogue was authentic, Lawrencean stuff, even though it was rewritten. Rare are the movies, for instance, in which the hero virulently denounces love and marriage as sordid and demeaning and a lie (Rupert Birkin rants walking through the crowd at the war memorial service, for instance, and in his conversations with Gerald, and when he and Ursula visit a street market). At these moments, D.H. Lawrence's voice came through – in its ferocity, but also its mistaken insistence on absolutes, its preachiness, and its occasional silliness.

Alan Bates also captures the way that Bertie Lawrence enjoyed playing the trickster and teaser – how, although he might have believed most of what he wrote and said, he also knew he was deliberately winding people up. Lawrence knew he was a pain in the ass at times, and the movie recognizes that.

Alan Bates' Rupert Birkin became the classic depiction of a Lawrence-like character on screen; lit'ry critics tend to identify D.H. Lawrence with Birkin, although if you're going to do that kind of author-character identification, there's much more of Lawrence in Ursula and Gudrun (who are the stars of both *The Rainbow* and *Women In Love*). But I guess some literary critics find it easier to think that a *male* author has equivalents with a *male* character, although these two novels, like *The Plumed Serpent, The Fox, The Virgin and the Gipsy* and *Lady Chatterley's Lover*, among others, are centred on women.

OLIVER REED.

If there's an actor who's most associated with playing Ken Russell's alter-egos on film, it is probably Oliver Reed (1938-99).[44] An actor with a dark, bullish, glowering look[45] (like a British Brando), and a cult following, Reed has appeared in leading roles in *The Debussy Film, Dante's Inferno, The Devils, Women In Love* and *Tommy* (as well as having cameos in other Russell movies, such as *Lisztomania, Mahler* and *Prisoner of Honor*.[46] Some filmmakers have actors who act as lucky charms in their movies, and they like to include them in every film, if they can; Reed in one of those lucky charms for Russell). Reed was an instinctive actor, who took his work seriously, and learnt his lines,[47] and who preferred to capture scenes in one or two takes.

Meeting Ken Russell was a turning-point in his career, Oliver Reed acknowledged. 'Working with Russell nearly always produced Ollie's best acting, and the reason for that was simple: Ollie believed in Ken' (R. Sellers, 288). Russell was very important to Reed's career. They liked each other, shared a similar sense of humour (and a taste for recklessness). As Glenda Jackson put it, 'there was real affection and real respect, I think, on both sides. Oliver would have done anything for Ken, absolutely anything'.[48]

One of Oliver's Reed's' finest performances prior to *Women In Love* was in *Dante's Infero* (Ken Russell, 1967). There are two sensational performances at the heart of *Dante's Inferno*: Reed in the title role, and Judith Paris[49] as his doomed lover, model and later wife, Lizzie Siddal. Both were roles of a lifetime, gifts to an actor to grab them and run to the stars with them. And Reed and Paris threw themselves into the BBC movie completely.

---

44 One of Ollie Reed's nicknames for Ken Russell was Jesus – Russell often wore sandals, had a beard and long hair.
45 Oliver Reed's voice was not a loud, shouty voice, but soft and often a whisper ('the whispering giant', he was called). When Reed played villains, he did it with a low, quiet voice, because a bad guy didn't have storm about and shout.
46 Ollie was paid in bottles of champagne, apparently (three Dom Perignon for *Mahler* [R. Sellers, 281]).
47 Many have attested to Ollie's drunken nights, only for him to turn up on set sober and well-prepared.
48 Quoted in R. Sellers, 180.
49 Judith Paris appeared in many Ken Russell works, including *The Devils, Lady Chatterley* and *Savage Messiah*.

There's plenty of physical acting for Oliver Reed and Judith Paris in *Dante's Inferno* – they are clambering over boulders and wading through freezing streams in the Lake District – which every Russell actor had to do – and Paris is floating in cold rivers, and also in the sea. And I bet they didn't have wet suits.

Oliver Reed is not merely stunning to look at and brilliant at playing moody, tortured souls (perfect for Gerald Crich in *Women In Love*), he is also acting up a storm in each of his leading roles for Ken Russell. Indeed, as Dante Gabriel Rossetti, there are very actors of the time who could've been so effective as Reed (Alan Bates, of course, and maybe David Hemmings and Terence Stamp, but not many others).

Oliver Reed had to undergo some tough acting tasks in *Dante's Inferno* – in his attempted suicide scene, he crashes through a door into the back garden, stumbling around caged birds (the symbolism is both intuitive and crushingly obvious – but it works), falling to the ground and having a snake crawl on his face (on *his face*, with his eyes open – there are not many actors who would do that! Would you let a real, live snake crawl over your face? No, nor me! And neither would Ken Russell – he hates snakes).

Following *Women In Love*, Oliver Reed turned in a career high with his portrayal of Urbain Grandier in *The Devils* (Ken Russell, 1971). The womanizing, devoutly religious and canny politico Granider was certainly a challenging role,[50] and one many an actor would jump at the chance to do[51] – these sorts of roles simply don't come along that often. Reed's performance was certainly Oscar-worthy, and maybe the finest performance of his career – although *The Devils* was probably just a tad too Out There for the Academy in L.A.

Altho' Oliver Reed recognized that Urban Grandier was his greatest role, he also thought that his performance

---

[50] Oliver Reed sometimes wasn't confident about his dialogue and his voice (he had the Latin quotations in *The Devils* reduced, for instance, and the lines hidden off-camera). Critics have wondered if Reed might've done some William Shakespeare – an aged King Lear, perhaps, or Macbeth (in the 1971 adaption which starred Jon Finch).
[51] Filming *The Devils* had been intense, Oliver Reed admitted – he likened working with Ken Russell on this challenging production to sitting on a firecracker.

had been swamped somewhat by the extravagance of the filmmaking: 'there was so much going on that it was difficult to make a performance live. The performances got lost in the tirade of masturbation, flagellation and kissing God's feet', Reed complained when the movie was released. But when you consider Reed's performance now, it seems magnificent.

Ollie Reed[52] was cast in the 1975 musical of the Who's rock opera, *Tommy*.[53] Reed was wonderfully lecherous, slick, rugged, devilish and humorous as the redcoat (or rather, greencoat) at Bernie's holiday camp who seduces Tommy's mother (however, Reed's singing was awful! I love Reed, but sometimes his singing in *Tommy* is soooo bad! Pete Townshend's reaction when he sat down at a piano in the recording studio to hear Reed sing was typical: 'are you fucking joking?' But Russell was adamant that Reed's performance as Uncle Frank more than made up for his lacklustre vocals. And it's true: Reed is fabulous in *Tommy*, and it's doesn't matter in the end that he can't sing at all, altho' some moments are fairly painful).[54]

Stories about Oliver Reed are many, some legendary, and many humourous. Ken Russell has often told the story of visiting Reed and getting into a drunken sword fight (Reed had wanted to do a film about Sir Thomas Becket, and launched into a rehearsal at his home with real swords). And everybody knows the showbiz story of preparing for and filming the nude wrestling scene in *Women In Love*. Really good parts for Reed dried up in his later career (*Castaway*, 1987, was a notable role, tho' a weedy movie), and in the 1970s and 1980s he appeared in many, many truly dreadful movies (purely for the $$$$$). Reed famously made a great comeback with *Gladiator* (2000), as the gladiator manager Proximo, but he died during the last part of filming (and even his demise – arm-

---

[52] Apparently casting Oliver Reed in *Tommy* was needed to ensure some of the financial backing. (Keith Moon apparently coveted the role – but that was never gonna happen!).

[53] When Ken Russell worried that some of the performances in *Tommy* were going to be too over-the-top, Oliver Reed retorted, ' me over the top? Have you ever seen any of your films?'

[54] Not only could Oliver Reed not sing, by any standards, he couldn't remember lyrics. Recording Reed's vocals was a nightmare, and had to be done line by line.

wrestling with a bunch of sailors in Malta – became part of the Ollie Legend).[55]

As well as being a well-known 'hell-raiser' and drinker, the Oliver Reed Legend also included flashing: he 'would take little persuading to produce his penis', according to biographer Cliff Goodwin.[56] Sometimes Reed's desperate need to play, to perform pranks and tricks on victims, seems not only childish but pathetic and occasionally violent (even more so when he teamed up with Keith Moon, another prankster who wore everyone out with his restless need to act the clown).

CHRISTOPHER GABLE.

Much less revered than Oliver Reed, and without his star status, but also important for Ken Russell's cinema, was Christopher Gable (1940-98) – Russell's dancing alter-ego, you might say (Gable can dance on screen what Russell would love to be able to do). Gable appeared in *Women In Love* as Tibby Lupton, a young husband who's killed by his new bride. Gable also appeared in Russell's *Delius: Song of Summer, The Music Lovers, The Boy Friend*,[57] *The Dance of the Seven Veils*, and *The Rainbow*.

JENNIE LINDEN.

The acting in *Women In Love* was strong, on the whole, though Jennie Linden (b. December 8, 1939) was too often weak and unconvincing as the amazing Ursula Brangwen.[58] Certainly Linden is by far the least convincing among the principal actors. Linden looked a little too late 1960s, too (though the whole film does too, just as any movie looks exactly like the year it was made).[59]

---

[55] As was the rewriting of the Proximo character, and the use of doubles and even digital visual effects to complete Reed's role.
[56] C. Goodwin, 2001.
[57] Twiggy might get all of the press attention for her role in *The Boy Friend*, but Gable is an essential part of the mix. And he can *really* dance!
[58] And following *Women In Love*, Jennie Linden did not achieve much, acting-wise, although she did appear in Russell's *Valentino*.
[59] Besides, that is partly down to the costume designer, the hair and make-up department, who have used a very late 1960s look.

URSULA BRANGWEN.

Ursula Brangwen is one of the great characters in modern fiction – a rebellious, polemical, mercurial, passionate woman. She's got to be on fire at times, a walking tornado of emotions, but that's the last thing you get from Jennie Linden, unfortunately. Linden is an uninspiring actress, which might be OK for soap opera on TV or a lightweight rom-com, but for D.H. Lawrence's fiction, you need actors who've got everything, and then some. And they *must* catch fire when needed. And they *must* be able to suggest depths and layers. (Ken Russell did express some reservations about Linden later).[60] And, as the 1969 film is about four characters in two couples, one weak performance affects all of the others.

Ursula Brangwen is way too meek in the 1969 movie of *Women In Love*: she is only really allowed to let rip against Rupert Birkin once (in the scene where her jealousy over Hermione Roddice explodes – beautifully staged by the filmmakers, in a classic Lawrencean setting of fields and trees). In the two novels, *The Rainbow* and *Women In Love*, Ursula is far fiercer – she's one of the most fascinating and powerful characters in modern literature. In the United Artists movie, she opposes Birkin, yes, but also demurs to him too often.

It might have been possible to lose Jennie Linden and re-cast the part, although from experience I know that it's very difficult and wrecks schedules. I would imagine that Ken Russell has had to fire actors over the course of a long career in film and television, but it's something everyone tries to avoid if possible.

GLENDA JACKSON.

Glenda Jackson was superb in *Women In Love*, as one would expect (and she rightly won an Oscar).[61] Jackson (b. 1936) is an unusual star, with unconventional

---

[60] Two of the actresses that Russell had passed on but had since worked with might have been better, he thought (Bax, 172). Russell also remarked that he let Linden see the rushes, which the actress said had altered her performance: she opted to play Ursula younger than agreed.

[61] I would say that both Alan Bates and Oliver Reed also delivered Oscar-worthy performances.

looks. She is one of England's major actresses, and she can act up a storm. As Ken Russell put it, 'sometimes she looked plain ugly, sometimes just plain, and then, sometimes, the most beautiful creature one had ever seen' (L, 71). Jackson was 32 when *Women In Love* was made: she was mainly known as a stage actress, in *Marat/ Sade* (1964-65, her big breakthrough), *Three Sisters, Henry VI, Hamlet, Collaborators, The Maids, The White Devil, Stevie, Antony and Cleopatra* and *Hedda Gabler*.

Glenda Jackson had appeared prior to *Women In Love* in movies such as *This Sporting Life, Marat/ Sade* and *Negatives*. After *Women In Love* and *The Music Lovers*, Jackson acted in *Sunday Bloody Sunday,* the BBC's *Elizabeth R* (one of her famous roles, which she also did in *Mary, Queen of Scots*), *A Touch of Class, The Tempest, Hedda, House Calls, Stevie, Return of the Soldier, Turtle Diary* and a couple of later Russell outings, *Salomé's Last Dance* and *The Rainbow*. Jackson later went into politics, and was elected a Labour MP in 1992 at the General Election.

Glenda Jackson was Ken Russell's first choice to play Sister Jeanne in *The Devils*. When she refused (not fancying the role),[62] Russell was furious – 'it produced the most bilious fury from him', as Jackson put it – it had seemed the perfect pairing, Reed and Jackson, and had proved so successful in *Women In Love*.

OLIVER REED AND GLENDA JACKSON.

Oliver Reed[63] was dark and troubled as Gerald Crich, smouldering under English sexual repression, giving a convincing impression of someone who desires something, but doesn't know exactly what it is (all of these characters are searching, questioning, examining). Certainly Gerald comes from a troubled family – his mother (played by Ken Russell regular Catherine Wilmer) is portrayed as mad (setting the hounds on miners coming to the house, for instance, or dropping a shovel on her

---

[62] 'I was worried about playing another neurotic, sex-starved lady, albeit a nun,' Jackson remarked in the *New York Times* in 1971.
[63] Ken Russell had wanted Michael Caine for the role of Gerald Crich, but Caine wouldn't do the nudity.

husband's coffin at his funeral), his sister Laura kills herself and new husband, Tibby Lupton, in the lake, and his father dies soon after.

Glenda Jackson and Oliver Reed were very different people, and they did not socialize off-camera in *Women In Love*.[64] As with Vanessa Redgrave in *The Devils*, Jackson was another strong woman that Reed couldn't dominate (and in their subsequent appearances in the same movies, Jackson and Reed continued to be chalk and cheese; but Jackson admired Reed's abilities as an actor).

It's called *Women In Love*, but there are quite a few deaths on-screen – and two suicides, no less – and all of them are within the Crich family. This is a tormented, dysfunctional family: one daughter simultaneously kills herself and murders her new husband; the mother is insane; the father loses his will to live after his daughter's death; and the son kills himself.

All of this's featured in *Women In Love* partly to set up the finale of the movie – Gerald Crich walking off into the snow to die.[65] The suicide has to be convincing – because Gerald is a powerful character, a strong man, now the head of his family, a tyro in the local community (and wealthy), and he's played by Oliver Reed, an actor with a commanding presence. You have to show, in *Women In Love*, how a character embodied by Reed would do something like that. And it works – you never question that Gerald's suicide seems unbelievable, or out of kilter with the rest of the movie, or added on, or false.

Indeed, it's more ironic that Gerald Crich's played by Oliver Reed as a physically confident, energetic man, but is brought low by the torment of a relationship with a strong-willed woman (and the family curse of insanity). Real strength is inside.[66]

---

[64] Reed had been a little intimidated by Jackson, as she was a celebrated stage actress by this time. But he found that Jackson was down-to-earth and not the snobby theatrical actress at all.
[65] DP Billy Williams: 'We were underneath the Matterhorn, it was very deep snow, it was quite a long sequence, and he walks a long way. And of course it could only be done in one take because there was no hope of ever doing another one. Everything was perfect, the lights, the camera, the performance, it was a great moment' (R. Sellers, 179).
[66] Even Gerald's suicide becomes a big physical act, however.

THE LOOK AND STYLE OF *WOMEN IN LOVE*.

Billy Williams,[67] who photographed *Women In Love*, said it was a 'very sumptuous looking film, very rich and colourful. It was very much a cameraman's film'. The photography in *Women In Love* is very beautiful; it has a lovely *quality* to it, a *texture* which's sadly lacking from some of the later works directed by Ken Russell (and most video photography simply can't compete).

Billy Williams said that Ken Russell was prepared to experiment (we knew that!). There were handheld Arriflex shots, zooms, slow motion, the camera on its side, and so on. Russell and Williams also experimented with a range of lighting conditions – soft, Summer light, dusk, candlelight, firelight.[68] *Women In Love* offered many opportunities for cinematography, Williams said, in terms of colour, different lighting effects, day-for-night, night-for-night, candlelight, firelight, twilight, dawn and snow scenes. 'It had everything going for it, all the opportunities'.[69] That's true of so many Ken Russell movies – a DP for Russell has to able to shoot in very low level conditions, or in firelight, or candlelight, or dawn, or magic hour, or night. (Indeed, one of the things that attracts cinematographers to historical movies is the opportunity to explore lighting that doesn't crop up so much in contemporary-set films – candlelight, firelight, etc).

The most memorable lighting effect in *Women In Love* occurred in the most famous scene in the 1969 movie, probably the scene most people associate with Ken Russell more than any other: the nude wrestling between Oliver Reed and Alan Bates in the billiards room, in front of a huge, log fire. As often in his films, Russell, Williams and the camera crew moved from medium shots to handheld close-ups (using two Arriflexes), as the action intensified.

In the scene in *Women In Love* where Gudrun Brangwen dances with the cattle (one of the first scenes filmed),

---

[67] As well as shooting *Women In Love* and *Billion Dollar Brain*, Billy Williams also lit *Sunday Bloody Sunday*, *The Wind and the Lion*, *Saturn 3* and *The Devil's Advocate*. He received an Oscar for *Gandhi*, and a nomination for *On Golden Pond*.
[68] D. Petrie, 1996, 155.
[69] B. Williams, in D. Schaefer, 1984, 271.

the filmmakers used handheld camera, intercut with images of Rupert Birkin dancing in front of Ursula and singing 'Oh, You Beautiful Doll'. Both Gudrun and Birkin seduce their partners by dancing, with Gudrun's dance having a much more elemental and animalistic aspect to it, emphasized by the way she dances with the cows then in front of Gerald (choreography was by Russell regular Terry Gilbert. Some of the scene was shot by Russell himself – you can spot the way that Russell handles the camera a mile off. So he was dancing in amongst his actors – that inter-relationship of the director, the camera and the actors is a key ingredient in Russell's cinema. Russell is not the kind of director who huddles behind the video monitors in a tent).

Ken Russell recalled that the physical aspects of the scene contributed to its impact: Glenda Jackson hated the cows and the cold and the mud, didn't get on with Oliver Reed, it was late in the day with the light going,[70] and she had the director operating the camera himself (Bax, 174). All of which added to the pressure – exactly the kind of thing that Russell thrives on.

Women In Love also contains perhaps Ken Russell's most extravagant mirror scene, in the duologue between Gerald and Birkin, which employs mirrors extensively for its close-ups, as well as the (inevitable) infinity mirror shot, famous from *Citizen Kane*. And, like all mirror shots in movies, it can mean anything, from the two men's lives or personalities being fragmented at that point onwards, to the multiplicity of selves that everyone possesses, to any psychological or psychoanalytical interpretation you fancy. Mirror scenes make film theorists go ga-ga, so we'll leave it to them to scrutinize the scene with their nerdy toothpicks and laser-guided spectacles.

Many of the costumes in *Women In Love* are taken from the book (like Gudrun's dark blue dress), but what *was* Jennie Linden wearing in that first scene? With that hat and colourful coat she might have just wandered out of the Biba store or Carnaby Street (it had bugger all to do with

---

[70] Directors and cameramen love magic hour photography, but everyone else is knackered at the end of the day, and feels the pressure to get the scenes done.

the character in D.H. Lawrence's 1920 story). Later on, Ursula sports a bright orange outfit, and Gerald has a jacket with orange and brown stripes (a nice touch has Birkin wearing the tie that goes with Gerald's jacket, suggesting the intimacy between the men). Orange, gold and brown form the colour scheme of the 1969 production, particularly in relation to the Brangwen sisters (Gudrun's bedroom, for instance, is gold and orange, and she wears a gold outfit). And often the two women are clad in bright colours (such as orange or blue) to contrast with the miners in black and grey or the grimy town, emphasizing their individuality and exoticism. Later, the palette shifts into blacks and whites, reflecting moral absolutes.

Jack Fisher wrote of the colours in *Women in Love*:

> Ranging from the dark, suffocating browns, through red-golds, through the lush warm exteriors, to the green-white of the snow, the colors constantly reaffirm Russell's visual attitude to the events. (1976, 43)

In their incredible book *Film Art*, one of *the* standard texts on cinema, David Bordwell and Kristin Thompson use the costumes and design in *Women In Love* to illustrate a good example of storytelling with colour:

> Ken Russell's *Women In Love* affords a clear example of how costume and setting can coordinate and contribute to a film's overall narrative progression. The opening scenes portray the character's shallow middle-class life by means of highly saturated primary and complementary colors in costume and setting. In the middle portions of the film, as the characters discover love on a country estate, pale pastels predominate. The last section of *Women In Love* takes place around the Matterhorn, and the character's ardor has cooled. Now the colors have become even paler, dominated by pure black and white. By integrating itself with setting, costume may function to reinforce the film's narrative and thematic patterns. (163)

Every costume drama says as much about the time it was produced as about the intended historical period, of course, and *Women In Love* is no exception. *Women In Love* is *very* Sixties, and very *late* Sixties. The characters could walk onto the set of *Blow-Up* or *The Magical Mystery Tour* or *Performance* and would blend in perfectly. Times change, fashions change, and by the 1990s and after for costume dramas, the wardrobe was much more restrained and muted, colour-wise, with blacks, greys, dark blues and creams predominating (in films such as *Sense and Sensibility, Emma, Wings of a Dove, Oliver Twist,* etc). Meanwhile, *every* friggin' movie and trailer and poster in the 21st century seems to be coloured in steely greys, blues and blacks, as if the warm end of the spectrum has vanished and left the planet.

THE WEDDING SCENE.

The first big scene in the 1969 adaption of *Women In Love* was the wedding of Gerald Crich's sister, Laura (Sharon Gurney) to Tibs (Christopher Gable). Some scene-setting was employed as Gudrun and Ursula walk through the streets of Beldover (cue images of a Lawrencean mining town – gotta have those in a film adaption of Lawrence, right?), and ride on a tram (when they arrive and walk through the streets, there are further environmental scenes of shops and extras). These scenes establish the 'women in love' of the title, two of the principal characters (and, importantly, also the lead actors), the setting, their relationship, and some of their desires. But already the film was shifting into different forms of narration (the dialogue between Gudrun and Ursula isn't heard – instead, there's George Delerue's music).[71]

And when the 1969 film of *Women In Love* reaches the church for the wedding, a montage form of editing is employed to depict some of the back stories of the characters (such as the scenes of Rupert Birkin's school inspector visiting Ursula Brangwen, and the introduction of Hermione Roddice – beautifully and extravagantly played with arch artifice by Eleanor Bron). Such montages were likely developed during the editing period, as they often do. The producers didn't like the opening, and asked for a

---

[71] There's a lot less music in *Women In Love* than one might imagine for a Ken Russell movie, and there are more popular songs than usual in a period movie about love and relationships. Delerue provides some terrific music cues, however.

re-edit. (Ken Russell and Mike Bradsell would employ the technique again and again – most famously and imaginatively in the *First Piano Concerto* sequence in *The Music Lovers*, a *tour-de-force* of exposition and editing). The montage form of editing is also a way of getting across exposition and back-story but keeping it lively (by not staying with one scene too long).

The wedding at the top of *Women In Love* is a big scene allowing the introduction of a bunch of characters, including the two men, Rupert Birkin and Gerald Crich (just like one of the most famous wedding scenes in movies – *The Godfather*). And, unusually, the 1969 movie constructs a sequence of women looking with erotic desire at men (the other way around is the norm in cinema). Indeed, *Women In Love* announces from its opening scene that it's going to be, in part, a 'woman's film'. Ken Russell making a 'women's picture'?! You bet: because the first two, major characters introduced here are Ursula and Gudrun. And the title has two terms linked to the 'feminine' and to 'women's films' – 'women' and 'love'.

Strategically, this was a good move for Ken Russell, at that stage in his career, because a movie titled *Women In Love* is probably going to bring in a female audience (the opposite of *Billion Dollar Brain*). Strategically good, because it meant that Russell wasn't typed as only producing male-oriented movies early on in his career (many movie directors, including many of the biggest names, rarely if ever include women in the title roles or main roles, and they would *never* produce a movie with the title *Women In Love*!).

Women In Love also announces early on that it's going to be about *relationships*. It is a 'relationship movie', without a doubt. What is the battleground of *Women In Love*? It's not war, or heroes vs. villains, or cowboys, or car chases in Paris, or samurai in Edo period Japan, it's about *relationships*. The first big scene, for instance, is (very ironically) a wedding (thus, it doesn't *end* with a wedding, like a conventional romantic yarn), with the four main characters discussing or thinking about erotic relationships (and set against the wildly enthusiastic lovers – Tibby Lupton races up the church path to embrace his bride and kiss her (she hares off up the path to escape him), and in subsequent scenes they are always shown madly in love, kissing and the like – which makes Laura Crich's desire to kill herself and her new husband even more tragic – and inexplicable).

Before the dinner party under the trees, there's a scene of Rupert Birkin and Hermione Roddice by a pool, which depicts their uncomfortable relationship (when Birkin spills his drink, and Hermione begins to lick it off, the awkward embrace/ kiss demonstrates clearly that the erotic aspect of their relationship is very dead – the movie also mocks Hermione, as well as the other characters, reinforcing the portrayal of her an eccentric and unfeeling soul). Ursula and Gudrun are invited to Hermione's place for a meal.

THE FIG SCENE.

If you don't think that Ken Russell is a good screenwriter, the fig scene proves otherwise (Russell and Larry Kramer co-wrote the script, but the fig scene seems to have been Russell's idea). It's good scriptwriting, because it's doing a bunch of things simultaneously (just as Russell said of D.H. Lawrence's poem): the fig scene shows:

(1) Rupert Birkin's unusual views, including the emphasis on sex and sensuality;

(2) Birkin's tendency to lecture his audience, and to be a bit of jerk when he's doing it;

(3) Gerald's bemused reaction (he's probably seen Rupert going on like this many times – we all have friends like that!);

(4) Ursula's fascination with Birkin, particularly the unspoken erotic link between them;

(5) the power games between Birkin and Hermione (and how their relationship is past its use-by date);

(6) and, lastly, it's pure D.H. Lawrence.

This is the poem 'Figs' in full:

The proper way to eat a fig, in society,

Is to split it in four, holding it by the stump,
And open it, so that it is a glittering, rosy, moist, honied,
                            heavy-petalled four-petalled flower.

Then you throw away the skin
Which is just like a four-sepalled calyx,
After you have taken off the blossom, with your lips.

But the vulgar way
Is just to put your mouth to the crack, and take out the flesh in
                                                                         one bite.

Every fruit has its secret.

The fig is a very secretive fruit.
As you see it standing growing, you feel at once it is symbolic:
And it seems male.
But when you come to know it better, you agree with the
Romans, it is female.

The Italians vulgarly say, it stands for the female part; the fig-
                                                                                      fruit:
The fissure, the yoni,
The wonderful moist conductivity towards the centre.

Involved,
Inturned,
The flowering all inward and womb-fibrilled;
And but one orifice.

The fig, the horse-shoe, the squash-blossom.
Symbols.

There was a flower that flowered inward, womb-ward;
Now there is a fruit like a ripe womb.

It was always a secret.
That's how it should be, the female should always be secret.

There never was any standing aloft and unfolded on a bough
Like other flowers, in a revelation of petals;
Silver-pink peach, venetian green glass of medlars and sorb-
                                                                                     apples,
Shallow wine-cups on short, bulging stems
Openly pledging heaven:
Here's to the thorn in flower! Here is to Utterance!
The brave, adventurous rosaceæ.

Folded upon itself, and secret unutterable,
And milky-sapped, sap that curdles milk and makes *ricotta*,
Sap that smells strange on your fingers, that even goats won't
                                                          taste it;
Folded upon itself, enclosed like any Mohammedan woman,
Its nakedness all within-walls, its flowering forever unseen,
One small way of access only, and this close-curtained from
                                                          the light;
Fig, fruit of the female mystery, covert and inward,
Mediterranean fruit, with your covert nakedness,
Where everything happens invisible, flowering and
                                                        fertilization, and fruiting
In the inwardness of your you, that eye will never see
Till it's finished, and you're over-ripe, and you burst to give up
                                                         your ghost.

Till the drop of ripeness exudes,
And the year is over.

And then the fig has kept her secret long enough.
So it explodes, and you see through the fissure the scarlet.
And the fig is finished, the year is over.

That's how the fig dies, showing her crimson through the
                                                        purple slit
Like a wound, the exposure of her secret, on the open day.
Like a prostitute, the bursten fig, making a show of her secret.

That's how women die too.

The year is fallen over-ripe,
The year of our women.
The year of our women is fallen over-ripe.
The secret is laid bare.
And rottenness soon sets in.
The year of our women is fallen over-ripe.

When Eve once knew *in her mind* that she was naked
She quickly sewed fig-leaves, and sewed the same for the man.
She'd been naked all her days before,
But till then, till that apple of knowledge, she hadn't had the
                                                        fact on her mind.

She got the fact on her mind, and quickly sewed fig-leaves.
And women have been sewing ever since.
But now they stitch to adorn the bursten fig, not to cover it.

They have their nakedness more than ever on their mind,
And they won't let us forget it.

Now, the secret
Becomes an affirmation through moist, scarlet lips
That laugh at the Lord's indignation.

What then, good Lord! cry the women.
We have kept our secret long enough.
We are a ripe fig.
Let us burst into affirmation.

They forget, ripe figs won't keep.
Ripe figs won't keep.

Honey-white figs of the north, black figs with scarlet inside, of
                                                                          the south.
Ripe figs won't keep, won't keep in any clime.
What then, when women the world over have all bursten into
                                                                          affirmation?
And bursten figs won't keep?

You can see that Ken Russell and Larry Kramer took many lines from the poem and put them into the 1969 movie. Seems simple, doesn't it? You get D.H. Lawrence to write your script for you. Yeah, but you can only do this if (1) you know how to put it in the movie, (2) it fits with the character and the story (and the theme), (3) you rewrite it so it doesn't sound like poetry, and (4) you have very good actors who can deliver this sort of material (trust me, not every actor could do this scene as excellently as Alan Bates. He makes it look effortless – because he is a *very* good actor).

The fig scene came from Bertie Lawrence's poetry, Ken Russell said: it was typical of Russell's approach to adapting books that he would take dialogue or ideas from an author's other works and incorporate them into the film. The dialogue about the fig works partly because the Birkin in the *movie* is closely modelled on Lawrence himself (and Lawrence's voice comes through loud and clear in his poems. There's a refrain in the scene where Birkin talks about catkins).

Women In Love is what you could call a 'subtext film'

– a movie in which everything really significant is played as subtext. What is the subtext of the fig scene (which Ken Russell added to the script)? Well, Birkin makes the subtext the centrepiece of the scene, it's not hidden at all: it's about women, sex, erotic relationships, etc. It's the kind of speech that has driven feminists nuts about D.H. Lawrence. Looking at the United Artists film again, Birkin comes across as a bit of a tit, and a pretentious tit, too (but quite a few of Lawrence's characters are twerps). And it's one of those odd scenes where a bunch of characters listen quietly to one character going on and on, and no one stops him and tells him he's a dick (you try delivering that speech at the next dinner party you go to!). But Alan Bates plays it beautifully.

Meanwhile, the editing is creating another network of reaction shots, to actors Jennie Linden, Oliver Reed, Glenda Jackson and others, and further hinting at the erotic attraction between the two couples. And there is another subtext, which's the dissatisfying erotic relationship between Birkin and Hermione.

Look at the 1969 movie of *Women In Love* again, and you'll see just how much the *editing* is contributing towards the piece (courtesy of Mike Bradsell and his team). Of course, the visuals are ravishing at times, and Ken Russell has always been known for being a master at creating intoxicating visuals. But it's the *editing* that is doing so much of the storytelling, especially in this movie about subtexts and relationships.

Thus, while the dialogue is doing one thing, and the actions within a scene are doing another (plus the *mise-en-scène*, costumes, sets, etc), it's actually the editing that is controlling the meanings and subtexts and emotions of the movie. D.H. Lawrence does spoil his novels sometimes by being way too obvious and insistent in his dialogue – continually, Lorenzo's characters tell each other how they're feeling, how they're reacting to the other person, what they want, what they don't want, etc.

That can work in a movie (or a stage play), but often it can also be too on the nose. Filmmakers like to *show* not tell (well, the good ones do, and especially the visual filmmakers). In *Women In Love*, it's the editing that is doing so much of the telling, although there is Lawrencean dialogue too (especially from Ursula and Birkin).

♣

THE MASQUE.

In the 1920 novel of *Women In Love*, the masque in the style of the then fashionable Russian ballet (Vaslav Nijinsky and Sergei Diaghilev) takes up not much more'n a page. In the 1969 interpretation, it becomes a major set-piece (Ken Russell was a big fan of Nijinsky (1890-1950), and planned a film about him). Russell & co. manage to stage a lengthy music and dance number in a literary adaption (maybe Russell was thinking, well, if Harry Saltzman isn't going to produce my Nijinsky movie, I'll just squeeze in a ballet scene in *Women In Love*!).

The episode is a battle of wills between Hermione Roddice and Rupert Birkin: Hermione is leading the scene, but Birkin takes over (much to Hermione's irritation). *Dramatically*, it's that simple. *Cinematically*, it's more complex, and includes many beats and bits of business. Piano music pounds throughout (like an audition for *The Boy Friend*), as Hermione leads the Brangwen sisters, Gudrun and Ursula, in a mythological dance, while the men watch. One can imagine that Ken Russell would be quite happy to make a whole film like this. Forget the dialogue – move into music and movement and dance: *Women In Love* as a ballet, or a musical, or an opera. Russell once joked that it might have been better to turn *Women In Love* into a musical – certainly music and dance play far more important roles here than in any other adaption of D.H. Lawrence's fiction.

As Joseph Gomez pointed out, the influence of Isadora Duncan, one of Ken Russell's heroes in dance, influenced the 1969 movie, particularly in the Greek ballet sequence at Hermione Roddice's, and also in the scene where Gudrun dances before the cattle (G, 82). Russell reckoned that Lawrence must've drawn on Duncan's elemental approach to dance: 'Gudrun would have liked to be Isadora, but a bit more intellectual with it... [Duncan] was the first woman to be aware of the elemental sense around her and respond to it. Lawrence must have been conscious of this'. (Bax, 174)

Halfway through, with Rupert Birkin's encouragement, the scene became a semi-drunken dance to modern music. Hermione Roddice's rage is carefully repressed (she's a little like a movie director who's furious when the organized chaos of the film set becomes disorganized chaos, and the actors are jiving to jazz or thrash metal or garage when they should be swanning around smoothly to Peter Tchaikovsky or Sergei Rachmaninov).

COMMUNING WITH NATURE.

The nude wrestling scene gets all the press coverage, but there is much more male nudity in *Women In Love* than that: Alan Bates goes nude in the previous sequence, where he communes in Lorzeno-style with the natural world. Hmmm; it's kinda D.H. Lawrence, but not really (it's a modern (or rather, a late 1960s) interpretation of what a Lawrencean character Communing With Nature might do). The scene is effective in its deployment of sound effects, however – the soft brushing sounds of walking through grass and bushes, with some nighttime sounds added. (Alan Bates rubs himself on a pine tree – surely an oak tree or a beech tree would be softer?! But maybe there wasn't an oak or beech nearby. He also lies down in the grass – classic images of a soul uniting with nature).

Or maybe rolling around in the grass and rubbing branches over his body was the kind of thing that Ken Russell got up to in the Lake District! What was Russell's direction to Alan Bates as they filmed that scene? 'Err, have a go at getting closer to nature, love, you know, roll in the grass for a bit!'

And Ollie Reed also appears nude – when he dives into the lake (once again while Gudrun and Ursula look on). So this movie sets up the male nudity early on – and it's unusual in that it's the guys who disrobe first (and that they are looked at by women, and women who are becoming attracted to them).

Women In Love captured a particular quality of the British landscape, John Baxter reckoned, which could also be found in the art of Charles Dickens, H.G. Wells, John Constable and especially J.M.W. Turner. Quaint, romantic, pastoral, but also 'a little threatening, a little absurd' (Bax, 142-3).

Then follows a scene which conjures classic images of the Brits being Brits: war and religion, a priest, hymns, and a war memorial. Rupert Birkin rails against it all, of course. This is more Lawrencean – or, at least, the didactic D.H. Lawrence who never missed an opportunity to lecture his readers, and give his five cents – well, three thousand dollars – of thoughts on the state of the world (Birkin can come across as a whinger, as many Lawrencean figures do – nothing is good enough, society is going to pot, the government are idiots, there's nothing and no one worth loving, etc etc etc).

Women In Love's coal-mining scene is very impressive, a big scene with plenty of extras; it has an earthy feeling of the hard labour that goes into hauling material out from the planet. Of course, a D.H. Lawrence adaption *has* have a coal mining scene, and *Women In Love* has one of the best (similarly the streets in the town, with its miners, alleys and pubs, are vividly depicted). There's a stunning high angle, long shot of the miners walking home at the end of the work day, with a steam engine thundering by, clouds of steam, and Gerald and his father in their white car moving through the workers.[72] (I'm not sure where it was filmed, but it looked like a plant that was still functioning; thirty years later, film companies in the U.K. had to go to coal mines that had been turned into heritage centres, places with that plasticky, cleaned-up, theme park look. In *Women In Love*, the scenes are authentically gritty and non-glossy).[73]

---

[72] The image of the big, posh car in amongst the throng of exhausted coal-miners going homeward was an old but effective commentary on the power relations between owners and workers. Steven Spielberg and David Lean – they've all used that scene.

[73] Such as the utterly abysmal adaption Britain's ITV made of *Sons and Lovers*.

GUDRUN DANCES BEFORE THE CATTLE.

The water-party scenes lay the groundwork for three of the most memorable scenes in *Women In Love*: the drowning of Laura and Tibs; Gudrun dancing with the cattle; and the parallel romances of Gerald and Gudrun and Birkin and Ursula. These are genuinely cinematic scenes, not talky,[74] not dialogue-led, not 'filmed theatre', not television. Ken Russell put down *Women In Love* continually, and insisted he'd done better work elsewhere, but these are all very fine scenes. (And he finally has a decent enough budget to mount a large-scale version of the historical scenes he'd filmed in *Dante's Inferno* and *The Debussy Film*. Altho', at $1.25-1.6 million, the budget for *Women In Love* is still tiny).

We're in the middle of the 1969 film, with a series of scenes that seem idyllic and lyrical – Gudrun and Ursula Brangwen go swimming nude (there has to be a nude, bathing scene in a D.H. Lawrence film); they have a picnic; and Gudrun decides to dance. Yes, Ken Russell has squeezed in *another* dance scene into the movie! It's one of his best, partly because of the way it's staged and choreographed, the way it's shot and cut (largely with the lake in the background, under some huge trees in full leaf), partly due to the superb way that Glenda Jackson plays it, and partly because it doesn't have strident music accompanying it (instead, it's Ursula singing 'I'm Forever Blowing Bubbles'. which's faded quietly into reverb). 'All my films are choreography. The camera moves and the people move', Russell remarked (Bax, 190).

It's a very effective scene, playing to that non-verbal, musical-movement realm which's Ken Russell's specialty. Indeed, this might be the most successful sequence in the 1969 film of *Women In Love*, this group of scenes – the shift from the picnic, to Ursula dancing, to the confrontation with the cattle, to Gerald's approach, to the colloquy

---

[74] In Birkin-mode, in *Women In Love*, D.H. Lawrence writes: 'What was the good of talking, any way? It must happen beyond the sound of words.' (327). Yes, but Lawrence still never shuts up!

between Gudrun and Gerald.[75]

When Gudrun Brangwen faces the cattle, and dances before them, the episode is a genuine piece of D.H. Lawrence's fiction – more so, perhaps, than the anguished lovemaking or the nude wrestling. The United Artists picture shifts from the lyrical images of Gudrun making shapes against the lake to much looser, handheld images and rapid cutting. And when Gerald arrives (running, more dynamic than his arrival with Birkin in the book), the film shifts its style of narration yet again, with lap dissolves between the shots.

THE WATER-PARTY SCENE.

The biggest scene in *Women In Love*, in terms of extras, costumes and budget, illustrated the novel's chapter XIV, "Water-Party", where rowing boats lit by paper lanterns floated on a lake at twilight (shot over three successive dusks,[76] at the 'magic hour', beloved of cameramen, because of the soft light it creates, making everyone look great, and hated by line producers, because it only lasts ten minutes). The water-party also featured details like fairground rides, miners drinking beer, and introduced Mrs Crich (Ken Russell is very fond of festival or masquerade scenes – anything with plenty of chaos and movement and colour. Producers, of course, know just how much these scenes cost, and what a headache they are).

As Joseph A. Gomez said of Ken Russell: he

is consumed by images, and his entire career could be analyzed in terms of his attempts to transform other people's words into his unique images. (1981, 249)

One of the most memorable images from *Women In Love* was the brilliantly-executed cut between the nude

---

[75] As well as 'I'm Forever Blowing Bubbles', *Women In Love* also employs other popular and folk songs, and includes brass bands, and a rendition of 'Jerusalem' by William Blake and Sir Hubert Parry (1848-1918) at the war memorial ('Jerusalem' is an alternative, British national anthem).

[76] 'With this being so long and complex it took three evenings to shoot it,' recalled DP Billy Williams. And Olly Reed and the other actors had to swim in the cold water time after time.

bodies of the drowned couple, Tibby and Laura Lupton, on the mud at the bottom of the lake, after the boating party, to the figures of Ursula Brangwen and Rupert Birkin after they have made love (lying in very similar positions). The cut suggested the Lawrencean (Western) preoccupations with sex and death, with death-in-love and love-in-death. That was when the 1969 movie came close to the spirit of the 1920 novel, or at least found images which seemed to be striking equivalents for what happens in the book.

Why include the death of the newly-weds, Laura and Tibby Lupton? They are a sub-plot and minor characters, but their story relates directly to the main plot of love and sex and relationships. We see Laura getting married to Tibby at the opening of *Women In Love*, and they seem madly in love with each other. Giggingly, laughingly in love. And in subsequent scenes (such as at the Russian dance), they are still all over each other.

Then, during the water party, the couple are still the happy, young lovers, fooling about on the water, and going skinny-dipping (creeping into the lake when they're naked). So when Laura calls to Tibs, chuckling, then disappears under the water and Tibby's splashing about in trouble, like Susan Backlinie at the beginning of *Jaws* when the shark attacks her, and yelling for help, the flipside of love – tragedy, destruction, death – is vividly revealed. The cut from the dead lovers in the mud to Ursula and Birkin after their clinch rams home the point.

So the sub-plot of Laura and Tibby Lupton in *Women In Love* – like a mini *Romeo and Juliet* play, with its doomed, young lovers – is included to throw light on the twin relationships of Gerald-Gudrun and Birkin-Ursula. The death of Laura and Tibby is all the more shocking, in dramatic terms, because they seemed so wildly in love, and, even more extraordinary, it was a suicide. It's also important that the 1969 film deliberately *doesn't* explain their death, or psychologize it. (But we note that it is the *woman* who drags the man underwater, further developing the theme of the predatory woman established in the fig scene; also, one of Laura's first acts is to rush away from

Tibs at the church, encouraging him to pursue her, like Daphne and Apollo in Greek mythology. And in that legend, Apollo was torn to shreds! We also note that in the previous scene, we saw the mentally ill Mrs Crich, suggesting that insanity is in the family– and, in true Lawrencean style, it's on the mother's side).

And the death and suicide of Laura and Tibby's included for another important reason: how it relates to Gerald Crich. Who is it who walks through the mud in the drained lake and stands over the drowned lovers? It's Gerald. Why? Because the picture has to set up that Gerald is going to kill himself too by the end of the story (*Women In Love* contains two suicides, no less).

BIRKIN AND URSULA MAKE LOVE.

Another memorable effect in *Women In Love* was the tilted camera – putting the camera on one side when filming the long lens close-ups of Ursula Brangwen and Rupert Birkin meeting in an overgrown field, accompanied by over-sumptuous (i.e., ironic) music (by Georges Delerue). It was Ken Russell in his satirical TV commercial mode, which he employed in films like *The Music Lovers* and *Tommy*. Again, I'm sure that some viewers (and movie critics) took that scene literally, rather than ironically, as was clearly intended (look at the sequence again – there's no way that it is meant to be taken straight; it's two lovers walking towards each other in slow motion! Also, it's gorgeously done, and still very unusual – the camera on its side, the actors moving towards each other, the slow motion, the close framing, the backlighting, the angle having the effect of two lovers lying on top of each other).

The best moments of *Women In Love* were, as so often in a movie directed by Ken Russell, non-dialogue scenes: images plus music, such as the superb scene where Gudrun Brangwen gets up and starts to dance in amongst some trees and cattle, while Ursula sings 'I'm Forever Blowing Bubbles', one of the most popular songs of 1920 (the music was also employed over the opening credits, and is one of the signature music cues in the 1969 movie). The handheld shots of Gudrun facing off the cattle came after this.

The familiar Ken Russellian counterpoint approach is used with the music sometimes – for instance, the song 'I'm Forever Blowing Bubbles' is about wishing or dreaming, and the characters in *Women In Love*, as in movies such as *The Music Lovers* and *Savage Messiah*, have dreams or desires which are unreal and cannot be fulfilled. Russell argued that although the music doesn't appear in the novel, the two young women would've been aware of the popular music of the time. And of course the music places the scene in the 1920s period.

The setting – the trees by the lake – is a brilliant use of locations (and magic hour photography). The move from long shots in silhouette to handheld close-ups is a classic Ken Russell cinematic technique, as is the use of near-silence as Gudrun Brangwen dances with the music coming in later, to accentuate the change in the mood and purpose of the scene – from Gudrun to an illustration of her eccentric and even perverse delight in startling the cattle (it wasn't meant to be 'real', Russell commented in *An Appalling Talent*, not 'real' for him, as the director, but 'real' for Gudrun, to embody her character and the novel [Bax, 175]). And dramatically the scene's impressive, in the way it brings Gerald Crich into the scene, and puts Gudrun and Gerald together romantically (notice, too, the unusual dissolves in the midst of the exchange of dialogue, as Gudrun lies on the grass below Gerald, a marvellous way of suggesting the strangeness in the developing relationship between the two. Indeed, the erotic relationship of Gudrun and Gerald has strangeness heightened at many moments – the way that Gudrun seems coolly indifferent to Gerald's advances when she's with him, but how fascinated she is when she watches him from a distance. As if he disappoints her at close quarters, and she'd prefer him to remain a fantasy, seen from afar).

THE NUDE WRESTLING SCENE.

The famous nude wrestling match in *Women In Love* had originally been conceived by Ken Russell & co. as taking place outdoors, at night, when Gerald Crich comes upon Rupert Birkin bathing nude in the lake. They lark about, and get to fighting. Russell told the story, many times, how Oliver Reed stormed into his house when he found out about the nude scene (from his wife – he apparently hadn't read the novel), and showed him how it should really be played (how Reed was in an unstoppable mood (i.e., drunk). Another time, Reed used swords in his demonstration, which ended with Russell cutting Reed on the chest). Russell also often related how the shoot went, how the actors had a few drinks to set themselves up, how Reed compared his genitals with Alan Bates in the restroom the night b4 when they went out for a drink, and how Reed nipped into a corner to masturbate to enlarge his penis during filming (all rubbish, but now part of the legend).[77]

Still daring today, *Women In Love*'s nude wrestling scene is Ken Russell's cinema at its finest (and it's also a tribute to Russell's standing as a director that he could get two major actors to do this scene. And still today there are plenty of stars who would *not* do that scene. Ever. For *any* money). Needless to say, nobody was looking forward to filming it – tough for the actors and for the crew.

In the chapter "Gladiatorial", the scene is described by Lorenzo thus:

> So the two men entwined and wrestled with each other, working nearer and nearer. Both were white and clear, but Gerald flushed smart red where he was touched, and Birkin remained white and tense. He seemed to penetrate into Gerald's more solid, more diffuse bulk, to interfuse his body through the body of the other, as if to bring it subtly into subjection, always seizing with some rapid necromantic foreknowledge every motion of the other flesh, converting and counteracting it, playing upon the limbs and trunk of Gerald like some hard wind. It was as

---

[77] Alan Bates dislocated his shoulder after shooting for 3 days, and Oliver Reed had bruises. The filmmakers had put rubber under the carpet, but that didn't look good, because they bounced on it. 'We took it out and they just landed crash bang wallop on the floor, time after time', Ken Russell recalled (Bax, 180).

> if Birkin's whole physical intelligence interpenetrated into Gerald's body, as if his fine, sublimated energy entered into the flesh of the fuller man, like some potency, casting a fine net, a prison, through the muscles into the very depths of Gerald's physical being. (348-9)

Plenty of *penetration*, then.

In the 1969 version of *Women In Love*, the nude wrestling scene begins with some dialogue, once again about the familiar Lawrencean themes of love and relationships, in particular male brotherhood and closeness. Importantly, it is a scene between equals – this is not Gerald seducing Birkin or vice versa: it's Gerald who suddenly stands up and asks Birkin to demonstrate, and it's Birkin who suggests that they should strip.[78]

That it's a gay sex scene the United Artists movie is in no doubt: this is two men at night in a room on their own, drinking by firelight, even before they get naked – i.e., it's already a very romantic setting (and the lighting – and intimate conversation – emphasizes that). But when the men strip off and begin wrestling, the scene becomes the longest love scene in the movie (and in much of Ken Russell's cinema).

The rapid cutting disguises long views of nudity, as per the censorship laws,[79] but it can't hide the fact that this is two men fully naked who're grappling each other (and men that we know are very friendly with each other). It might have been called 'Men In Love', as Ken Russell admitted. Only when the men have wrestled for some time do editor Mike Bradsell and director Russell bring in the music (and take down the local sound of pants and slaps). The scene climaxes – literally – with the two men face to face, very close together, with the kiss apparently inevitable. And when they slowly collapse to the floor, with Gerald on top of Birkin, the poses again suggest

---

[78] Note the cutaway to the large, white bear skin – more animalistic, Lawrencean flesh and spirit.
[79] In the early Seventies, films such as *Zabriskie Point*, *M*A*S*H*, *Fellini Satyricon* and *Women In Love* escaped the 'X' rating, which was death at the box office, when the MPAA under Jack Valenti raised the 'R' rating from 16 to 17.

lovemaking.[80]

For feminists such as Luce Irigaray and Andrea Dworkin, women become commodities traded between men. In Irigaray's view of the narcissistic, phallocentric economy, women are not the endpoint of desire, but the means or carriers of male desire. As it's between men, this sexual economy is homosexual, governed by and for men. This is certainly at work in *Women In Love*: the book and the film may be about 'women in love', but it's men who have the final say, and the women for some feminists are commodities. And D.H. Lawrence's 1920 novel also makes clear the homoerotic relationship between Birkin and Crich – so clear, in fact, that there's a nude wrestling scene between the two guys! Lawrence doesn't depict gay sex, but has the nude wrestling scene stand in for it (with all the motifs pointing towards sex – the nudity, the sweat, the closeness, and even the fireside, nighttime setting). All of that is brought out in the 1969 movie.

Women In Love is unusual among mainstream commercial cinema in depicting not one but two gay relationships. That Herr Loerke and his companion are gay nobody can be in any doubt (or that Loerke swings both ways, having his eye on Gudrun from the get-go. But he is also the kind of personality that would try to seduce Gudrun Brangwen simply to cause trouble).

Some critics have chosen to see the central relationship in *Women In Love* between Rupert and Gerald as brotherhood or a Platonic ideal or companionship or whatever the current euphemism is for gay relationships. But no, this is a homosexual relationship. It might be unreciprocated fully from Gerald's point-of-view (he appears reluctant to go the whole hog), but Birkin certainly wants it. It's Birkin, of course, that's talking about wanting more than companionship and love with a woman. There must be something more, for Birkin – and the movie keeps

---

80 Ken Russell commented that when the censors in Argentina cut out much of the scene, but included the opening section, where Gerald and Birkin shake hands, and the final shots, where they are lying on the carpet together, it suggested the scene was even more erotic ('it became known as the great buggering scene and filled cinemas for months', according to the maestro).

coming back to that (to the point where it closes the picture).

So *Women In Love* portrays the courtship and intercourse of two heterosexual couples, but also the courtship and near-sexual relationship of two men. But one could argue, because of all of the devices and tropes employed, that the nude wrestling scene is a sex scene between two men in all but name. And once you combine those dramatic, romantic elements with some terrific performances, a great cast, and innovative and beautiful filmmaking, you can see why *Women In Love* is many folks' favourite Ken Russell movie.

SWITZERLAND.

The Swiss scenes in *Women In Love* were impressive – the endless reaches of snow contrasting dramatically with the soft undulations of the English countryside (they were filmed below the Matterhorn in Switzerland, including the Riffelberg Inn in Zermatt). Character actor Vladik Sheybal, another Ken Russell regular, as Loerke, added to the atmosphere of decadence, stifled sexuality, boredom, and impending doom.

Herr Loerke is a cliché of the decadent, purist artist, right down to his bisexuality – the first time he's introduced, in the German dance sequence, he's already got his eye on Gudrun Brangwen, but his blond lover (Richard Heffer) gets to dance with her first. Loerke also embodies the darker, sensual side of life that Gudrun hankers after (and all that's lacking in her relationship with Gerald Crich) – in the 1969 movie, Gudrun's depicted as someone who's simultaneously attracted and repulsed by violence and eroticism (or violent eroticism, or erotic violence). For instance, in the famous scene (superbly staged) where Gerald rides his white horse[81] right at a passing train,[82] Ursula freaks out but Gudrun is

---

[81] The horse is pure nature in motion in D.H.L.'s art – majestic but also destructive, heavy and dark. In *Women In Love*, the horse is associated with death and violence. Gerald tortures his mare (on one level it's a stand-in for Gudrun, just like Alec d'Urberville rides his mare (in *Tess of the d'Urbervilles*).

[82] And it does seem to be Oliver Reed riding the horse at a gallop beside the train – though the stunt in front of the train is likely a stuntman.

fascinated.[83]

In the movie version of *Women In Love*, it's partly Gerald Crich's powerful physicality and drive that attracts Gudrun Brangwen (not, for example, his economic wealth or powerful job as mine manager). But after they've got together, Gudrun finds out that Gerald is not what she expected, and maybe he can't love her (and maybe she would've been better off admiring Gerald from afar). The scenes between them in the Swiss chalet are beautifully performed (and written) – Gudrun systematically (and quietly) demolishes Gerald and his idea of love and relationships. And in the lengthy master two-shot, Oliver Reed plays his moodiness at Moody Three, and simmers brilliantly. You know that Reed's Gerald is not going to sit back and take all this dressing down, even if it is the truth (Gudrun's right about Gerald's brutal form of loving – because in the next scene he fucks Gudrun like he's murdering her – and it's the first appearance of the characteristic, handheld, up-and-down, Ken Russell camera movement, which simulates sex).

The Swiss episode in *Women In Love* has a genuinely apocalyptic feel to it, a relentless surge towards self-destruction that seems unstoppable – like an ocean liner that can't stop and crashes into a harbour. The urge towards self-absorption which leads to self-immolation, the United Artists movie suggests, is a fatal flaw in the Crich family: the mother is insane, the daughter (Laura) killed herself *and* her new husband Tibby, and the son, that the family now relies upon, stalks off into the mountains to die.

And Ken Russell, Larry Kramer and the team find the perfect embodiment of the insanity of Gerald's act, as well as the desperation and sadness of it, by showing Oliver Reed trudging through the pristine snow. And, rightly, editor Mike Bradsell holds and holds on that shot. And this is just one of many, many memorable images in *Women*

---

[83] For Linda Ruth Williams, the scene in the book has a cinematic quality, with D.H. Lawrence shifting points-of-view from the third person to Gudrun's p.o.v., and the shot-counter-shot pattern of the text helps to render the movie version successful (*Sex In the Head*, Harvester Wheatsheaf, 1993, 66).

In Love. It might be for Russell one of his least-liked movies, but it contains numerous vivid images.

▼

In conventional drama characters are usually changed at the end of a play or a novel. In *Women In Love* (the novel) there is no great change. Ursula Brangwen seems no different: instead, the characters are wearier, more cynical and more bitter. The war between love and solitude is not resolved, partly because D.H. Lawrence always sees things in terms of opposition, rather than two, complementary sides. Eugene Goodheart writes in *The Utopian Vision of D.H. Lawrence*:

> Lawrence opposes an ecstatic, onanistic aloneness (don't be deceived by his insistence that he is not alone) in which the self absorbs and is enhanced by the cosmos to the romantic cult of passion, the dissolution of the identities of lovers into a death-like unity. Lawrence discovers the terror at the heart of sexual passion.[84]

The 1969 United Artists film does reflect that sense of circularity,[85] and characters getting nowhere. There is a tragic ending to *Women In Love*, with Gerald walking off into the mountains to expire, but Ursula and Birkin, it seems, haven't advanced spiritually or psychologically at all. As Joseph Gomez remarked, Ken Russell and Larry Kramer were much more sceptical and satirical about Ursula than D.H. Lawrence was, and it doesn't seem that Ursula has altered much at all (whereas she most definitely has in the 1920 novel). *Women In Love* ends with the lovers disagreeing. (The levels of satire and scepticism in the movie are thus further ways in which it misrepresents the novel).

MARKETING AND RECEPTION.

Women In Love was marketed cleverly in North America by United Artists, according to Ken Russell: they

---

[84] E. Goodheart. *The Utopian Vision of D.H. Lawrence*, University of Chicago Press, 1963, 78.
[85] There are repetitions and rhymes throughout the picture. For example, there's a visual rhyme where Gudrun takes Gerald to the same place under a bridge where she saw a miner and his girl embracing (which expresses her fascination and fear of sex and love).

went down the academic/ literary/ college route, and showed the movie to psychologists, students, and intellectuals (Bax, 182). The tactic has been used many times with prestige or literary movies, to build strong word-of-mouth, b4 opening the movie wider.

Though not his favourite movie, or his most typical movie, Joseph Lanza is right to point out that *Women In Love* contains many of Ken Russell's key themes, and was:

> perfect for summarizing Russell's courtships and inevitable conflicts between the sexes; his conflicted sympathies with homosexual relationships; his so-called love of nature and his phobias about its slimier side; his desire to tell a serious story while simultaneously slipping into farce; his love of art and his penchant for destroying art's mystique; his battle between visceral, irrational sensations and the more intellectual approach to life that Lawrence once derided as "sex in the head"; and spells of anger, pessimism and even nihilism that belie his frustrated love of life. (2)

D.H. LAWRENCE AT THE CINEMA

> The film is only pictures, like pictures in the *Daily Mirror*. And pictures don't have any feelings apart from their own feelings. I mean the feelings of the people who watch them. Pictures don't have any feelings except in the people who watch them. And that's why they like them. Because they make them feel that they are everything.
>
> D.H. Lawrence, *The Lost Girl* (p. 144)

Ken Russell has contributed more than most to the D.H. Lawrence film and television industry, taking on three of Lawrence's biggest works. Films of Lawrence's work, up to the period of *Women In Love,* include: *The Rocking Horse Winner* (Anthony Pelissier, 1949, GB), with Valerie Hobson and John Mills, a real British curio; the superb *Sons and Lovers* (1960, Jack Cardiff, GB), with Dean Stockwell, Trevor Howard and Wendy Hiller; and *Lady Chatterley's Lover* (Marc Allégret, 1955), a French version, starring Danielle Darrieux; a North American version of *The Fox* (Mark Rydell, 1968), with Keir Dullea and Sandy Dennis; and *The Virgin and the Gipsy* (Christopher Miles, 1970, GB), with Franco Nero and Joanna Shimkus.

The 1960s was a decade of significant D.H. Lawrence movies and influence: there was the *Lady Chatterley* trial in 1960 (a version of *Lady Chatterley's Lover* had appeared in 1955); *Sons and Lovers* in 1960; then, in the late 1960s, when Lawrence was associated with counter-culture, the Summer of Love, free expression, hippy ideals and so on, there were three pictures: *The Fox, Women In Love* and *The Virgin and the Gipsy* (the 1970 *Virgin and the Gipsy* might not have been commissioned by producers inspired by the success of United Artists' film, but it was definitely of a similar type, and may have been influenced by it).

1960's *Sons and Lovers* was a terrific, if drastically curtailed, version of the 1913 D.H. Lawrence novel, and one of the first, major movies of a Lorenzo book. It enhanced the picture enormously by filming in many of the locations that inspired Lawrence for his novel (that doesn't automatically work, of course – because movies are pure illusion, but here it paid off).

Being directed by one of the great British cinematographers, Jack Cardiff (most famous for his collaborations with Mickey Powell), *Sons and Lovers* was always going to look great, and of course it did, with pin-sharp, contrasty, black-and-white photography (the DP was Freddie Francis). And although it missed out reams of Lawrencean prose and incidents, it did capture some of the erotic and psychological tensions in the relationships surrounding Paul Morel.

Dean Stockwell, an American Method actor who's made 100s of appearances in TV and movies, delivered an intense and convincing Paul Morel, as if James Dean had grown up in 1910s Nottinghamshire. Stockwell's Morel avoided the pitfalls of the role (such as not coming over as a smug, self-satisfied know-it-all, or someone wallowing in depression and narcissism, which's how some of Lorenzo's characters can appear. Because, let's face it,

Morel can seem like a stuck-up prig in *Sons and Lovers*).

▼

Since the Sixties the number of D.H. Lawrence adaptions has grown: there have been BBC TV versions of *Sons and Lovers* (1981, adapted by Trevor Griffiths); *The Captain's Doll* (BBC, 1982); *The Trespasser* (Colin Gregg, 1981, GB); *The Boy in the Bush* (Rob Stewart, 1984, Channel Four); *The Rainbow* (Stuart Burge, 1989, BBC), with Imogen Stubbs; an Australian *Kangaroo* (Tim Burstall, 1986), with Colin Friels and Judy Davis; *Priest of Love*, about Lawrence's life (Christopher Miles, 1981, GB), with Ian McKellen, Ava Gardner, Janet Suzman and John Gielgud; soft porn versions of *Lady Chatterley's Lover* (Just Jaecklin, 1981, GB/ Fr) with Sylvia Kristel and Nicholas Clay, a Czech TV version – *Milenec lady Chatterleyové* (1998), *The Young Lady Chatterley* (1977), and a sequel (1985).[86] Britain's ITV channel produced a version of *Sons and Lovers* in 2003 (it was scripted by Simon Burke and was truly awful).

Other Lorenzo adaptions include: *You Touched Me* (1949 and 2014, short), *Samson and Delilah* (1959 and 1985, short), *The Stocking* (1955), *The Widowing of Mrs. Holroyd* (1961, 1974, 1976 and 1995), *The Stories of D.H. Lawrence* (1966-67, ITV Playhouse, 12 stories), *The Princess* (1968), *The Daughter-in-Law* (1969, 1971 and 1974), *A Collier's Friday Night* (1976), *The Rocking Horse Winner* (1977 and 1983), *The Horse Dealer's Daughter* (1983, short), *The Story of Lady Chatterley* (1989), *Earthly Disturbance* (1993), *La fidèle infidèle* (1995), *The Rocking Horse Winner* (1998, short), *Odour of Chrysanthemums* (2006, short), *The Blind Man* (2011, short), *Inside the Mind of Mr D.H. Lawrence* (2013), and *The White Stocking* (2014, short).

It's a testament to the power of *Women In Love* that film and TV companies held off remaking it for such a long time. Finally, the BBC (inevitably) took up *Women In Love* for a TV rehash in 2011 (the year that Ken Russell died), combining it with *The Rainbow* (for a mini-series of two

---

86 Movies using the *Lady Chatterley's Lover* monkier or source material have been either prestige/ literary productions or softcore porn flicks.

episodes).[87] The crew included William Ivory (script), Miranda Bowen (direction), and 9 producers; the cast included Rory Kinnear, Rachael Stirling, Rosamund Pike and Joseph Mawle.

It was horseshit: I got thru 20 minutes before giving up. I loathed the writing (characters standing about pontificating in boring reams of dialogue), I loathed the zero energy in the drama, I detested the horrible, shaky, quasi-documentary camerawork, the hopeless, 'impressionistic' approach to staging scenes, the inept direction (treating D.H. Lawrence like a crummy soap opera), and the useless, embarrassed, snippy interaction between the characters (why do so many Brit TV shows have this same crappy, downcast, apologetic, sarky style of performance?). Revolting.

A dire version of *Lady Chatterley's Lover* and *John Thomas and Lady Jane* was produced by Pascale Ferran in 2006. A French production, it completely missed the essence of Lorenzo's famous novel of sex and liberation. What was interesting about *Lady Chatterley's Lover*, looking at it from the viewpoint of British cinema and English literature, was to see how a French film production took on a 'British' subject. Oh, *Lady Chatterley's Lover* looked fine (most movies do), because the French locations easily stood in for the English Midlands. But it was fascinating to see the French film industry trying to reproduce the idiosyncrasies of the English way of life, how people talk to each other, how they move. In other words, although the subject and setting was English, *Lady Chatterley* couldn't help but be thoroughly *French*.

What's striking about the list of films made from D.H. Lawrence's work is that nearly all of them, apart from the Australian *Kangaroo* and the 1968 version of *The Fox*, and the 1993 *Lady Chatterley*, are British adaptions (well, 'British' in the sense of being made in Britain with mainly British casts; the money for some of those films was of course American, including for Ken Russell's 1969 and 1988 movies). Hollywood has steered clear of adapting

---

[87] The events of *The Rainbow* were placed into a flashback structure, with the TV series concentrating on *Women In Love*.

Lawrence; and most of the adaptions of Thomas Hardy have also been British. William Shakespeare has had many more big budget Hollywood adaptions, as have Charles Dickens (and, to a lesser degree, Jane Austen, the Brontës and E.M. Forster).

Perhaps Thomas Hardy and D.H. Lawrence are too regional, too 'British'. Emily Brontë and Charles Dickens, like James Joyce, Graham Greene and Joseph Conrad, seem to travel outside Britain. There have been 'international' versions of Lawrence's contemporary E.M. Forster; these films (*A Room With a View, Howard's End, A Passage to India*), and the spate of Jane Austen adaptions, are part of British 'heritage' cinema, the sort of pictures made by the Merchant-Ivory team, and favouring Forster and Henry James.

And most adaptions of D.H. Lawrence have been for television, where they are typically put into the 'classic' or 'prestige' bracket. Lawrence's short stories have been turned into one-off TV films (resembling the TV play for the day), and the novels have sometimes become mini-series (like *Lady Chatterley* directed by Ken Russell in 1993).

It's also striking that many of the adaptions of D.H. Lawrence have been influenced by the 1969 *Women In Love*. And the biopic of Lawrence, *Priest of Love*, is very much a Ken Russell-style movie.

D.H. Lawrence's novels have not so far been part of the heritage film industry. It's no surprise that many of the adaptions of Lawrence's novels have been on television (it's the same with Austen, Dickens, Hardy and Brontë), like Ken Russell's last Lawrence adaption, in 1993.

In amongst all of these D.H. Lawrence film and TV series (there are others), the United Artists *Women In Love* has been one of the most significant. It may not be Ken Russell's favourite among his films, but it's certainly had a lasting impact on how Lawrence's fiction has been adapted for the big and small screen. It's simply one of those movies anyone has to take into account if they're adapting D.H. Lawrence, and you can bet that anybody who has adapted Lawrence for the screen has seen *Women In Love*, and you can bet that if someone's seen a Lawrence adaption, it will be *Women In Love*. In short, *Women In Love* is probably *the* premier adaption of a Lawrence text.

▼

Probably the single most challenging aspect of a D.H. Lawrence adaption is the script. Get that right, and you have *so much* of your work already done (but *no* adaption has cracked the screenplay, in my opinion).

Closely followed by the *casting*. Not the casting of the grotesques and the eccentrics in a D.H. Lawrence adaption, nor the children, nor the old coots and crones (much easier to cast). I'm talking about the lead characters; that is, the Lawrencean men and the Lawrencean women – Ursula, Gudrun, Birkin and Gerald in *Women In Love*, Ursula and Skrebensky in *The Rainbow*, Mellors and Lady C in *Lady Chatterley's Lover*, Paul Morel, Clara and Miriam in *Sons and Lovers*, Kate and Cipriano in *The Plumed Serpent*, Aaron in *Aaron's Rod*, and so on. You can take your pick from the talent from the whole history of cinema, but I bet you won't find too many actors and actresses who can really pull off those lead roles and embody Lawrence's characters.

Why? Because they're practically unplayable.

And that's why I reckon *Women In Love* was among the more successful of adaptions of Lorenzo, because the casting (aside from Jennie Linden as Ursula), was spot-on, among well-known British actors of the time. And it's also one reason why *Lady Chatterley* and *The Rainbow* are so much less satisfying. (Casting *Women In Love* wasn't easy, though: Ken Russell said he and Larry Kramer saw dozens of women for the roles of Ursula and Gudrun [Bax, 171f]).

▼

I had a go at adapting D.H. Lawrence for the stage in 2006 – a version of his short story *The Horse-Dealer's Daughter*, which we put on at a theatre in London (as well as preparing it for a film adaption). Lawrence is supremely inspiring to adapt – partly because it's such an immense challenge – to reach those psychological, emotional and spiritual zones that Lawrence himself is striving for.

So I can appreciate the difficulties in adapting D.H. Lawrence's fiction for drama. For a start, you've got to have great actors who can deliver rock-solid performances, and the actors have got to be able to deliver lines which, although they're not as intricate as William Shakespeare, do need special care.

And then you try to use all the means at your disposal to explore the feelings and themes in D.H. Lawrence's text – so we had music, lighting, props, movement, etc. And the elements you'd expect in a Lawrence piece: the pre-World War One setting, the symbolism, the elevated dialogue, and of course some nudity. (I added some characters and scenes to the short story *The Horse-Dealer's Daughter*, partly because it wasn't long enough for a play). It's a challenge because you're dramatizing and visualizing feelings, philosophies, metaphysical ideas, and social and religious concepts, rather than 'characters' in 'real' situations.

On the set of Women In Love
(from an ATV documentary,
this page and over)

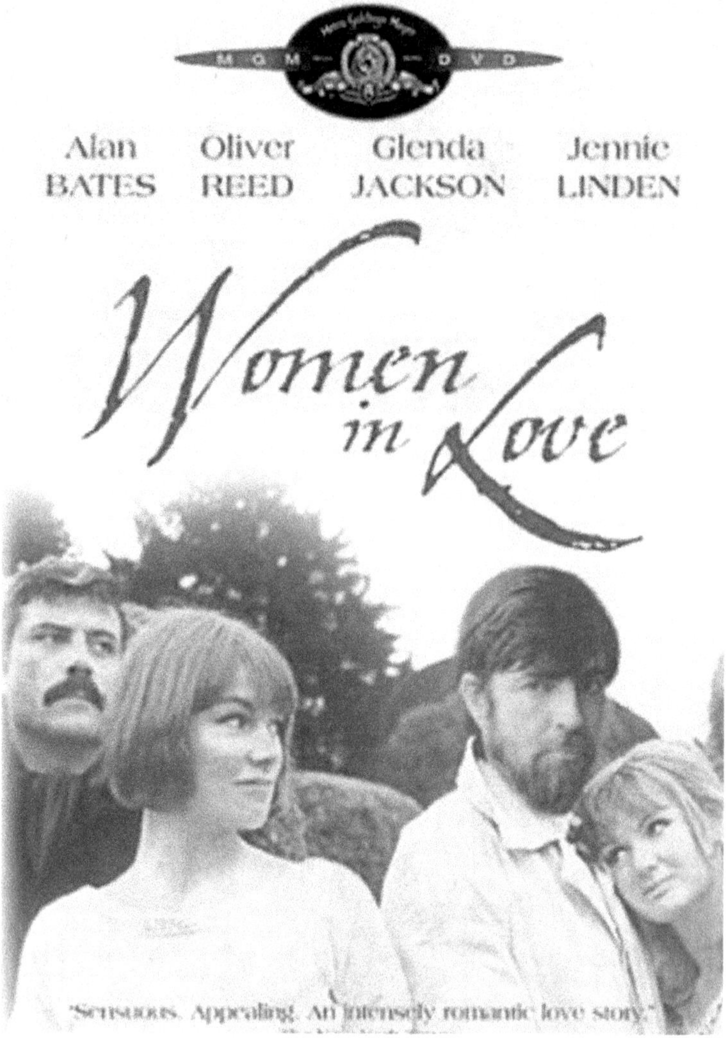

Alan **BATES**   Oliver **REED**   Glenda **JACKSON**   Jennie **LINDEN**

Women in Love

"Sensuous. Appealing. An intensely romantic love story."

The stunning match cut in Women In Love
from the dead lovers at the bottom of the lake
to Birkin and Ursula after sex.
It's a good illustration of an invisible but
vital ingredient in Ken Russell's cinema: editing.

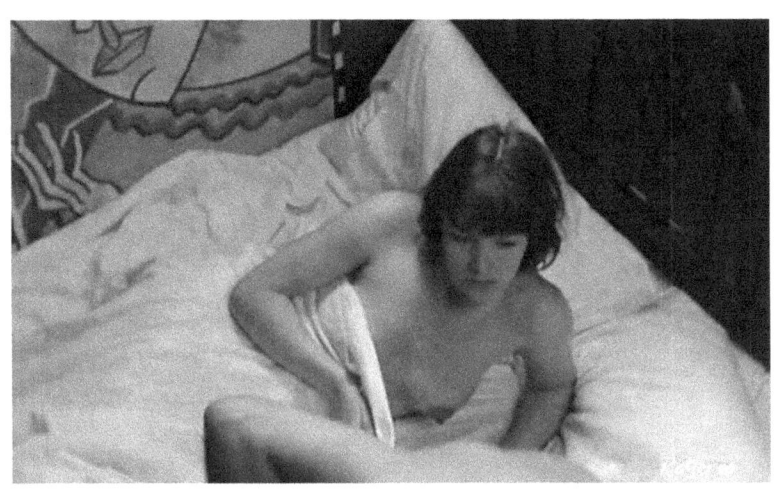

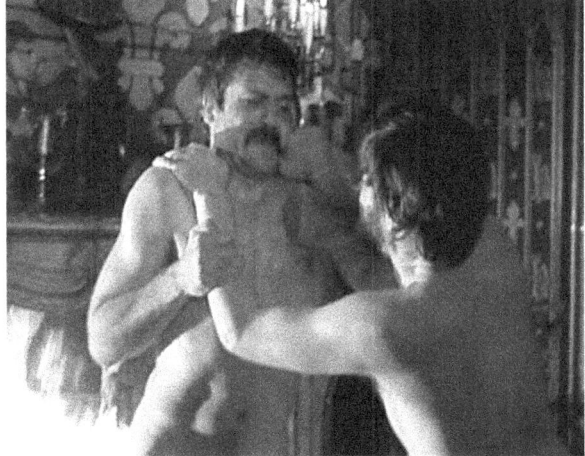
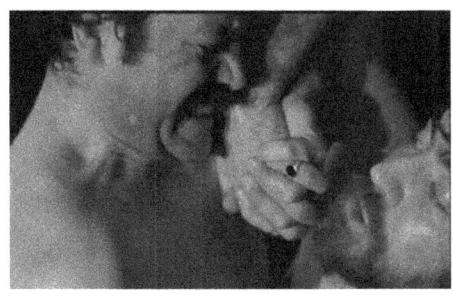

4

INTRODUCTION TO KEN RUSSELL

WHY DO I LOVE KEN RUSSELL?
For me, Ken Russell is the greatest living filmmaker in Britain. Even though he died on November 27, 2011, he's still somehow very much alive. After the death of Michael Powell in 1990, who else was there? As an image-maker, Russell is not only a total natural, he has very few peers among filmmakers – not only in Britain, but also around the globe. Russell's inventiveness seems to know no bounds, and his films are cascades of images, so much so that it can't all be taken in on the first viewing of a picture. Russell does everything a great director and a great artist should do, and then he does so much more.

Why do I love Ken Russell's movies so much? For many reasons: the spirituality, such a rare commodity in recent British cinema: Russell's films are not afraid of addressing spiritual issues. • The poetry. • The music – no other filmmaker of the same era in Britain has been such a tireless and enthusiastic promoter of music. • The dancing – no other British film director has included so much dance in their output (and *very few* directors anywhere!).[1] • The British popular culture elements. • The English landscape.[2] • The romance and romantic sensibility. • His stories of artists and creativity. • His interviews and public persona, appearing on everything from websites and YouTube to silliness like British TV's *Big Brother*. • His

---
[1] Yep, there ain't a lotta dancing in the flicks of James Cameron, Ridley Scott, Michael Bay, Jerry Bruckheimer, Wolfgang Petersen, Roland Emmerich *et al*.
[2] Ken Russell's Britain is much more *England* than it is Scotland, Ireland of Wales.

encouragement of young filmmakers and his teaching.[3]

England... Britain... Wouldn't it be wonderful if British or English movies could be made about England or Britain that were as awe-inspiring as recent Japanese movies made about Japan, like *Princess Mononoke* or *Spirited Away*? Or wild, flamboyant, enormously imaginative *animé* series such as *Fullmetal Alchemist, Escaflowne, Ghost In the Shell: Stand Alone Complex, Moribito: Guardian of the Spirit* or *Mushishi*? Instead, what do we get? Crappy heritage movies, horrible and vicious gangster movies, smug, self-satisfied rom-coms, and dull-as-shit soap operas!

Where are the great filmmakers who can make mythical, visionary works about Britain?

Ken Russell has got closer than most.

▼ Why isn't there a Ken Russell Film Festival every year? (in the New Forest or Southampton, naturally – come as your favourite Ken Russell character! Dress up as a nun or a Nazi or a hooker or a WW1 soldier or a Decadent dandy!).

▼ Why aren't the BAFTAs re-named the Russells?

▼ Why isn't the Royal Albert Hall re-dubbed the Imperial Russell Palace of Music?

▼ Why isn't there a Ken Russell radio station, playing Russell's beloved classical composers and folk songs (but without the inane blather of BBC Radio 3 and Classic FM)?

▼ Why isn't there a Ken Russell chain of cinemas, showing German Expressionist masterpieces, British naval WW2 pictures, MGM musicals and Charlie Chaplin shorts? (And why is every friggin' movie released in Britain today on a wide scale in a first-run cinema North American?).

▼

Ken Russell has been dubbed 'the *enfant terrible* of British cinema', 'the Wild Man of the BBC' and 'a fish and chips Fellini' (no, no, it' vice versa – Fellini is a 'pasta and pizza Russell'!). I've been calling him The Greatest Living

---

[3] Ken Russell has contributed to many educational courses and film courses. He has been happy to give lectures or help out with workshops. He has been a visiting tutor at Newport Film School and the University of Southampton.

British Filmmaker for ages.[4]

We all have our favourites. For me, Ken Russell's cinema ranges from the completely stupendous and spellbinding – *The Devils, Tommy, The Music Lovers, Dante's Inferno, The Debussy Film, Delius: Song of Summer, Isadora Duncan, The Dance of the Seven Veils* – to the sheer fun – *Crimes of Passion, Women In Love, Billion Dollar Brain* – to the flawed but majestic – *Lisztomania, Altered States* – to the flawed and disappointing – *The Rainbow, Lady Chatterley, Gothic, Valentino, The Lair of the White Worm* – to pieces I just find flat – *Always On Sunday* and *The Fall of the Louse of Usher*.

Part of problem of assessing the works of Ken Russell is availability and accessibility. If you mention Ken Russell, many people will have seen *Women In Love* and *Tommy* and maybe one or two other flicks, such as *The Music Lovers* or *Billion Dollar Brain*.[5] If they're older, they might have seen some of the pieces for television, including the *Monitor* programmes, and will talk fondly of *Elgar*. But that's about it.

Which's better than some filmmakers – at least many viewers will have some idea who Ken Russell is, or they will link Ken Russell to particular movies or TV shows. Most film directors don't have that kind of recognition: *very* few film directors have a high profile media image, and are recognized by the general public (even so-called 'major' film directors still get sold as 'from the director of' on the trailers and ads, rather than being referred to by name).

But beyond that, I would guess that the general viewing public (whoever the hell they are) wouldn't have seen or know much about Ken Russell's many, many other projects.

And that is in Britain. Outside of the green, sceptred isle, Ken Russell's star will fade rapidly, I would imagine. For instance, he would be known in parts of the United States of America, and in France (where they love movies

---

[4] One of the only other people to agree with me is critic Mark Kermode: 'Russell is Britain's greatest living director', Kermode asserted in *Hatchet Job* (34).
[5] But they likely won't realize that *Billion Dollar Brain* was directed by Russell.

and filmmakers more than anyone), but not much beyond that. However, many more movies directed by Russell are available in the U.S.A. – not least because he directed most of his movies for North American producers and studios.[6]

Carl Theodore Dreyer, Ingmar Bergman, Andrei Tarkovsky, Rainer Werner Fassbinder, Luis Buñuel – these are European filmmakers revered by the film *cognoscenti*, but Ken Russell's name would not be placed among that company by many film critics. As Russell himself remarked, if he'd been called 'Russellini' he might be more accepted in movie circles.[7] (But no, folks, it's the *other way around*: Federico Fellini is 'the Italian Ken Russell'!).[8]

In a way, it doesn't matter... but it does if you've evaluating cinema and a particular filmmaker. There are whole books, for instance, on filmmakers who have only made three or four movies! Quentin Tarantino, Peter Jackson, Steven Soderbergh, Terry Malick, etc. By comparison with them, Russell is a major filmmaker with an incredible body of work.

Yet to fully appreciate Ken Russell's cinema, you need to have seen films such as *The Devils* and *Savage Messiah* and *Mahler* and *Delius: Song of Summer* and *Crimes of Passion* and *The Rainbow* and so on. You also need to have caught a good proportion of Russell's TV work. Russell's output is truly staggering and mind-boggling: in television and cinema, he has produced a huge number of pieces.

For instance, if you think that Ken Russell turns out brash, vulgar, self-consciously excessive and dumb movies, you must see *Delius: Song of Summer* or *Savage Messiah* or *Prisoner of Honor*. The problem is, only a handful of Russell movies are broadcast on TV, and most of Russell's TV programmes have hardly been seen at all

---

[6] However, filmmakers with an encyclopedic understanding of cinema, such as Martin Scorsese, wrongly believed that more of Russell's BBC work was available in Britain than the U.S.A.
[7] Sometimes Russell is 'Russellini', often he's 'Russellstein' (Eisenstein) and 'Russellelles' (Welles), and sometimes he's 'Russell-lin' (Chaplin).
[8] M. Kermode, 2013, 34.

since their original air date.[9]

It's true that most TV shows aren't usually repeated anyway.[10] Some are, but it's a tiny proportion of the whole output of television – even of a small country like Britain. It's also true that TV shows are very rarely exported. So viewers in Argentina, say, or South Africa, will probably never have seen a TV show directed by Ken Russell. Similarly, most theatrical films are *not* shown outside of their country of origin. A Jean-Luc Godard movie or an Ingmar Bergman movie might travel to other European countries, or to the U.S.A., but only because they are well-known filmmakers with a very high critical standing. But most movies made in, say, Poland, will only ever be seen in Poland, and only ever on Polish TV (if they are lucky enough to be broadcast at all. Many movies are made but never shown anywhere).

So a full appreciation of an important filmmaker such as Ken Russell cannot take place unless viewers have seen most of his major works. I discovered this when recently writing books on Jean-Luc Godard and Walerian Borowczyk.[11]

With Ken Russell, you'd think that, in Britain at least, his films would be readily available. Many are, but many are not. There are numerous reasons for this – to do with money and sales, obviously – but also legal issues, who owns what, etc. It's probably true that if Warners or MGM or United Artists or the BBC or whoever found out that a Ken Russell movie might sell 30 million units on DVD, it would be in Wal-Mart or Tesco's this afternoon.

Some filmmakers never produce audio commentaries

---

[9] The BBC's newer cable channel, BBC Four, has re-broadcast some of the early Russell works.

[10] One aspect of television that Ken Russell liked was that shows were repeated, whereas movies were released, did the rounds of the theatres, then disappeared. Sometimes they might pop up on TV. As he remarked in 1973: 'if I could feel that films I did for television were shown all over the world at frequent intervals I'd probably never make a so-called feature film again' (Bax, 138). Those views were expressed before home video and DVD, which Russell embraced, and before the rise of the internet, which Russell also embraced wholeheartedly.

[11] Andrei Tarkovsky was easy – he only directed seven feature films, all of which are available. But many of the movies of Godard and Borowczyk (including key works) are *not* available, not on video or DVD. The advent of video, and later DVD, has certainly made many works obtainable, but even then often only in particular territories or in sub-standard versions.

to DVD versions of their movies, and one wishes they would: Woody Allen, Ingmar Bergman and Steven Spielberg, for example, are some filmmakers I really wish would provide commentaries. Happily, Ken Russell does, and I highly recommend buying the DVD versions of his films for the commentaries alone. Russell is a wonderful commentator on his own movies, offering all sorts of priceless stories and snippets about the productions.[12]

The American DVD release of some of Ken Russell's 1960s BBC films (*Ken Russell At the BBC*) is absolutely indispensable (it's the period of *Women In Love*): the box set includes *The Debussy Film, Isadora Duncan, Dante's Inferno* and *Delius: Song of Summer*. If you haven't seen some of these masterpieces, get this box of DVDs. You won't believe your eyes.

I have been amazed many times in writing this book about Ken Russell's cinema. He's astonishing, as we all know, but until only recently have I realized just *how* astonishing. *Delius: Song of Summer* has been available for some time, and it's one of Russell's finest works. But I hadn't seen three of the 1960s TV films, *The Debussy Film, Isadora Duncan* and *Dante's Inferno,* before (collected on the BBC Video DVD).

OMG, this man is a genius! I simply can't believe how Ken Russell achieved it all. The level of imagination and flair is just astounding. Russell proves for all to see that with a group of dedicated actors and film crew, a masterpiece can be attained on a tiny budget (and you need a ton of ideas, a strong screenplay and lots of food – plus a tipple or two).

▼

Ken Russell has never been establishment as a film director like, say, Alfred Hitchcock, David Lean, Carol Reed or Michael Powell, some of the film directors continually wheeled out as the best of British talent. However, one of Russell's films made it into the Top 100 British movies collated by the British Film Institute in 1999 (guess which one? Yeah, *Women in Love*. Let's ignore the

---

[12] On the internet, the Savage Messiah site is a good place to start: iainfisher.com/ Russell.

fact that the studio was North American (United Artists), that the money was American, that the co-writer and producer and originator of the project (Larry Kramer) was also American).

But, as this book insists, Ken Russell as a filmmaker is every bit as fascinating, as talented, as stylish, or as crazy as Hitch, Lean, Reed or Powell & Pressburger. And his pictures are just as extraordinary.

▼

Quite a few film critics as well as film fans criticize Ken Russell's later work in the light of his earlier work. It's unfair, but it's difficult not to do it. Thus, *Mindbender* or *Dogboys* will be compared with *The Devils* or *Tommy*. It's unfair because the context and conditions of each project are different: the production of, say, *Altered States*, was pretty tough, and *Women in Love*, for instance, was produced in a different cultural as well as cinematic context from, say, *Prisoner of Honor* or *The Fall of the Louse of Usher*.

And we should always remember that it's *extremely difficult* to make films as good as the finest of Ken Russell's movies – *The Devils, Tommy,* or *The Music Lovers.* To demonstrate that, you could have a go yourself. Assuming you can raise the finance for a movie about nuns and priests in Loudun or a classical composer, you'd have to tackle by far the toughest task on any movie: developing a script that did everything you wanted to do (also within a particular budget, also satisfying your backers, also something filmable).

Which's why some movies – including the best of Ken Russell – seem miraculous. How did they get the money and resources and actors to produce *The Devils*?! Or other filmmakers' work, like *The Wind Rises*?! Or *Chimes At Midnight*?! It's completely remarkable.

The best movies seem as if they have always already existed. As if they came from nowhere but should always have been there. As if you have always known them, to the point where you seem a part of them (almost as if you had made them yourself).

But not every movie can be that miraculous (if only!).

And so not every Ken Russell picture can be *Savage Messiah* or *Mahler* or *Delius*.

The vitriol that Ken Russell has personally attracted from critics is striking, as if he's become the whipping boy for whatever is pissing off the critics. But a large number of 'major' film directors have produced turkeys.

Recent duds include:

Steven Spielberg, *Tin-Tin* (some would add *Hook* and *1941*)

Ridley Scott, *Hannibal, Kingdom of Heaven, G.I. Jane, Black Hawk Down*

Sam Raimi, *Spider-man 3*

Peter Greenaway, *8 1/2 Women*

Peter Jackson, *The Hobbit, King Kong, The Frighteners*

Alan Parker, *Evita*

Brian de Palma, *The Bonfire of the Vanities, Snake Eyes, Mission To Mars*

Terry Gilliam, *The Brothers Grimm, Fear and Loathing In Las Vegas*

Quentin Tarantino, *Kill Bill*

Paul Thomas Anderson, *Punch-Drunk Love*

(Of course, one wouldn't class Jackson, Raimi, de Palma, Parker, Tarantino, etc, as 'major' film directors).

And how about these disasters? –

The Lion, the Witch and The Wardrobe (cost: $180m), *Prince Caspian* (cost: $200m), *Voyage of the Dawn Treader, Spider-man 3* (cost: $300 million), *Home On the Range* (cost $110 million), *Snow White and the Huntsman* (cost: $170 million!), the *Bourne* series, *Quantum of Solace, Casino Royale, The Hunger Games, Batman Begins, The Beach, 8MM, Alien vs. Predator, Chocolat, The Da Vinci Code, Speed 2, Lolita, Vanilla Sky, Amélie, About a Boy, Billy Elliot, The Hulk, Oceans 11*, the *Charlie's Angels* movies, *Unbreakable, Jungle Book 2, Lemony Snicket, Sin City, Lara Croft, King Arthur, The Village, X-Men Origins: Wolverine*, the *Bridget Jones* films and *Where the Wild Things Are*.

So, sure, Ken Russell has directed some financial flops, and some very disappointing pictures, but many of the flops I've noted above (there are *plenty* more!) are shockingly inept and misconceived (and *very* expensive): *Snow White and the Huntsman,* a travesty of a movie... *Casino Royale,* the 2006 *James Bond* re-boot which had the sophisticated, world-weary super-spy acting like a ditzy, love-sick teenager... *Where the Wild Things Are,* Universal's cretinous movie-as-psychotherapy, offensive on every possible level... *Alien vs. Predator,* a shocking devaluation of a once-entertaining horror franchise... *The Hulk,* simply awful and woefully misjudged (despite the high-calibre talent involved)... *X-Men Origins: Wolverine,* a deeply disturbing cesspit of a movie... and *Chocolat,* a gruelling two hours of insipid shit.[13]

Some of those movies are truly abysmal (some are even offensively bad, with their insidious pro-military, pro-war, pro-American ideology). And the sum total of the budgets and P & A and marketing of just this handful of turkeys amounts to – $4 billion? $5 billion? $10 billion? (Just *one* of those crappy movies would've paid for *all* of Ken Russell's unmade projects! Ack!).

▼

In one respect Ken Russell is far ahead of the critics, and that is in the realm of music. No *major* film critic, alive or dead, has the anything like the knowledge that Russell has about music. Thus, they simply *can't* assess the depictions of music and composers accurately. (Music critics, tho', have taken Russell to task for his representations of composers and music, particularly, of course, the assassinations. But even they would also have to (grudgingly) admit that Russell contributed towards the dissemination of classical music in popular culture).

▼

I have refrained from quoting too many critics who dislike Ken Russell's cinema: you know who they are, and you know what they've written. There's no point really in bringing those complaints and attacks back to life. Russell's films polarize people as few other British filmmakers' works do. It does seem that people either love his movies or hate 'em.

---

[13] Despite starring two gorgeous actors, Johnny Depp and Juliette Binoche.

Besides, Ken Russell himself has found the sheer number of critics who have come out against him daunting and upsetting. In his review of Joseph Lanza's 2008 study of himself, Russell said that when Lanza piles up so many negative reviews, it has the effect of depressing the hell out of the director. And Russell wondered if the sheer number of bad reviews might influence the undiscerning reader.[14]

I'm reminded of England's greatest painter, J.M.W. Turner. *Every* major art critic of the day came out against Turner's art: William Hazlitt, John Taylor, James Boaden, Richard Westmacott, William Thackeray, Leigh Hunt, *The Times, The Athenaeum, Tatler,* etc. It deeply distressed the painter (though he was a tough character, a working class Cockney).

But all of the critics of Joseph William Mallord Turner were *wrong. WRONG.* And no one remembers what Hazlitt or Thackeray said (except the animosity between, say, James Whistler and Turner). But no one can forget Turner's extraordinary paintings. I've been to exhibitions in New York City of Turner's art which have been packed with punters, and lectures on Turner which fill a giant auditorium at the Met.

J.M.W. Turner's art lives on... But the critics fade into *utter oblivion.*

---

[14] Ken Russell stated in the London *Times* in 2008: 'But because Lanza feels compelled to reprint the worst of every bad review my films have received as a coda to each chapter, I can only surmise that I'm damned on every page. It has taken some nerve for me just to keep reading. More than once the temptation to retire to bed with the covers over my head reared up like a phantom holiday in the park. Did I do that? Did I say that? And more to the point, did they say that?'

5

KEN RUSSELL: ENGLAND'S GREAT VISIONARY FILMMAKER

> We do live on a magic island, without doubt, but so far as British films are concerned there is precious little evidence of this. By and large, contemporary filmmakers seem to revel in squalor, glorify ignorance and extol violence. There is another kind of life outside of this which many people in this country would like to celebrate, if only they were given the opportunity and not made to feel guilty about it. It has nothing to do with religion; it is to do with the spirit of the land in which we live, that elusive quality touched on by the music of VW (Vaughan Williams) and his contemporaries such as Arnold Bax, Frank Bridge and John Ireland: music expressing the majesty of nature, forgotten rituals, pagan goddesses and ancient heroes.
>
> Ken Russell, *A British Picture* (238-8)

ENGLAND'S GREATEST LIVING FILMMAKER.

Ken Russell is England's greatest living filmmaker; I've been saying this for years, and even now he's staging musicals featuring angels and great artists on heavenly clouds,[15] it's still true. Russell seemed to have always been around.

After the deaths of Michael Powell and David Lean, Ken Russell was The Man.

Who else was there? Oh, yes, there are many other British film directors who have become more successful, commercially, than Ken Russell: Ridley Scott, Tony Scott,

---
[15] Nothing's changed there then! – Ken Russell would be right at home in heaven (chatting with his favourite classical composers, for instance) – but he'd probably ask for a transfer to somewhere hotter and wilder!

Alan Parker, Adrian Lyne, Mike Newell, *et al*. And there are the 'important' or 'serious' Brit filmmakers, like Mike Leigh or Ken Loach or Alan Clarke. And the mavericks, like Peter Greenaway and Derek Jarman.

It's true that filmmakers like the Scotts, the Parkers, the Hudsons and the Lynes can make big, glossy movies with tons of action and pretty people and all, and it's true that I love many of the films of the above film directors...

...But there's something about Ken Russell's films that makes him, ultimately, a more fascinating filmmaker than pretty much *all* other British filmmakers of recent times. It's do with, I think, the subjects that he's chosen and how his movies seem to be reaching for something. Often they don't reach it; often they don't deliver on their promise or their goals. That happened more with the later pieces... But the group of movies that Ken Russell produced from the late 1960s to the end of the 1970s are remarkable on so many levels (with *Women In Love* in the middle). Part of it is to do with the sheer *joy* of making cinema, which the films of that period are full of. And then there is the enormous *ambition* of those subjects (even more extraordinary bearing in mind that these works were mainly made for low budgets). And there's the way that Russell tackled those subjects and themes and stories. Visually, they are stunning. The muse of music has no superior in British cinema. And there are some outstanding performances.[16] It's all quite remarkable.

Henry Kenneth Alfred Russell was born in Southampton in Southern England on July 3, 1927;[17] he grew up in Southampton. He died in Lymington, Hampshire, on November 27, 2011. As well as being associated with Southern England, where he lived (in the New Forest), and where many of his movies have been filmed (all along the South Coast), and with London and the Home Counties

---

[16] For a film director often derided for emphasizing visuals and spectacle too much (unfairly and mistakenly, I think), Russell managed to provide the creative context on set for numerous great performances in his movies.

[17] Ken Russell is of the generation of Stanley Kubrick (b. 1928), Jean-Luc Godard (b. 1930), Bryan Forbes (b. 1926), Kenneth Anger (b. 1927), Andrzej Wajda (b. 1927) and Andy Warhol (b. 1928).

(where Britain's film production is centred), Russell also has strong links to the Lake District in Northern England.[18]

Ken Russell studied at Pangbourne, as a cadet at the Royal Naval College, from 1941; and later at Walthamstow (the Technical College and School of Art, where he met Shirley Kingdon, his first wife). He spent time in the Merchant Navy[19] and the Royal Air Force. He worked in an art gallery (Lefèvre Art Gallery) in Bond Street, London. In the 1950s, he was a stills photographer, for magazines such as *Picture Post* and *Illustrated*. He became fascinated by ballet, and studied evenings in Hampstead, at the International Ballet School.[20] He toured with dance companies (both photography and choreography would feature prominently in his movies).[21] By the late 1950s, Russell was working for the BBC, making arts documentaries (the first was in 1959 – having impressed the BBC with his homemade movies).

Ken Russell was married four times – to Shirley Kingdon (married between 1956-78), Vivian Jolly (1983-91),[22] Hetty Baynes (1992-99) and Elize Tribble (2001-2011). Jolly, Russell's second wife, was a film student and assistant on *Savage Messiah*. Russell met his fourth wife, actress Baynes, when he was casting a *South Bank Show* documentary. Russell met his fourth wife Tribble when she answered a lonely hearts ad he placed in *The Times*: 'Unbankable film director Ken Russell seeks soul mate – mad about movies, music, and Moët and Chandon champagne'.

Every biography, autobiography, interview and study of Ken Russell agrees that in his youth movies played a huge role. Russell consumed thousands and thousands of

---

[18] For many years Russell had a place in the New Forest, and also a bungalow near the ocean. A fire in recent years burnt up numerous belongings. Russell has also lived in his beloved Lake District, and in London.
[19] He left the Navy, according to Joseph Gomez, due to a nervous breakdown (1976, 18).
[20] Russell acknowledged that he wasn't the greatest of dancers, and dancers were some of his (many) heroes.
[21] Ken Russell has written at length in his autobiographies and interviews of his time in the Merchant Navy, his tours with dance companies, and his early attempts at amateur filmmaking.
[22] Anthony Perkins officiated at Russell's wedding to Vivian Jolly – the ceremony took place on the *Queen Mary*, included extracts from Thomas Hardy and William Wordsworth, and doubled as a wrap party for *Crimes of Passion*.

movies in his childhood. He has cited so many cinematic influences, so many film icons he worshipped, so many movies he saw, some repeatedly: William Boyd Westerns... *The Fleet's Inn* ('drooling over Dorothy Lamour' a dozen times)... Betty Grable in *Springtime In the Rockies* ('lots of Grable musicals')... giant, German Expressionist epics like *Metropolis* and *Die Niebelungen* and of course the crazy, abstract *Cabinet of Dr Caligari*... Andy Clyde, Old Mother Reilly... *The Secret of the Loch*... *Citizen Kane*... Mickey Mouse... Charlie Chaplin... Felix the Cat... Snub Pollard... Betty Boop... *Of Mice and Men*... *The Westerner*... and 'almost every Warner Brothers film'...

Going to the movies was not just every week, but several times a week for Ken Russell (often with his mom or aunts or relatives). Sometimes 2 or 3 times a day. As he recalled: even when he was stationed out of town in the military, he 'still managed to see almost every film released in the early Forties', and sometimes would bicycle 30 miles to Salisbury to catch a movie (which gives an idea of his passion for cinema, which never left him).

CLASSIC RUSSELL.

The two periods of 'classic' Ken Russell work would be the TV documentaries of the early-to-late 1960s (with 1962's *Elgar* as the highpoint that everyone remembers), and the feature films of the late 1960s to late 1970s (with *Women in Love* and *Tommy* being the high watermarks among audiences if not critics).

Certainly, it's with *Women in Love*[23] that Ken Russell begins that extraordinary run of feature-length movies: *Women In Love* thus helped Russell's career enormously: *Women in Love* was followed by *The Music Lovers* (his favourite movie), which was followed by *The Devils*, which was followed by *The Boy Friend*, which was followed by *Savage Messiah*, which was followed by *Mahler*, which was followed by *Tommy*, which was

---
[23] D.H. Lawrence himself had not been opposed to the idea of making *Women in Love* into a movie, when it was suggested back in the 1920s.

followed by *Lisztomania*. That's a run of eight amazing movies. You could add *Valentino* and *Altered States* (many wouldn't).

'OUTRAGEOUS', 'VULGAR', 'ENFANT TERRIBLE'.

Over the course of his film career, Ken Russell has been asked the same questions again and again. Like Alfred Hitchcock or Charlie Chaplin, Russell is one of the very few film directors that the general public might have heard of and who also has a recognizable media persona. As he put it in *A British Picture*:

> Am I difficult to work with? Do I hate actors? Am I a misogynist? Do I set out to shock just for the sake of it? Do I distort facts? Does it bother me that many of my films are flops? Is it true that I never go to the cinema? What does it feel like to be the oldest *enfant terrible* in the business? (BP, 161)

In short, people – film critics too, who should know better – believe and endorse the legend (and Ken Russell, like Orson Welles or Werner Herzog or Michael Powell, certainly helps along the legend with his anecdotes and chat show stories).[24] But maybe he recounts those stories because it's expected of him, and it's what people want, and it's easier than sitting in silence.

Ken Russell was known as an 'outrageous' filmmaker, delighting in 'shock' tactics – as Joe Gomez succinctly put it in his excellent mid-1970s study of Russellini: 'his films are outstanding examples of the 'kick 'em in the crotch' school of overstatement' (1976, 70) – including extremes of sex,[25] temperament, behaviour and violence;[26] his style employed flamboyant camerawork, rapid cutting, anti-naturalism, and extravagance; he preferred out-size acting,

---

[24] Ken Russell is the film director as 'Mr De Thrill', the director in *The Boy Friend*.
[25] Glenda Jackson defended the depiction of sex in a Ken Russell movie: it wasn't exploitative, she affirmed, it was part of the characters and the drama. And eroticism is so personal anyway.
[26] Later filmmakers, such as Peter Greenaway or Derek Jarman, were sometimes dubbed 'controversial' by the media. But how tame the works of Greenaway and Jarman appear beside those of Ken Russell!

often camp[27] and self-mocking; his themes were art, sex, death and the individual (usually the artist) in society; his films seemed to be apolitical, far more interested in depicting the many strands of an artist's life than social comment or ideology. If Russell had any political views, they were formed in the middle of the 20th century (Existentialism, bohemia, the artist as rebel, psycho-analysis, and a profound 18-19th century Romanticism), and rounded off by the hippy ideals of the 1960s. Russell's one overriding theme or driving philosophy was Romanticism, and the myth of the Romantic artist informed most of his work (meaning Romanticism in the 18th and 19th centuries, with its tenets of infinity, going to extremes, the sublime, subjectivity, emotionalism, ecstasy, paganism, mythology, poetry and art, mysticism and spirituality, unity, idealism, the individual over/ against society, and so on). 'He's a very romantic man', Glenda Jackson said (1972).

The psychology that Ken Russell employs in his cinema is of the Freudian school, as if Russell picked up a book on Sigmund Freud in the 1950s, and applied it to everything he did after that. Russell's philosophy and approach is very much of the mid-20th century, of the 1940s and the 1950s, *not* the 1960s (he was 33 when the Sixties began). That is the mid-20th century of Existential philosophy (with its emphasis on outsiderness, alienation and the individual), the Parisian *avant garde,* Surrealism, psychoanalysis, the American Beat Generation, jazz and early rock 'n' roll (tho' classical music has always been Uncle Ken's rock music). Over that all, World War Two dominates.

Ken Russell's films were just as often set in rural landscapes, including the wild reaches of Cumbria, as in towns and cities; his pictures were not London or Home Counties-biased, like so much of British cinema; Russell's cinema enshrined the myth and dream of England/ Britain, like the work of Derek Jarman, John Boorman and Michael

---
27 Ken Russell is so camp he out-camps many gay filmmakers, as Raymond Murray pointed out in his guide to gay and lesbian cinema. Critics have noticed that homosexuality is sometimes sent up or denounced in Russell's cinema. This campest and gayest of heterosexual filmmakers often portrays homosexuality negatively.

Powell, a place rich in history, poetry, art and culture.

What is a filmmaker, in the realm of commercial, entertainment cinema? A storyteller. *A filmmaker is a storyteller* (among many other things). And I guess I like the stories that Ken Russell tells, and I like most of his characters. It ain't the same with many contemporary filmmakers – I don't like (or want) their stories or their characters.

Yes, the *way* that Ken Russell tells his stories and presents his characters is wild, unusual, flamboyant, colourful – and sometimes crude and hysterical. But I still much prefer his stories and characters to so many of contemporary Western cinema's stories and characters. Who cares about violent gangsters and drug dealers and the banal, stupid, smug, arrogant, vain white heroes and heroines of so many contemporary Hollywood or British movies? Not I.

Anti-Russell critics are many; some critics just can't get on with Ken Russell's form of cinema. British critics especially don't seem to know what to make of him. David Shipman said in *The Story of Cinema* that while Russell is 'capable of spectacular and *outré* images on the screen... he has no gift for character, situation, pacing, rhythm, tension or tone' (1130).

That is *junk*!

Critics saw Russell's cinema as self-indulgent, excessive, pretentious, boorish, coarse, and simplistic. D.H. Lawrence's champion, the (over-rated but influential) critic F.R. Leavis, hated Russell's interpretation of Lawrence (*Women in Love*), calling it an outrage and 'an obscene undertaking'. Russell's movies are not what critics expect, or want: and they don't offer a pretext for the things that critics like to write about. As Jack Fisher put it, 'the critics, confronted with work which doesn't stimulate what they are prepared to say, flounder and react negatively'.[28]

'The cult of Ken Russell really depends on an act of faith, a willingness to believe in the master's integrity in what he does,' remarked Peter Webb in *The Erotic Arts* (290). That applies to virtually any artist. You have to go

---
28 J. Fisher, in T. Atkins, 40.

along with what they're doing. Otherwise there's no exchange at all.

Asked about the notion of being 'indulgent' in movies, a critique often hurled at Ken Russell, the filmmaker replied:

> Films are hard to make and I think the word indulge really leads one to believe that it's an easy sort of business and it's really extremely difficult. You'll be standing out there in the rain thinking that it's not an easy job being a film director. But the director is the director and if he feels for whatever reason, perhaps under great delusion, that he wants that scene and he can get away with it even though it might be questionable in terms of taste then he should be allowed to do it. It's his movie. But if the committee steps in and says you can't do that because we're going to cut it out then it's a waste of time.

Excessive? Well, *duh*, of course Ken Russell's cinema can be excessive. As Michael Gallagher pointed out, in reference to *The Devils* and *Lisztomania* (in the *Catholic Film Newsletter* of all places), 'to accuse Russell of excess when he is working in this area, however, is very much like accusing Rubens of sensuality'.[29] Yes – being excessive is what Russell does for a living.

Huw Wheldon on Ken Russell:

> Ken needs a strong producer or a strong script-writer, or both, because without them his own powers of invention and imagination are so enormous that he's like a bird being driven along on a huge gale. It was this gale that made him such a marvellous colleague. Most of my colleagues in those days were drivers but Ken was like a team of stallions. He had a leaping imagination and, as frequently happens with people of this kind, great tenacity and determination. He would go through a stone wall to get the proper location. If it's necessary to be on the 54th floor then you go to the 54th floor, and *certainly* you walk up the stairs. (Bax, 123)

Entertainment came first in movie-making for Ken Russell: 'to entertain first, and the preaching comes second. Most of my films are based on that premise'. Russell said that he made his films for himself, and hoped that someone else was entertained (RC, 247).

---
29 Quoted in PF, 7.

There are times when you're watching a Ken Russell work and you think, oh crap, he's not going to do *that*! And he does. Yep, Russell delights in delivering some really simplistic symbolism or gestures, stuff that a fifth grader or 14 year-old kid getting hold of a video camera might think was really cool.

◆

Ken Russell's public persona was also larger-than-life, and often threatened to undermine the attention given to his movies. He had run-ins with censors and film critics (famously attacking Alexander Walker with a newspaper on television in 1971 on the late night discussion programme *24 Hours*); he was a regular (and entertaining) guest on TV chat shows and documentaries (talking about Oliver Reed, for instance, or Keith Moon, or the current state of the British film industry). He was on TV and radio and in print so often his stories, such as one about how the naked wrestling scene in *Women in Love* was shot, became very familiar (Russell has discussed that scene so many times, it would make a movie longer than ten *Women In Loves*). He often appeared in his films (*Lady Chatterley, Whore, Gothic, Valentino, Tommy*, and so on), and presented TV documentaries (part of Russell's personality is definitely the frustrated actor).

Approaching someone from the outside as a subject for a movie, from the media, from books and magazines and newspapers, would all be lies, Ken Russell asserted: he didn't want the everyday facts about someone, what time they woke up, but the spirit of their work: 'the spirit of music, the spirit of Mahler, the spirit of D.H. Lawrence, that's what I'm into. That's the truth, the artistic truth' (RC, 245).

No one had really got to grips with the real Ken Russell, the director complained: 'nobody knows the real me and I've never seen the real me written about' (RC, 245).

His reputation as the Bad Boy of British Cinema, a rebel, an iconoclast, etc, was ill-founded, said Ken Russell. In person, he said he was quite mild-mannered and shy, which disappointed and upset people when they met him

(BP, 156). That Russell is shy and quiet is attested by numerous colleagues: Huw Wheldon recalled that when he met Russell in the late 1950s, he was 'shy and quiet… A little watchful, but silent and extremely modest' (in PF, 36). The abrasive Russell emerged after he left the Beeb, Wheldon remarked: but although 'singularly quiet, gentle and modest', Russell was also very confident from the beginning, knew what he wanted, and would walk through walls to get it (Bax, 121). Of course: only someone with incredible drive, energy and ambition could've produced that huge amount of work. You don't make movies and TV shows by sitting on your ass at home complaining that nobody returns your calls or reads your scripts! Russell is the classic filmmaker as self-taught artist, where the philosophy is: *fuck it, let's grab a camera and go do it already!*

The more flamboyant, dandy and outspoken aspects of Ken Russell's media persona developed in the late 1960s. Before that, Russell was often seen as introvert: as his stature increased with the successes of *Women in Love* and *The Music Lovers,* the familiar Ken Russell – camp, loud, OTT – came to the fore in media appearances.

As well as shy and reserved, Ken Russell has also been described as temperamental and mercurial, occasionally given to outbursts of anger on set. But also very generous, and a lot of fun – there can be a lot of laughs on a Russell set.

John Baxter described Ken Russell in the familiar terms of an emotional, volatile personality: those whom he discovers to be enemies are resented, but loyalty and friendship and devotion are rewarded – with loyalty, friendship and devotion (Bax, 124).

Despite occasionally falling out with some people on his crews, and one or two actors, and the odd writer or producer, during the most successful times of his career, Ken Russell had plenty of people eager to work on his movies. There was a regular bunch of filmmakers and actors, for instance, who would turn up to work on each subsequent production. If a Ken Russell movie really was a tough experience, with the director being overly demanding and given to prima donna outbursts, and the hours long, and the pay low (and the food terrible), many performers and crew wouldn't come back. But they did.

One thing was sure with a Ken Russell movie: you got to do stuff, in front of or behind the camera, that you hardly did anywhere else. (There are things that actors have done on a Russell movie/ TV show that they will only have done that once: running along a field waving the Czech flag while naked, dressing up as a combination of Wagner, Hitler and a storm-trooper and mowing down Jews in the street with a machine gun, and of course wrestling in the nude!).

THE FILM CAREER.

Writing this book, I am struck again and again by the sheer amount of work that Ken Russell has produced, by the quality of it, by the breadth of subjects in it, by the number of genres he has tackled, and by the torrent of images he has created. 'Putting pictures to music has always been a pleasure,' Russell wrote, 'like being paid to screw your favourite film star' (BP, 268-9).

Simply to consider Ken Russell's television work would require a hefty book in itself. Russell is probably always thought of a film director first, but he has actually produced many more TV shows than feature films.

In 2000, Ken Russell (aged 73) ventured into the world of very low budget filmmaking, a return to home movies, based in his New Forest home, edited on computers, with friends and helpers working for next-to-nothing (Russell embarked on an ambitious interpretation of *The Fall of the House of Usher*, and hoped to sell his movies on the internet). Other short films of the 2000s included *A Kitten for Hitler* (2007), *Hot Pants* (2006) and *Boudicca Bites Back* (2009). *Hot Pants* comprised 'three sexy shorts': *Revenge of the Elephant Man* (2004), *The Mystery of Mata Hari* (2004) and *The Good Ship Venus* (2005). That Russell couldn't obtain backing for his later projects was awful, Glenda Jackson complained after his death, for a filmmaker with his incredible talent and body of work.

The 23 feature films directed by Ken Russell and

released theatrically (with *Women In Love* his third feature release) are:

French Dressing
Billion Dollar Brain
Women In Love
The Music Lovers
The Devils
The Boy Friend
Savage Messiah
Mahler
Tommy
Lisztomania
Valentino
Altered States
Crimes of Passion
Gothic
Aria (segment)
Salome's Last Dance
The Lair of the White Worm
The Rainbow
Whore
Mindbender
Lion's Mouth
The Fall of the Louse of Usher
Hot Pants

The films directed for television include:

Isadora Duncan
Dante's Inferno
The Debussy Film
Delius: Song of Summer
The Dance of the Seven Veils
Clouds of Glory
The Planets
A British Picture
Road to Mandalay
The Strange Affliction of Anton Bruckner
The Insatiable Mrs Kirsch (from *Tales of Erotica*)

The Mystery of Dr Martinu
The Secret Life of Arnold Bax
Prisoner of Honor
Lady Chatterley
Ken Russell's Treasure Island
Alice in Russialand
Classic Widows
In Search of the English Folk Song
Dogboys
Elgar: Fantasy of a Composer On a Bicycle
Brighton Belles

Ken Russell favoured films about classical composers (Tchaikovsky, Mahler, Strauss, Prokofiev, Debussy, Delius, Elgar, Liszt, Sir Arnold Bax, Bruckner), and artists (Gaudier-Brzeska, Byron, Shelley, Wordsworth, Coleridge, Rossetti, Valentino),[30] and literary adaptions and allusions (D.H. Lawrence, Lord Byron, Percy Bysshe Shelley, Oscar Wilde, Dr Polidori, Aldous Huxley, H.S. Ede, Bram Stoker, Edgar Allan Poe and Len Deighton). Most of Russell's films have been based on novels or biographies[31] (as with many film directors, including the greats): *The Music Lovers, Savage Messiah, The Lair of the White Worm, Valentino, The Rainbow, Women in Love* and *Lady Chatterley*. Plays have also been favoured by Russell: *Whore, Salomé's Last Dance, The Devils, The Boy Friend,* and the musical *Tommy*. Ken Russell filmed three D.H. Lawrence novels (*Women in Love, The Rainbow* and *Lady Chatterley's Lover*) – something, I think, no other director has done.

The most celebrated of Ken Russell's early films, made for the BBC (where his mentor was Huw Wheldon), were about classical composers (Edward Elgar, Claude Debussy, Sergei Prokofiev, Béla Bartók, Richard Strauss, Frederick Delius). He also directed films about Antonio Gaudi, James Lloyd, Dante Gabriel Rossetti, Lotte Lenya, Isadora Duncan, Marie Rambert, Shelagh Delaney, Gordon Jacob, and painters Robert McBryde and Robert Coquhoun.

---

30 Ken Russell said he might like and revere artists, but he also recognized that they were people too, and he saw their flaws (RC, 246).
31 The biopic is one of Russell's key forms – but fictionalized, highly theatrical versions of biographies.

Ken Russell called his film on Richard Strauss, *The Dance of the Seven Veils,* 'an irreverent comic strip, as lurid as his music' (1993, 101). Russell wanted to pop Strauss's pompous ego, but the resultant film was controversial, with questions being asked in the House of Commons. Russell noted that he wasn't employed by the BBC after the Strauss film for 21 years (until *Lady Chatterley*). It was only screened once, and never since. What a shame! It's *wild*!

An early trip to Haworth, centre of the Brontë cult, when Ken and Shirley Russell were newly-weds in 1957, resulted in a series of b/w photographs of Kingdon impersonating the Brontë sisters in costumes she'd made. For Russell, it was

> the beginning of a lot of things I still attempt on films. I still enjoy location, for instance. The recce trip is one of the most enjoyable things about filmmaking. And the do-it-yourself approach has carried on. We still beg, borrow and steal props and make do and mend and improvize a lot. It might be rough and ready but it pays off in a kind of intangible authenticity. (Bax, 92)

Ken Russell's *Monitor* and *Omnibus* documentaries of the late 1950s and 1960s included *Bartók, London Moods, Mr Chester's Traction Engines, Old Battersea House, Architecture of Entertainment, Cranks At Work, The Light Fantastic, Marie Rambert Remembers, The Miner's Picnic, Shelagh Delaney's Salford, Gordon Jacob, Guitar Craze, McBryde and Coquhoun: Two Scottish Painters, Poet's London, Portrait of a Goon, Variations On a Mechanical Theme, The Debussy Film, Elgar, Lotte Lenya Sings Kurt Weill, Dante's Inferno, Always On Sunday, Diary of a Nobody, The Dotty World of James Lloyd, Lonely Shore, Watch the Birdie, Pop Goes the Easel, Preservation Man, Antonio Gaudi, Don't Shoot the Composer, Song of Summer* and *Dance of the Seven Veils.* (Remember that many of the *Monitor* and TV pieces were only ten or fifteen minutes long).

Ken Russell had a long-standing friendship with Melvyn Bragg, presenter of ITV's *South Bank Show* in

England. Russell made a few documentaries for *South Bank Show*, and other TV slots, in the 1980s and 1990s. Bragg (b. 1939 – now Lord Bragg) is one of Russell's most important collaborators – not only has he been one of Russell's strongest supporters, he has, with the London Weekend Television *South Bank Show* team, given Russell many opportunities to present documentaries and film essays on national television.

And Melvyn Bragg[32] wrote one of Ken Russell's most significant movies: *The Music Lovers,* the one Russell regards as a masterpiece, a long-cherished project which he wouldn't change at all. And Bragg also co-wrote TV films such as *Always On Sunday*,[33] *Clouds of Glory,* and *The Debussy Film.* (It must be significant, too, that Bragg shares with Russell a passion for British Romantic poets and artists, and also for the Lake District – for a while they were neighbours up in Cumbria).[34] Following his early film scripts, Bragg worked chiefly in televison and radio (a pity, because his movie scripts are excellent).

Ken Russell produced a documentary on Georges Delerue in 1966, who had scored his first feature film, *French Dressing* (and went on to compose the music for *Women In Love)*. Delerue (1924-92), along with Henry Mancini and Michel Legrand, was one of the chief composers of the French New Wave films (he wrote the scores for *Don't Shoot the Piano Player, Contempt, Hiroshima Mon Amour, La Peu Douce, Day For Night, The Conformist, Anne and Muriel, A Man For All Seasons* and *Anne of the Thousand Days,* for example. Many of those movies are regarded as classics).

Joseph Gomez identified two traditions of filmmaking that were forerunners of Ken Russell's cinema: the film biography, such as those about Émile Zola or Louis Pasteur or Abraham Lincoln or Glenn Miller or General George Patton or Sir Thomas Becket. Russell has made the biopic

---

[32] Bragg's movie credits include *Jesus Christ Superstar, The Music Lovers, Isadora, Play Dirty, Orion* and *A Time To Dance.*
[33] With Melvyn Bragg, Ken Russell wrote a portrait of the French painter Henri Rousseau, the misunderstood 'primitivist' – *Always On Sunday* (1965).
[34] Bragg has included the Lakes in his fiction, with Thomas Hardy as an obvious touchstone.

his own genre. Russell's films draw on the biographical filmic tradition but depart from it radically. They might begin with research and facts, but they don't bother with historical contextualization,[35] for instance, or with a chronology.[36] And they reserve the right to veer off into fantasy, nightmare, dream and more fantasy: Russell has never let anything hold him back when he wants to explore the inner life of his subjects. If they're hankering after sex, or fame, or spiritual oneness in their dreams, Russell will show that, rather than have 'em talk about it to someone else, or muse wistfully in voiceover.

The other tradition is the British documentary – first on film, then, from the 1950s onwards, for television. But the British documentary tradition is closely linked with socialist-realist approaches, of which the 'kitchen sink' dramas of the 1960s are an off-shoot. Ken Russell, needless to say, is *not* part of the left-wing or left-liberal political school of filmmaking in Britain, the Mike Leighs and Ken Loachs. (For instance, altho' Russell has included scenes of hard labour such as mining (in *Women In Love*), or scraping a living in poverty (in *Savage Messiah*), it is not in the naturalistic/ realistic mode of the 'kitchen sink' brigade).

Focussing on an individual in the biopics cleverly combines two strands in Ken Russell's *œuvre*: document-ary/ history and fantasy/ fiction. A point that Russell has made time and time again is that reality is always more fantastical and unbelievable than fantasy. It's true: real life is *far stranger* than anything anyone can imagine. Any time critics or studio executives have questioned whether this or that crazy event really occurred, Russell has responded with photographs and written evidence to say, yes, that crazee stuff *did* happen. 'People are always saying my films are bizarre,' Russell said, 'but they pale beside reality'.[37]

---

[35] But the first question for everybody (cast and crew) in the team would be: '*what year* is this?'
[36] Some of Ken Russell's historical films simply dispense with many of the conventions of the genre. For instance, bustling street scenes or long shots or cities, to set the scene. There are none at all in *Liszto-mania*, and very few in *Mahler*.
[37] Quoted in J. Baxter, 1976, 22

Ken Russell is among the most accomplished filmmakers at stretching budgets.[38] Many of his films were made in the region of $400,000-$1,500,000.[39] And, considering many were historical films, that meant that Russell and his production team had to find all manner of ways of enhancing the movie within strict limits. Working in the same arena of historical films on very low budgets (and in the same era) were filmmakers such as Werner Herzog, Luis Buñuel and Pier Paolo Pasolini.

Although Ken Russell disliked historical films for their romanticized, nostalgic look, he wasn't against doing lots of historical research. For pictures such as *The Devils* and *Savage Messiah*, Russell said he conducted tons of research. Russell remarked that it was impossible to use every bit of information that research turned up, 'so you may as well use the ones that suit your concept best' (Bax, 223). Russell smarted from critics attacking his historical films for something that was actually accurate (often it was the things that seemed the more ludicrous that were actually true).

One of Ken Russell's notions was a kind of cinematic simulacrum, a re-animation of the dead and of the past: to use the real locations if possible,[40] and to use the dialogue that people really said, and to cast actors who looked like the originals. Then 'there is a chance that one will get some resonance, capture the elusive, ghostly moment when it all happened' (Bax, 134). At the same time, Russell also acknowledges that the idea of dressing modern actors up in old costumes and having them pretend to be real, historical people was also bogus – and he sent up that way of making documentaries in his wild, OTT *The Dance of the Seven Veils*.

One could extend the study of Ken Russell's films into areas like Russell's cinema in the international market-

---

[38] Ken Russell enjoyed having a high budget on *Altered States* – his biggest (RC, 249).

[39] Look at what Ken Russell and his film crews put on screen for budgets of $1-2 million, compared to other movies of the period of *Women In Love*, like *Paint Your Wagon* (1969, 26 million bucks), *Catch 22* (1970, $24m), *Fiddler On the Roof* (1970, $40.5m), *Dr Doolittle* (1967, $20m), and *Star!* (1968, $14m).

[40] Over the course of his career, Ken Russell must've filmed in more of Britain's country mansions and churches, as well as 100s of picturesque spots in the landscape, than almost any other film director.

place, and how they have fared at the box office. If Russell's films had been huge hits, he probably would've been given more money to spend on his films. At the same time, there would have more studio (and producer) interference. One of the advantages of low budget filmmaking is the independence. It's all about balances: even with their modest budgets, Russell had many run-ins with studios and producers who disagreed with how he'd put his movies together.

Part of the context of Ken Russell's work of the late 1960s and early 1970s, for instance, which's the golden age of Russell's cinema, is that North American studios were still investing in European (and British) film production (that is, timing played a significant role in Russell's career: had he entered feature film production 7-10 years later, it would have been a different story).[41]

Sometimes the American film studios got more than they bargained for from some of their British productions (such as *Performance*, *The Devils* and *The Music Lovers*). Ken Russell remarked that American studios wanted to have it both ways: they wanted to come to Great Britain and produce movies – which they did more of in the 1960s than any other time (and the British film industry never really recovered when they pulled out) – but they also wanted them to conform to their conservative values. And when they saw the more out-there movies they'd paid for, such as *The Devils* or *Performance* (both funded by Warners), they reacted badly.

And when Hollywood pulled out of Albion, partly due to its own crisis, around 1970-71, bang went the backing of studios like United Artists and Warner Brothers. For some commentators, including me, the British film industry has never really recovered from that collapse.[42] It was certainly much more of a struggle for many British

---

[41] For instance, you can only make a series of stupendous movies like those of Ken Russell's if you have decent financial backing, the resources of a fully-equipped studio, a terrific crew, amazing performers, and talented collaborators.

[42] Yeah – when was the last time you saw a British movie about a British subject in a first-run British movie house? I don't mean *James Bond*, *Harry Potter* or something filmed in Britain, or using British actors and crew, and I don't mean on television, DVD, Blu-ray, video or online, I mean a properly, fully *British* theme and subject in a British cinema.

filmmakers after the early Seventies, including Ken Russell. His films *Mahler* and *Savage Messiah*, for instance, were made on much smaller budgets ($268,000) than *The Devils*, *Women in Love* or *The Music Lovers*, which were backed by Warners and UA.

One of the striking things is that, although most of his productions were financed with North American money, the casts were usually all-Brits (one or two Americans were cast in the earlier movies, such as *Billion Dollar Brain*, and increasingly from *Tommy* onwards; but Ken Russell's movies avoid token Americans or international casts). Not only that, but many of the key roles were taken up by relatively unknown British actors: nobody in the U.S.A. would've heard of Dudley Sutton, Georgina Hale, Christopher Gable, Judith Paris, Max Adrian or others in the Russell Repertory Company). If *The Devils* or *The Music Lovers* or another historical movie of the 1960s and 1970s were made today, roles such as Count Chiluvsky in *The Music Lovers* or Baron de Laubardemont and Father Barré in *The Devils*, would definitely be cast using prominent American or international performers.

Ken Russell had a deal with the small, North American company Vestron in the 1980s which allowed him to make lower budget films without interference (Dan Ireland, Vice President at Vestron in acquisitions, was a big fan of Russell's work).[43] The budgets were very low – 'so tight it hurts', complained Russell (BP, 274). However, Russell was a wayward talent, and even when he was given free rein, he still occasionally produced low quality films. His movies of this 1980s period – *The Rainbow*, *Gothic*, *The Lair of the White Worm* and *Salomé's Last Dance* were for some critics low-power pictures. Many had literary origins (Bram Stoker, John Polidori, Mary Shelley, Oscar Wilde and D.H. Lawrence).

I have to admit, each of the four pictures of 1986-1989, from *Gothic* to *The Rainbow*, failed to amaze me in the same way as *Tommy* or *The Music Lovers* or *The Devils* did. They are not in the same class, I reckon.

---

[43] The Vestron deal of 3 movies came about partly due to the success on video of *Gothic* (released in the U.S.A. on Vestron Video), according to Joseph Lanza (PF, 272).

However, repeated viewings uncover all sorts of treasures in those four movies: the most significant aspects are that they are all about *British* subjects, they were based on material that was British, they were made in Britain, they were produced by a (mainly) British cast and crew, they were directed by a Brit, and, perhaps most importantly, they were in a *British* style of filmmaking (OK, the finance was North American – but the money is American for most of the 'British' movies you've seen or heard of. And, sad to say, any movie that appears to be 'British' that you've seen in a first-run theatre will be backed by American or foreign money).

Disregarding the $$$$$, this is the 'British picture' of Ken Russell's ideal philosophy: movies made about British subjects. But they weren't bleedin' gangsters in white Jags, not silly heritage melodramas, and not 'realistic' dramas about miserable lives on housing estates.

COMMERCIALS AND CAPITALISM.

Selling your soul to commercial television, commercials made for television, is one of Ken Russell's *bête noires*. He reckoned he produced about 20.[44] Everybody remembers the famous and amazing scene in *Tommy* where Ann-Margret rolls around in a sea of baked beans, washing powder and chocolate. It's a send-up of mass advertizing, which is a recurring theme in Russell's cinema: he distrusts the idealizations of advertizing, and reckons that they create gulfs between desire and attainment in Western society. The ad men show one thing, but the consumer can never attain it.

Commercials for Ken Russell are

> fantasies on life which promise a romantic solution but which can only lead to disillusionment, disappointment – death! To me, commercials are the twentieth century's greatest crime against man. I hate the insidious brainwashing effect they are having on our society. (Bax, 192)

---

[44] Meanwhile, Ridley Scott was happy to boast that he had made about 2,000 commercials before he went into features.

HUMOUR AND SATIRE.

There is a *lot more* satire and irony and send-up, some of it vicious and unmerciful, in Ken Russell's cinema than many critics as well as many audiences realize. There is an anger, too, especially in the films of the 1968-1975 period. That *Women In Love* is satirizing the characters leads to some confusion about Russell's cinema: are his movies investing in the charas seriously, or sending them up? Well, it's both – throughout Russell's cinema. (I am reminded of friends of Jean-Luc Godard, including Anna Karina, who were shocked sometimes by just how angry Godard was – at everything, not only America and capitalism – but most of all at himself. The rage erupted in movies such as *Weekend*, *La Chinoise* and *Masculine Feminine*). Russell's cinema is sometimes as caustic and vitriolic as Godard's: *The Devils,* most especially, but also *The Music Lovers, Women in Love, Savage Messiah* and *Mahler*. The anger certainly gives those pictures a tremendous energy, as with Godard's work. (Anger is also a key element in the work of Ingmar Bergman, Oliver Stone and Hayao Miyazaki).

The *Monty Python* team satirized Ken Russell's films a number of times (their famous TV shows were first broadcast between 1969 and 1974, the time of Russell's 'golden age' of filmmaking). In one send-up, entitled *Ken Russell's Garden Club, 1958* (1971), a bunch of people in silly costumes (including a pantomime goose), a Gumby and a naked woman cavort in a tangle of bodies on a flower bed (part of the Pythons' series 3, programme 1, *The Money Programme*). In another sketch (in series 3, programme 9, *The All-England Summarize Proust Competition*), a group of language students (wearing headphones, in booths) do a dance routine, Sandy Wilson's version of *The Devils*. And in the blindingly brilliant comedy *Monty Python and the Holy Grail,* they took on the plague scenes in *The Devils* – 'bring out your dead!'

Ken Russell's kind of cinema has always been easy to parody, because it's extravagant, over-the-top and ambitious (and *distinctive*, which makes it easier to parody). Actually, it's *already* parodying itself. No one can out-

Russell Russell. (Really, it wasn't the Pythons spoofing Russell's movies so much as loving that kind of filmmaking themselves – the Pythons weren't averse to having people dressed in animal costumes or doing silly dances in their sketches).

KEN RUSSELL AND BRITISH CINEMA

Ken Russell isn't usually placed with the European New Wave filmmakers by critics. Some filmmakers working in Blighty, such as Dick Lester, Lindsay Anderson and Ken Loach, had consciously taken up some of the French New Wave's techniques. You can see the influence of the New Wave on Russell's films, though. And there are direct links to the French *nouvelle vague*: Russell had Georges Delerue compose the music for *French Dressing* and *Women in Love* (he scored New Wave classics like *Jules et Jim, Shoot the Pianist, Hiroshima Mon Amour* and *Contempt*); and Jeanne Moreau was Russell's first choice for *Savage Messiah*.

British cinema – both François Truffaut and Jean-Luc Godard denounced British cinema, claiming that it didn't even exist. Those bastards! Well, OK, they do have a point. But to counter their oh-so French sneering, their oh-so arrogant denunciations, I would put forward some names:

Alfred Hitchcock
Charlie Chaplin
David Lean
Michael Powell
and Ken Russell

Oh, for certain, Truffaut and Godard (and all of the Parisian film *cogniscenti*) would dismiss David Lean as lightweight and populist, and Michael Powell as too fey, arch, self-conscious and pretentious, but they couldn't ignore Alfred Hitchcock or Charlie Chaplin – oh no, they are two filmmakers that French ciné culture absolutely reveres (along with Tsui Hark, Jerry Lewis, Woody Allen *et al)*. And, *no,* Hitchcock was *not* American, even though many of his most famous and celebrated movies were made (and set and financed) in the Land of the Free. Nope, Hitch is *British* through and through (and he didn't even go to make movies in the U.S. of A. until he was 40!).

I've added Ken Russell to that list. Why not?

In the 1960s and the 1970s, when Ken Russell was at the height of his power as a filmmaker in the theatrical release arena, his series of films (and TV shows) could certainly hold up well against *anything* that continental Europe or North America was turning out. True, Godard, Rohmer, Chabrol, Truffaut and their ilk in the Nouvelle Vague have been the darlings of film critics, and Russell has never had a similar solid, gushy critical following.

Of all the countries of the world, it is *Italian* filmmakers that I think of most often in connection with Ken Russell. And three Italian filmmakers in particular: Federico Fellini,[45] Luchino Visconti and Pier Paolo Pasolini (you can certainly spot the influence of Fellini on Russell, though Russell is virtually anti-Pasolinian; yet the poetics of cinema, which Pasolini continually evoked, are fundamental to Russell's movies). Closely followed by Germans such as Fritz Lang and F.W. Murnau (there are 100s of links between Russell's cinema and the great German filmmakers – but that's also true of just about anybody, as their influence has been almost universal). And of course Hollywood: Vincente Minnelli, Gene Kelly, Stanley Donen and MGM musicals, but also Busby Berkeley musicals of the 1930s, and RKO Fred Astaire musicals of the 1930s and 1940s. Orson Welles, always (*Citizen Kane* in particular). Among fellow Brits, Michael Powell above all, but also Charlie Chaplin, and maybe a little Alfred Hitchcock from time to time (but not much).

But although Ken Russell is one of the very few international filmmakers who evoke an authentic 'British' culture and society, who has been devoted to aspects of art

---

[45] Ken Russell liked Federico Fellini's movies, and wrote in 2007 in praise of Fellini's classic 1954 picture *La Strada*, which 'features the director's wife, Giulietta Masina, in a heartrending performance as a female clown, Gelsomina, who partners a hard-hearted strongman in his act after her mother sells her to a carnival'. In turn, Fellini enjoyed *The Devils*.

and culture in Britain, he is not really a 'British' filmmaker. Neither is he American, or international: he is his own genre and category: Russellian. Just like Orson Welles or Alfred Hitchcock created their own niches within world cinema – watch two or three successive shots from Hitch or Welles, and you can tell it's them, out of 1000s of movies. It's the same with Russell.

In short, Ken Russell has always been an outsider figure (a maverick, an oddball, an individualist, an eccentric even), in many respects.[46] From the kind of movies (the subjects, the approach) he makes... to the way of working.

> Maybe I was born in the wrong country. I'm not into small-time no-hopers and the dull and boring things that seem to interest English film directors. I don't see any point in making films about people painting electricity pylons in northern England. It's ludicrous, and that's the British film industry. (2009)

Similarly, within the British film industry, Ken Russell has not been one of the establishment figures: in 2009 he commented:

> I don't really consider myself part of the industry here, and never have, because all my films but one have been financed by Americans.

That's a point worth considering, but it's true of many of the most celebrated filmmakers in Britain or born in Britain: many of their movies are financed by North American companies (certainly that's true of filmmakers like Ridley and Tony Scott, Mike Newell, Alan Parker, Paul S. Anderson, etc).[47]

Often thought of as a *British* film director making *British* movies about *British* subjects, Ken Russell has actually directed most of his movies for North American film studios and North American film producers, with,

---

[46] 'I've never played the game. I have my own game and I'm very happy playing that', Ken Russell said in 2009.
[47] That most of Ken Russell's features are North American-financed is part of the reason why his movies are much more available in the Land of the Free than in many other territories. As Russell says, there are shelves devoted to his films in the U.S.A., but not in Blighty.

crucially, *North American* money, and most of his feature-length movies have been about non-British subjects.

KEN RUSSELL THE *AUTEUR*

Is Ken Russell an *auteur*? I don't know for sure, but I bet he doesn't like the term or the concept – and I don't know of *any* major filmmaker who does. It's entirely an idea cooked up by film critics, many of whom haven't much of a clue about what really goes into making a movie (indeed, film critics, who are presumably *professional* writers, have very poor knowledge about movie production, marketing and distribution. For example, they continually emphasize dialogue, the easiest thing to put into a film review (like the lyrics of a pop song – you just quote them), and also the easiest thing to denigrate. But all major filmmakers stress that dialogue is a very small part of the overall scheme and impact of a movie).

To the extent of conceiving, writing, producing and directing his own films, Ken Russell is only partially an *auteur*; he does not write all of his own films, for instance (*Women In Love* is *not* an *auteur* movie, and is not really 'a Ken Russell movie'). But in the sense of exercising a huge amount of control over most of the stages of production, yes (down to operating the camera (those distinctive tilted, kinetic, handheld camera moves come directly from the way that Russell wields the camera),[48] sometimes lighting scenes, and being closely involved with all of the other principal aspects of filmmaking).

In the sense of producing *as well as* directing his films – yes (and that is absolutely vital: Orson Welles, for instance, also acted as a producer on most of his twelve completed feature films he directed, and that makes a huge difference). Being his own producer meant that Russell was able to exercise more control over the pre-

---
[48] Ken Russell likes to operate the camera on his films (unions and DPs permitting). Like filmmakers such as David Lean, Steven Spielberg and Walerian Borowczyk, Russell works very closely with the cinematographers of his films.

production – such as casting, and commissioning writers to create a script. (However, Russell, like just about *all* major filmmakers, has rarely had final cut on his films, and has also had to trim back movies due to censorship – for instance, *The Devils* and *Crimes of Passion*).

In the sense of having particular themes, concerns, and even images, Ken Russell is definitely an *auteur*. At the level of the æsthetic, the visual, the aural, and the technical, Russell is most definitely an *auteur*, a filmmaker whose imprint is all over his films. Let's face it, there are *very few filmmakers* that you can look at and say, yep, that was definitely made by so-and-so. And you can do that with A Ken Russell Film – and you can recognize A Ken Russell Picture from very early on in the proceedings, too. Very few filmmakers would begin a film with a scene of a man kissing a woman's tits back-and-forth, faster and faster, speeding up a metronome and music, and following it rapidly by a semi-naked sword fight (and without a title, credits or explanation).

Ken Russell explained in 1973 how he worked with screenwriters:

> I usually tell [writers] how I would like the story. We discuss it; they will say why they don't like something or how they think something can be improved or come up with their own idea. They read it to me, and we revise as we go along. Usually, when I'm shooting, I revise yet again according to the necessities of the day. I believe in using what is available, and when I've changed my mind, I rewrite the whole thing.[49]

It's very significant that Ken Russell has co-written many of his movies and TV programmes, and has also had sole writing credit on many of them. Although the general view seems to be that film directors do everything on a movie – it's the *auteur* theory plus laziness (it's just easier to talk about one artist instead of 100s) – most directors do *not* write their movies (and I maintain that the writing, the concept, the creation of the characters, and the structure, are things the *screenwriter* does, *not* the director, the producer, the studio executives or the second unit clapper

---
49 In T. Fox, 102.

loader's dog).

Ken Russell acknowledged that he couldn't write as well as his writers, certainly when it came to dialogue.[50] But I'd say when it comes to getting across ideas in written form so they can be translated into images and sounds and music, Russell did just fine.

KEN RUSSELL AND THE CENSORS

It's tempting to get into a lengthy discussion of movie censorship and ratings, but there are good studies elsewhere which do so.[51] Ken Russell is one of those film directors who have become well-known for their run-ins with the film censors (and not only censors, but also media watchdogs, such as the National Viewers and Listeners Association and the Festival of Light in Great Britain (and their most prominent spokesman, Mary Whitehouse), and right-wing and religious groups in North America). *Women In Love* was of course a problematic movie for film censors.

As well as run-ins with the censors on movies such as *The Devils* and *Crimes of Passion* (or the British government with *Dance of the Seven Veils*), some of Ken Russell's films have been re-cut by the studios: *The Boy Friend* had fifteen minutes taken out of it for the U.S.A. release by the studio (MGM). And Warners re-cut *The Devils*, and that was after the parts had been lopped off it by the censors.

On the Hollywood practice of re-editing movies after the filmmakers have delivered them to the studio, Ken Russell hated the butchery:

> They're handed over to some Hollywood "cutter" who does a quick hatchet job on something I've slaved long and lovingly over for months. One company who didn't have an editor actually got their lawyer and the project-

50 In J. Walker, 1974.
51 M. Barker, 1984, M. Barker & J. Petley, 1997, E. De Grazia & R.K. Newman. *Banned Films: Movies, Censors and the First Amendment*, Bowker, New York, NY, 1982, T. Matthews, 1994, P. Keough, 1995, G. Phelps, 1975, and J. Lewis, 2000.

ionist to cut one of my movies. (BP, 103-4)

Very few filmmakers have 'final cut', even among film directors one would regard as masters, and even among film directors who have helped generate billions. Once a movie's been shot, control over it is given over to studios and executives (a movie, for example, will be edited on the studio lot). And it's the *studios* who *own* the film – a director might write and direct (and co-produce) a movie, but it's the studio who owns it and its rights.

One of the chief benefits of making movies on a low budget is that the filmmaker can retain (more) control of the project throughout its production. And filmmakers such as Ken Russell are so individual and unusual, it requires a good deal of sensitivity to re-cut their movies. They are simply not your average factory products churned out by mainstream, commercial film industries. So to cut a Ken Russell movie, you really have to be in tune with what the filmmakers were trying to achieve. And clearly some film studios weren't. (Film editors are thus sometimes caught in the middle of a struggle between the film directors, the producers, the censors and the studios. No wonder that many film studios take away a movie from the producers and director, and assign their own editors to projects. Some studio editors are loathed by filmmakers because they're butchering their babies).

Ken Russell's movies have often been positioned on the borders of the 'X' classification, particularly in the early 1970s. It's where Russell likes to operate – in the 'R' or 'X' zone. Adopting the 'R' rating and moving away from the 'X' classification, which occurred in the early 1970s, helped Hollywood reposition itself in the marketplace (distancing itself from the negative connotations of the 'X' certificate); it also meant that those who were criticizing Hollywood for turning out sleaze, violence or porn could be assured that Hollywood was producing fewer 'X' rated films.

However, the entire ratings system is all about money: it's about categorizing movies for the marketplace: who pays for the MPAA (Motion Picture Association of

America) and the ratings and censorship boards around the world? The film studios do. (In the 1990s and after, the members of the MPAA were seven: Sony, MGM, Universal, Paramount, Fox, Warners and Disney).

ACTING AND PERFORMANCES

> He's not doing it, thinking, "This'll bring 'em in, this'll make more money." He's exorcising demons of some kind.
>
> Glenda Jackson (1972)

Ken Russell isn't known as an 'actor's director' like Ingmar Bergman or Robert Altman. But he sure did coax some great performances from his cast: Ann-Margaret was nominated for an Oscar for *Tommy*, Glenda Jackson won an Oscar for *Women In Love*, and Oliver Reed delivered his career best in *The Devils* (and was also incredible in *The Debussy Film*, *Women In Love* and *Dante's Inferno*). There are sensational performances throughout Russell's work: Christopher Gable in the Richard Strauss satire, Kathleen Turner and Anthony Perkins in *Crimes of Passion*, Vanessa Redgrave in *The Devils,* Scott Anthony in *Savage Messiah,* Roger Daltrey in *Lisztomania* and *Tommy*, Twiggy in *The Boy Friend*, Stratford Johns in *Salome's Last Dance,* Amanda Donohue in *The Lair of the White Worm,* Robert Powell in *Mahler,* Max Adrian in, well, everything (but *Delius* especially), and of course an astonishing, incendiary performance by Richard Chamberlain (and Jackson again) in *The Music Lovers*.

Ken Russell acknowledged that he wasn't an 'actor's director', and didn't really know how to direct actors (I think he was being too modest). Instead, he said, he aimed to cast the film as well as he could, and to establish a creative atmosphere[52] on set. Many directors have said similar things:

> I don't know how to direct actors. I can talk to them and tell them what *I* think it's all about but I can't *make* them act and I'm not interested in doing so. That's up to them. What I *can* do is choose people and put them in an atmosphere that brings something out of them they didn't think they had. (Bax, 189)

Ken Russell could create a wonderful environment on the set, Richard Chamberlain said, in which actors were encouraged to experiment. Alan Bates remarked: 'I don't think Ken would listen to anything an actor said'. Glenda Jackson maintained that Russell could not direct actors much; instead, he would focus all his attention on some minor visual detail. Certainly Russell found working with Jackson 'a very great experience'. He discovered that she was so good he didn't need to say much to her about direction (Bax, 189).

What Ken Russell did best, Glenda Jackson remarked, was 'intensely emotional scenes', and for those he would create a strong atmosphere for the actors (1972). Rather than great acting, Russell said he was often after atmospheres. It wasn't about great speeches or dramatic ability. He has remarked that the initial discussion with an actor is where it all happens, is the really crucial meeting, where he lays out the story and the character.

The performances in Ken Russell's films have the appearance of improvization and spontaneity. But no: as with many another film director (Jean-Luc Godard, Ingmar Bergman and Francis Coppola come to mind), it's all actually carefully orchestrated. There might be suggestions from the actors, but the moves, the lines, the gestures, the blocking and so on are all worked out beforehand (and then rehearsed). The result may *look* effortless and spontaneous, and to viewers and to (too many) critics it can *look* as if it's 'just happening' there and then, but that's

---

[52] 'In a lot of my films it's the atmosphere I'm after and acting ability doesn't have a lot to do with that', Russell remarked (Bax, 190). Sometimes Russell would deliberately deflect attention from the scene or the actors or ramp up the tension by focussing on some minor detail, like a chair, or a costume, in order to 'create a tension, an atmosphere, a charge of electricity' (Bax, 189).

great art.

Sammi Davis, the star of *The Rainbow,* told me:

> Mostly if a scene didn't flow, Ken would say, 'Do it better', and I would say, 'You're right, I'll do it better'. He was fun to me in that way, he just said it like it was. In the film business there are many ways to inspire or gain a reaction or connection. With Ken, his ability to always just be himself is his key form of inspiration.[53]

I don't know for sure,[54] but I imagine that being an actor in a Ken Russell movie means throwing yourself into it whole-heartedly and trusting the director. If he tells you to take off your clothes and roll around in the grass, you do it. I bet Russell isn't the kind of director who's going to get into a two-hour discussion about your motivations for being nude in this particular scene.[55]

> I don't talk to my actors too much. I explain as much as I can to them but life isn't to do with explaining or manipulating. There's a danger of killing an instinct by analysing it. (Bax, 128)

And again, Ken Russell explained that often it was on his first meeting that everything about the character was laid out for the actor:

> I really direct an actor's performance during that first hour when I explode my concept of the character into his head for good and all. That is the moment of the creation of the character – the rest is rhubarb. (Bax, 184)

If Ken Russell has a reputation for being tough sometimes on his performers, so have other directors: Stanley Kubrick, Jean-Luc Godard and Federico Fellini, among many others, are also known for pushing their actors.

Ken Russell could be 'very demanding', 'very headstrong' and 'emotionally exhausting to work with', remarked DP Billy Williams.[56] Dorothy Tutin commented,

---

[53] S. Davis, letter to the author, 2007.
[54] But I have chatted to Sammi Davis about it.
[55] Actress Diana Laurie (in *The Lion's Mouth*) remarked of working with Ken Russell: 'He is a mix, he's such a mix of generous and stingy, relaxed and control freak, warm and then at times quite suspicious or untrusting of you, and comfortable and uncomfortable with himself.'
[56] B. Williams, in D. Schaefer, 1984, 271.

as many actors have done, on Russell's eagle eye for detail, for the visuals.

> Somehow Ken was the eye. He worked like a sculptor, using film as his material. The crew felt this too. I've never known a crew so on the ball. They had to be. Ken has an eye like a hawk. (Bax, 196)

And Dorothy Tutin also recalled, pace *Savage Messiah*, that the actors felt like they were performing not for the camera, but for the director. It's a common attitude among actors: they love to get a response from directors, to make them laugh or cry.

> He knows *exactly* what the film will be like, and we weren't doing it for the camera – we were doing it for *him*. It was often a question of catching up with Ken and his conception of the film. (Bax, 196)

Ken Russell has said he can talk to the actors about the characters and the story, but after that it's up to them. Sometimes he will deliberately keep an actor uninformed about aspects of a role (a common tactic).

Ken Russell has also employed psychological techniques that some would regard as harsh, tactics where a director will secretly manipulate a performer in order to obtain a particular result. For instance, not allowing Dorothy Tutin to have pins in her hat on a windy day, and also telling the crew that nobody was to help with her hat. Or making actors wear under-garments even if they won't show up on camera (a common gripe among actors). And you would have to accept that, going in, knowing it was a Ken Russell movie.

SEX AND NUDITY.

I'm sure that many actors would have not even bothered to go to a casting session if a role was advertized in the trade papers thus: 'this role will require full nudity'. And in Hollywood there are clauses in some actors' contracts about which bits of the body can be shown. That can be worked out by agents and producers months beforehand – much better than getting cold feet the day before filming.

But there's a starchy, British nervousness about nudity and sex in cinema, isn't there? Somehow, it's OK for Jean-Luc Godard or Pier Paolo Pasolini to ask for actors to go nude or simulate tupping in their movies, 'cos they are masters of the Euro art film, right? They're bleedin' *French* and *Italian*, ain't they? Intellectual and arty and oh-so sophisticated.

But for a British film director, it seems, well, just not done, old boy. Fine for porn, or stag reels, or a saucy seaside postcard (one of many bizarre British traditions), but not for a movie that you and your maiden aunt might go and see at the local fleapit of a Friday evenin'.

But a Ken Russell movie doesn't think like that – it's not that Russell was setting out to upset or shock the bourgeoisie (though there is an element of flaunting bad taste in his movies) – rather, it's what was required for the piece. I'm sure it was not the filmmakers thinking along the lines of, 'shit, this is going to really *annoy* people, isn't it?', but, 'you get your clothes off for this scene, dear.'

That's all it is. It's a body, it's a bit of fooling around, it's people fucking (like they have to do for there to be people at all: no sex = no humans). As Spike Milligan put it: 'People like to fuck'. The fuss about sex and nudity and 'bad language' and 'bad taste' comes from film critics, media watchdogs, broadcasters, and one or two irate people who live in Tunbridge Wells in England and read the *Times* (i.e., arch conservatives, who usually happen to be white and middle-aged and middle-class, too).

There's plenty of gay and lesbian material in Ken Russell's cinema too, from lesbianism in *The Rainbow* and *Dante's Inferno* (but cut from the final show), to homosexuality in *The Music Lovers, Women In Love,* and *Salomé's Last Dance*. Russell has also worked with gay writers such as Barry Sandler and Larry Kramer. As Russell has quipped, maybe he is gay. 'I don't think anyone knows themselves. We can all pretend, but I have no idea what I am. I'm me!'

RUSSELL'S WOMEN.

Ken Russell's cinema is full of beautiful women – so many amazing people have appeared in his movies and TV shows, including models Gala Mitchell and Twiggy, and actresses Fiona Lewis, Annette Robertson, Kathleen Turner, Françoise Dorléac, Ann-Margret, Tina Turner, Michelle Phillips, Nell Campbell, Blair Brown, Leslie Caron, Sammi Davis, Amanda Donohue, Helen Mirren, Theresa Russell, Vanessa Redgrave, Natasha and Joely Richardson.

Compared to all of his contemporaries, Ken Russell's cinema has offered more significant roles for women. The above list is just a small selection of the actresses who have worked for Russell. And let's recall again that Russell's works feature once-in-a-lifetime roles for actors: *Dante's Inferno, The Debussy Film, Isadora Duncan, The Dance of the Seven Veils, Delius: Song of Summer, Women in Love, The Devils, The Music Lovers, Savage Messiah, Mahler, Tommy, Lisztomania, Valentino, Altered States, Crimes of Passion, The Rainbow,* and *Lady Chatterley*. Those kind of ultra-challenging star roles don't come along very often.

ACTORS.

Among the actresses who appeared in Ken Russell's movies, the stars receive the most comment – Glenda Jackson, Vanessa Redgrave, Ann-Margret, Kathleen Turner, etc. But there's a group of actresses who have been essential to the success of Russell's cinema – such as Georgina Hale, Judith Paris, Imogen Claire, and Fiona Lewis. They are less well-known or praised, but they form a key group in Russell's work.

Some among Ken Russell's regular actors were first dancers: Christopher Gable was a dancer with the Royal Ballet (and apparently gave up his dance career to be in Ken Russell's films), Hannah King and Judith Paris. And of course the biggest diva in the dance world starred in *Valentino*.

Regular actors in Ken Russell's films and TV shows were members of the 'Russell Repertory Company': they included: Oliver Reed, Christopher Gable, Glenda Jackson, Georgina Hale, Vladek Sheybal, Judith Paris, Catherine Wilmer, Iza Teller, Ben Aris, Max Adrian,, John Justin, Fiona Lewis, Andrew Reilly, Antonia Ellis, David Collings, Peter Vaughan, Imogen Claire, Ken Colley, Murray Melvin, Dudley Sutton and Andrew Faulds. And most of his children have appeared in many of his films (as well as working on them as crew – Victoria, Xavier, Alex, James, Toby, etc).

Sammi Davis told me about a time making *The Lair of the White Worm* when she wanted some hints at her characterization:

> I asked him one day on the set of *The Lair of the White Worm* what I was meant to be thinking whilst peering into the mirror to check out a big wound on my neck. He said something like, 'Well obviously, you're feeling quite sad having just found you're missing mother, realising she has turned into a vampire and then shocking you by taking a huge chomp on your neck'. That did the trick, very simple, nothing more needed![57]

Ken Russell has often taken cameos in his movies, sometimes reluctantly, when no one else was available (or the actor cast turned out to be unsuitable or uncooperative, as in *Valentino*),[58] and sometimes joyfully, as in *Lady Chatterley*. And in the more recent, low budget movies, such as *Hot Pants* and *The Fall of the Louse of Usher*, Russell seems to be enjoying himself hamming it up in front of the camera (as well as behind it).

Ken Russell has also appeared in other people's films – in *The Russia House* (1990) and *Brothers of the Head* (2006). And on TV shows such as *Marple, Color Me Kubrick, Waking the Dead, Celebrity Naked Ambition, Big Brother, Open House, Carry On Darkly, Legends, Great Composers, Light Lunch, A History of British Art, Masterchef, Denton, Without Walls, The Last Resort*, and numerous news shows, chat shows and documentaries.[59]

---

[57] S. Davis, letter to the author, 2007.
[58] One of Russell's best cameos was as the legendary film director Rex Ingram in *Valentino*, shooting in the California desert.
[59] Such as documentaries on censorship: *X-Rated* and *Empire of the Censors*.

A few of Ken Russell's film influences: clockwise from top right:
Betty Grable. Leni Riefenstahl. Metropolis. The Fleet's In.
The Cabinet of Dr Caligari. Die Nibelungen.

Some of Ken Russell's favourite composers clockwise from top right: Claude Debussy. Franz Liszt. Dimitri Shostakovitch. Ralph Vaughan Williams. Gustav Mahler. Igor Stravinsky.

Ken Russell on set
(This page and over)

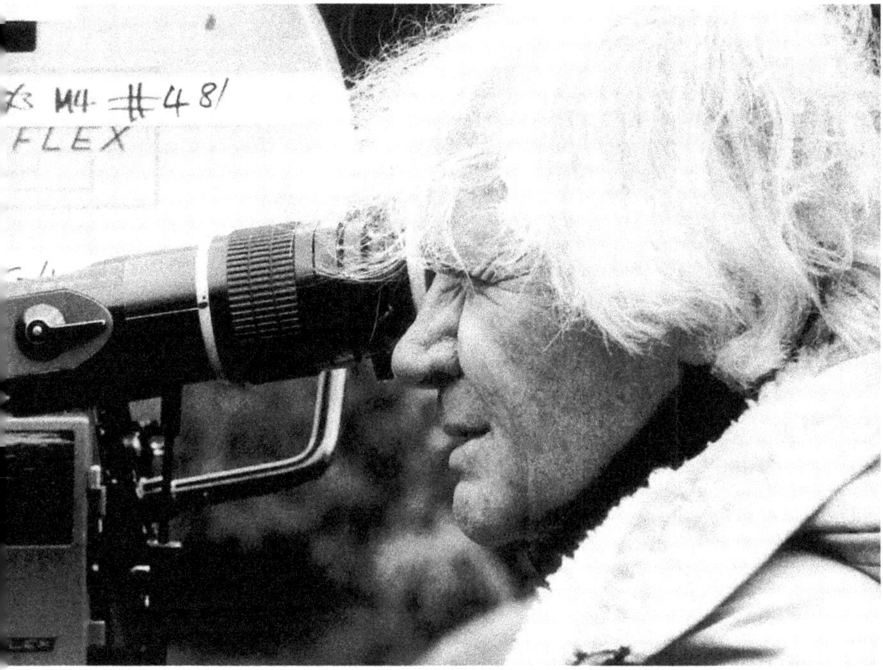
M4 #481
FLEX

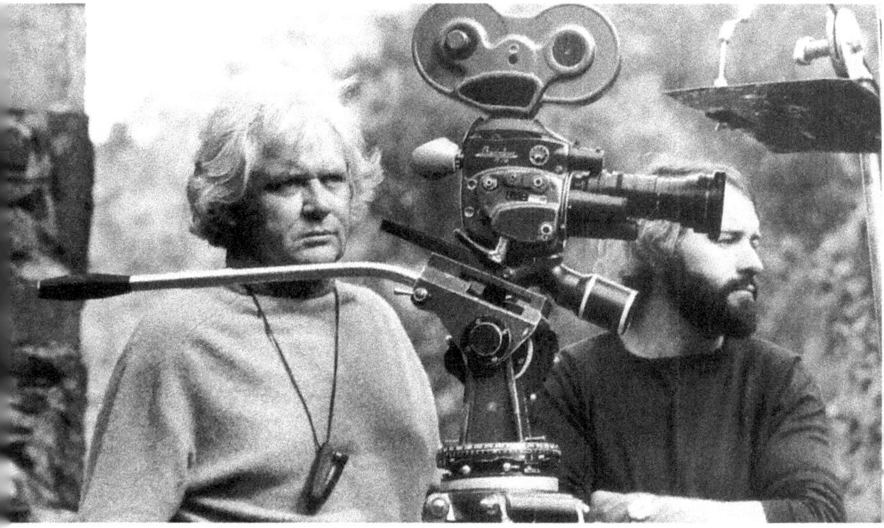

KEN RUSSELL AND THE CRITICS

> Pay no attention to what the critics say. No statue has ever been put up to a critic.
>
> Jean Sibelius

Ken Russell has been well served by the writers who've written book-length studies of his cinema: John Baxter, Joseph Gomez, Ken Hanke, and Gene Phillips. All excellent, all highly recommended. Other supporters of Russell's cinema include Stephen Farber, Mark Kermode and Paul Joyce. (More recent books include: Kevin Flanagan, Joseph Lanza, and Richard Crouse).

Ken Russell has written books about cinema – *Fire Over England: The British Cinema Comes Under Friendly Fire* and *Directing Film* – as well as his memoirs. His autobiography – essential reading – is *A British Picture* (a.k.a. *Altered States*). Russell's books are to be treasured, even if some folk might disagree about how he remembered some of the famous stories. What comes over strongly is his passion for movies (note, for instance, how many movies he cites seeing in his childhood, and where, and when. Like Jean-Luc Godard, Ingmar Bergman and Martin Scorsese, Russell has an insatiable love of cinema).

KEN RUSSELL'S CINEMATIC STYLE

THE CAMERA.

When it comes to shooting a scene, in terms of camera angles and movement, Ken Russell in his audio commentary to *Delius: Song of Summer* said there was only one way to shoot a scene, and he never had any hesitation about it. Steven Spielberg and Orson Welles have made the same remarks: they just *know* where to put the camera, and how to move it. Stanley Kubrick commented that choosing the camera angles and such like was relatively easy compared to the rehearsals.

Thus, Ken Russell does not walk onto the set and run through the standard master shot, medium shot, close-up, over-the-shoulder shot, etc, that film students are taught and that so many filmmakers persist in employing. Instead, Russell tended to shoot in single master shots, covering a scene from one, main viewpoint, sometimes adding close-ups or reaction shots. Of course, if a scene required a simple set-up of two close-ups or two medium shots, of two actors, Russell would do that (and some of Russell's later work for TV does resort to conventional shooting, partly no doubt because the schedules for TV are *much* tighter than for movies. You won't find a television production shoot running a 100 days for a two-hour movie! Or 18 months for 1980's *The Shining* and even more for 1963's *Cleopatra*! Shit, TV would've nailed *Heaven's Gate* in three weeks!).

At its best, though, Ken Russell's cinema is not a jog through standard camera angles and movements. Russell used the comparison with choreography – if the actors weren't moving, then the camera would be.

This has an effect on the editing, of course: it means that many scenes in Ken Russell's pictures are not shots of three or four seconds in a standard shot-reverse-shot pattern. It means that scenes are often broken down into single, mobile shots, sometimes peppered with reaction shots or insert shots. Although sometimes Russell and his editors will employ rapidfire montages, much more often they will allow the master shots to run on, so that some shots are quite long.

Actors love that, allowing them time and space to get into a scene, instead of lots of short shots (but they have to be good actors to concentrate over a lengthy take). However, Ken Russell's cinema is not known for *very* long takes, such as the films of Andrei Tarkovsky, Orson Welles, Jean-Luc Godard or Theo Angelopoulos.[59]

Ken Russell enjoys actors looking into the camera, in

---

[59] What would happen if Russell had filmed in long, ten-minute takes, like Theo Angelopoulos, or Hitch's *Rope*? Instead of people meandering and staring forlornly into space, as in Angelopoulos's eternally downbeat, Euro-Greek cinema, actors wouldn't be able to stop themselves breaking out into a Busby Berkeley dance routine, or getting freaky.

particular moments where actors turn to wink at the camera or glance at it in fun. Another aspect of Russell's style is self-conscious anachronisms, particularly the ones which pop out of the screen in the historical movies. Some viewers find them jarring, taking them out of the moment. For instance, while he found the anachronisms in *Dante's Inferno* jarring and in dubious taste, Richard Schickel also praised Russell for trying to push the medium of television.[60]

EDITING.

Ken Russell likened editing to composing music, inevitably. It was a case of mixing scenes with different tempos and moods, so the result was like a classical symphony, moving through a variety of moods. Getting the flow of scenes right, and the structure of a film, was very important for Russell. Editing is always an aspect of filmmaking that film critics tend to miss. With a filmmaker of eye-popping visuals, as with Oliver Stone or Pier Paolo Pasolini or whoever, it's easy to be distracted by the other technical aspects of the filmmaking. But it's clear with Russell, as with Stone or Pasolini or whoever, that editing is absolutely central. Because if the editing is wrong, the other elements won't work so well either.

I have drawn attention to editing many times in this study of Ken Russell's cinema, because it is *so important*. Yes, the visuals are extraordinary, and the sets, the costumes, the performances, and all the rest. But it's editing that puts all of this together. 'I like editing,' admitted Russell; 'it's very much a hands-on process' (DF, 98).

Like Orson Welles, Ken Russell doesn't like to hang about: his movies cut rapidly from one scene to another, once the point has been made. Welles hated those s-l-o-w movies (i.e., Michelangelo Antonioni), which showed someone walking right to the end of a road. No. Welles would *cut, cut, cut*! Dorothy Tutin remarked of *Savage Messiah* that it would have benefitted from a slower, quieter scene (which she was expecting to be in there

---

60 R. Schickel, "Great Lives On TV", *Harper's*, Jan, 1971.

somewhere), but perhaps was better without it: 'with Ken the instant an impression's made, it's off; gone. He never dwells on *anything* and I think that's right' (Bax, 195).

PUTTING ON A SHOW.

Many of Ken Russell's films contain scenes of theatricality and putting on a show. You could hire Russell to stage the Oscars or Grammy's, for instance, and I bet it'd be fab television (there would be *loads* of dancing, for example, and glittery costumes, and at least two or three orchestras on stage as well as in the pit, and the climax would involve four hundred naked performers doing the tango with live snakes).

There are shows-within-shows too, and films-within-films. *Valentino*, for instance, contains numerous examples, ranging from informal dances to big, theatrical performances, plus screenings of films for a couple of people or a theatre full of women. *The Devils* opens with the King of France camping it up as the Goddess Venus in a theatre. Characters dance for one person or put on shows for guests (as in *Women in Love*). Sometimes whole movies involve putting on a show (*Salomé's Last Dance* and *The Boy Friend*). Russell's movies portray backstage dramas, recreations of silent films, and plenty of painting and photography, too. Voyeurism is a constant theme, particularly the eroticism of looking, of scopophilia ('we are all voyeurs', Russell says).

MEN AND WOMEN.

Generally, the main characters in the films of Ken Russell have been men – in common with the vast majority of films, written or directed by men or women. However, some of Russell's films have featured women in the lead roles: *The Boy Friend, Whore, The Devils, Crimes of Passion* and *Women In Love*, for instance, as well as TV work such as *Isadora Duncan, Lady Chatterley* and *Shelagh Delaney's Salford*.

Ken Russell would not be regarded as a leading light in feminism, however, and sometimes his movies have been criticized for being sexist, chauvinistic or even misogynist. One could counter that the objectification of women in his films is also applied to men as many times, and there is plenty of male nudity (though more female nudity, I guess). Another defence would be that many of Russell's films are set in periods going back to the Middle Ages (in *The Devils*).

TIME AND HISTORY.

Ken Russell is very fond of using framing devices and multiple narrative layers in his movies.[61] They occur in, for instance, *The Debussy Film, Salomé's Last Dance, The Boy Friend, Valentino,* and *Mahler*. Russell explores the self-conscious, modernist device of one layer of narrative (a theatre company in *The Boy Friend* or a group of amateurs in *Salomé's Last Dance* putting on a play), commenting upon and reflecting the content of the play itself (belying the view that Russell's works are narratively simplistic).

As to time periods, Ken Russell's films long favoured the 19th century and early 20th century. That's partly because so many of his films are about classical composers: Mahler, Wagner, Martinu, Tchaikovsky, Liszt, Bartók, Debussy, Strauss, Elgar, Prokofiev, etc. *Women In Love* is set in 1920; *Savage Messiah* and *The Rainbow* in a similar First World War period; *The Boy Friend* in the 1920s; *Lady Chatterley* in the late 1920s; *Delius Song of Summer* in the 1920s; and *Gothic* in the early 1800s. *Prisoner of Honor* goes back to the late 19th century and early 20th century. *The Devils* goes furtherest back, to 1623-34 (altho' the setting might also be regarded as the High Middle Ages – and Sister Jeanne's erotic fantasies go back to the era of Christ).

The movies set in the present day include *Altered States*,[62] *Crimes of Passion, Mindbender, French Dressing, Whore, The Lair of the White Worm, Dogboys* and *The Fall of the Louse of Usher*. This means that Ken Russell is

---

[61] Russell self-consciously aped the narrative structure of *Citizen Kane* a few times.
[62] In *Altered States*, tho', Edward Jessup goes back to the dawn of time!

very at home in the 19th and early 20th centuries: that is his time period.[63] It has freed his imagination, perhaps, to be able to go back to the mid-19th century or to the period of the Great War. It also means, from a production point of view, that most of his films have been historical pieces, requiring period costumes, props, sets, vehicles, and all the rest. That also means they are going to cost a little more than films set in the contemporary world.

Ken Russell – despite the look and feel of some of his films, with their Pop Art and pop culture visuals and references, their pop promo and MTV-like montages – is not a fan of pop music. His passion is classical music. For instance, although Russell agreed to direct the Who's rock opera *Tommy*, he didn't like the music, and didn't like it after the film was made.[64] Russell is not, for example, a baby boomer, or of the hippy generation: he is a generation older than baby boomers (his formative years were the 1930s and 1940s: he was out of his teens by 1947, and was 33 in 1960). Russell didn't make documentaries about pop musicians, for instance (tho' I wish he had! – he was ideally placed in the boom in British music in the 1960s to produce documentaries on the Beatles, the Stones, the Kinks, the Who, etc), but about classical music (with the odd foray into folk).[65]

But Ken Russell has become associated with rock music – not least because he directed one of the great rock operas, *Tommy*. He has also helmed some pop promos (for acts such as Elton John, Sarah Brightman, Cliff Richard and Bryan Adams; the music videos were made mainly between 1985 and 1993).[66] And Russell's form of rapid montage cut to music certainly foreshadows MTV and music videos of the 1980s (that is, he films classical music like rock music – and if you've heard Ludwig van Beethoven, Dimitri Shostakovitch or Guiseppe Verdi,

---

[63] Other filmmakers have gone back to the early part of the 20th century repeatedly: Woody Allen and Francis Coppola come to mind.
[64] D. Sterritt, 1975.
[65] However, some of his documentaries contain pop music – *Pop Goes the Easel*, for instance.
[66] Pop promos were easy money for someone like Russell, and meant only one or two days for shooting (like commercials! Unlike commercials, tho', music videos were based around music, Russell's undying passion).

you'll know that classical music can be *way* heavier, *more* violent, *more* intense and *more* visceral than Led Zep, Black Sabbath, Napalm Death or the hardest of hardcore, the deadliest of death metal, or the scariest of speed metal music).

ROMANTIC STYLE.

A recurring motif in Ken Russell's approach to the natural world is to put a single figure in amongst the sublime beauty of the world and completely dwarf them. Often Russell will instruct his camera operator to frame the figure at the end of the zoom, then zoom out slowly. An apparently simple technique, yes, but immensely effective. It crops up in *Dante's Inferno*, in *Tommy,* in *The Dance of the Seven Veils*, in *The Devils,* in *The Debussy Film,* and in many Russell works. In *The Debussy Film,* there's a memorable scene where the camera frames the composer swimming in the English Channel and holds it for a long time: the human figure is a tiny speck in the immensity of the natural world. In *Dante's Inferno,* the camera begins on William Morris in Iceland (actually the Lake District), and pulls back and back, revealing the epic scenery of mountains and lakes, dwarfing the figure. The memorable climax to *Women In Love* features Gerald Crich trudging off into a wilderness of snow and ice (a one-take shot).

The concept clearly draws on the Romantic artists, on British artists such as John Martin and J.M.W. Turner, and on German artist Caspar David Friedrich. It's about Romantic ideas such as the Sublime, the Transcendent, the Infinite, and Nature. Ken Russell's images are direct inheritors of Romanticism (and some of his images are celluloid versions of a Friedrich painting).

OVER THE TOP.

I've mentioned how exotic and weird some of Ken Russell's movies can be, but there were many films made in the 1960s through 1980s which were just as Out There – I mean those films labelled 'mondo cinema', or 'exploitation cinema', or 'sexploitation', or 'underground cinema', or 'horror cinema' (movies which developed cult status, and had re-runs at midnight screenings, and later came back from the dead (like re-animated zombies) on video cassette, and yet again on DVD and Blu-ray or online streaming).

Spoofing Catholic themes and imagery is a big part of those European mondo/ exploitation/ horror flicks (understandable, being as many were made in Italy, France and Spain, and even lapsed Catholics or anti-Catholics still lerrrve to exploit the imagery). There are films about Dracula, Frankenstein, monsters, vampires, occultism, horror, Satanism, the Devil, nuns, and on and on, in 100s of pictures made in Europe between the 1960s and the 1980s, the era when Ken Russell was directing his feature films. And Russell's films, with their eroticized nuns, their sex scenes and nudity and flashcuts and all, are very much part of low budget, European filmmaking of the 1960s-70s, part of the clutch of horror, sex, exploitation and *fantastique* films – the vampires, aliens, serial killers, babes and freaks.

Part of the reason is that horror, thriller and occult flicks are cheap to make. And that's also why so many of those films include nudity – all you have to do is get people to take off their clothes: instant special effects! (Even better if they possess super-gorgeous bodies). You don't have to build vast sets or have costly costumes. It's the same with porno films (and also why porn often takes up horror or sci-fi or occult genres).

So although we exalt filmmakers such as Ken Russell or Pier Paolo Pasolini or Walerian Borowczyk or whoever – because they are 'serious' filmmakers, filmmakers who've made some 'serious' work which can be properly called 'art' – there are hundreds of other filmmakers and films of that period which contain just as much outrageous imagery. I mean filmmakers like José Bénazéraf, Jess Franco, Jean Rollin, José Larraz, Massimo Pupillo, etc. Or maybe it's because, somehow, the works of filmmakers like Pier Paolo Pasolini, Alain Robbe-Grillet and Ken Russell have survived, while so many others have been forgotten.

CATHOLIC STYLE.

Ken Russell's pictures are awash in Catholic imagery,[67] so much so it constitutes a style of its own (no other British filmmaker has produced so much Catholic and Christian material – tho' European ones have). If there's an opportunity for putting in a reference to Catholicism, Russell will take it. If there *isn't* a chance, Russell will invent one! Russell's Catholic style tends towards the extreme end of Catholicism, where sex and the sacred, sin and spirit, merge: lusty nuns (*The Devils*), randy, insane priests (*Crimes of Passion*), Nazi stormtroopers writhing in front of crucifixes (*Mahler*), Christ figures kissing nuns (*The Devils*), phallic worms sliding over crosses (*The Lair of the White Worm*), Satanic goats (*Altered States*), and so on.

THE KEN RUSSELL SCHOOL OF FILMMAKING: RUSSELL'S COLLABORATORS

Ken Russell's films, like those of Francis Coppola or Orson Welles, were somewhat family affairs: for many years his costume designer was his wife Shirley Kingdon. His children (by Kingdon) appeared in and worked on many films (Victoria (b. 1963), Alex (b. 1959), James (b. 1958), Toby (b. 1964), Xavier (b. 1957), and Victoria and Xavier were part of the crew on later productions (as well as her dad's movies, Victoria Russell has also designed the costumes for *Color Me Kubrick*).[68] Molly has acted in US TV shows. Alex is a painter.

Among the most important collaborators on Ken Russell's films were his producers – Roy Baird and Harry Benn and Ronaldo Vasconcellos and Dan Ireland (and also

---

[67] 'All my films have been Catholic films, films about love, faith, sin, forgiveness, redemption', except for *The Boy Friend*, Ken Russell remarked.
[68] Most memorably, Victoria appeared as Sally Simpson in *Tommy*. Ken Russell's other children – Alex, Molly, Rupert, etc – have also appeared in his movies.

Sandy Lieberson and David Puttnam). Baird acted as producer, with Benn often doing production manager duties. (Baird co-produced *Women In Love*).

SHIRLEY KINGDON.

The influence of Ken Russell's wife Shirley Ann Kingdon (1935-2002)[69] should not be under-estimated: presumably they would have discussed Russell's projects in great detail, with Shirley contributing all sorts of suggestions.[70]

And the importance of costume in Ken Russell's movies cannot be over-stressed: *all* of his movies are costume movies – not only in the usual sense of being historical films – but because they emphasize costume in every single shot (Russell described *Lisztomania,* for instance, as a costume film, a movie in which costume assumed prime significance; so is *Women In Love*). Taken as a whole, Russell's movies constitute some of the most impressive expressions of costume design in film history.

And while we are mentioning *costume*, it's vital to include *hair* and *make-up* too: for *Women In Love*, it was Charles E. Parker (make-up) and A.G. Scott (hairdresser). That is, as well as being *costume* films, Ken Russell's films are also *hair* films, and *make-up* films.

Although he questioned the practicality and tensions of a husband and wife working together professionally (it's still very rare in cinema), there's no doubt that Ken Russell appreciated the enormous contribution that his wife Shirley Kingdon made to his movies. She was known as 'Second Hand Rose', someone who could find treasures in second hand (used) stores. In *A British Picture*, Russell writes:

> Undoubtedly, one of her greatest talents was the ability to sort through mountains of old clothes and unearth a Fortuni dress – the equivalent of coming across a Stradivarius in a junk shop. In fact, some of our happiest moments together were spent in junk shops with me as her willing assistant. And one has only to look at *Savage*

---

[69] I have referred to Shirley Russell as Shirley Kingdon in this study to differentiate her from Russell when using just the surname.
[70] John Baxter remarked that Kingdon was in on every stage in a production, and a vital member of Russell's coterie (Bax, 56).

Messiah, *The Music Lovers* and *The Boy Friend* to see that it all paid off. (BP, 95)

MICHAEL BRADSELL.

One of Ken Russell's regular editors was Michael Bradsell: he cut *Women In Love*, *The Devils*, *The Music Lovers*, *The Boy Friend*, *Mahler*, *Tommy* and *Savage Messiah*. And Bradsell cut later movies such as *Gothic*, *Aria* and *Hot Pants*. Which makes Bradsell one of the absolutely vital contributors to Russell's cinema, because editing is a particularly important ingredient in Russell's filmic style. It's Bradsell and his team who would have worked out in detail the counter-pointing that Russell likes to employ, where one section or scene is played against another, and the editing techniques such as the famous, Russellian shock cuts.

THE OPENING SCENE

One of Ken Russell's specialities is the strong opening sequence. Many filmmakers, such as Orson Welles and George Lucas, have also cultivated the technique. It's the opposite of employing a s-l-o-w opening sequence which takes five minutes to get into the narrative. Not for Russell a montage of fifteen 2nd unit shots of the principal setting of the story, for example, accompanied by slow, depressing music. Or lengthy quotes or captions. Or a lot of exposition upfront. Russell gets right into it.

Orson Welles said that a movie should open powerfully, because the screen was dead, the thing was just film projected onto a screen. Theatre could get away with slower openings, as the audience settled into their seats. But a movie had to grab the audience right from the beginning – the 'riderless horse' must enter the scene, as Welles put it. Hence the beginning of *Othello* (1952), with that extraordinary funeral on the battlements, or the unbeatable start of *Citizen Kane*.

The Big Beginning was a lesson that Ken Russell learnt

from his television days,[71] when his documentaries for *Monitor* were broadcast in a Sunday evening slot after a movie. As Russell explained:

> I gradually learned that as we followed the main feature film on Sunday night when anyone saw *Monitor*, the average viewer would take x number of seconds to get up and turn it off, so if I had a film on we would drop the logo thing at the beginning and put it at the end and I would devise an opening sequence for my films which would stop them turning off.

So *Lisztomania* starts with composer Franz Liszt and one of his lovers fucking (swiftly followed by a comic duel with swords); *The Debussy Film* (1965) has a beautiful woman being shot with arrows, in a St Sebastian skit; *Mahler* opens with a building by a lake exploding; *Tommy* starts with a man silhouetted against a mighty, orange sun; and *The Devils* launches with a high camp musical number. Russell also acknowledged that viewers tended to be desensitized by so much television viewing. They'd be talking while the news was on, or eating supper while watching a movie. Hence the shock effects, to wake up the audience.

SOME OF KEN RUSSELL'S INFLUENCES

SYMBOLIST ART.

An important influence on the cinema of Ken Russell is late 19th century literary and artistic culture in Europe, including, in Britain, Oscar Wilde,[72] Aubrey Beardsley, and the Pre-Raphaelites. Wilde and his play *Salomé* and the figure of Salomé herself (particularly as enshrined by Beardsley), crop up in many places in Russell's output (even in unlikely places, such as a Michael Caine *Harry Palmer* movie).

---

[71] The device comes from television, where it's called the 'short hook', typically a murder, car crash, or explosion, designed to stop people changing channels (A. Block, 433).
[72] Oscar Wilde became enamoured of French Symbolism, and employed its influences (Moreau, Huysmans, Louÿs), in his *Salomé*.

SURREALISM.

Ken Russell was a fan of Surrealism, and wanted to make a film about Salvador Dali. Jean Cocteau was another big influence on Russell's cinema, and it's easy to spot Cocteau's heightened, theatrical and fantastical elements in his films.[73]

Jean Cocteau's influence can be discerned all over the place – in the work of Jean-Luc Godard, Donald Cammell, Derek Jarman, Orson Welles, Francis Coppola, Kenneth Anger, and of course the Walt Disney Studios, who updated *Beauty and the Beast* in 1991 (as a Broadway musical). It's probably impossible to watch *La Belle et la Bête* or *Blood of a Poet* or one of Cocteau's *Orpheus* films and *not* be influenced. They are so beautiful and enchanting, they can't help but throw a spell over you.[74]

THE LAKE DISTRICT.

The Lake District was used many times by Ken Russell: his beloved Skiddaw, Castle Crag, Derwent Water and Borrowdale Valley (Russell first visited the Lakes in 1965, looking for locations for his Dante Gabriel Rossetti documentary, and later lived there for over 20 years). Cumbria was used for the crag Roger Daltrey climbed at the end of *Tommy* (and the opening picnic scene); Robert Powell's lakeside retreat in *Mahler*; Oliver Reed solemnly consecrates Mass in the mountains and lakes in *The Devils*; and the waterfall where Sammi Davis and Paul McGann made out in *The Rainbow* (and where Reed as Dante Gabriel Rossetti contemplated suicide in Russell's *Monitor* programme about the Pre-Raphaelites).

The Lakes also featured in *Dance of the Seven Veils, Dante's Inferno, Song of Summer, A British Picture* and films on Wordsworth and Coleridge. The area stood in for Norway, Iceland, Bavaria and France. In *A British Picture*, Ken Russell described his first sight of the mountain Skiddaw:

---

[73] 'His films (*La Belle et La Bete, Orpheus*) made a big impact on me. The third amateur movie I made, *Amelia and the Angel* was heavily influenced by Cocteau. It was the one that got me into the BBC', Russell later said.

[74] *The Red Balloon* (Albert Lamorisse, 1956) was also an inspiration for the young Ken Russell.

> I jumped out of bed, pulled the curtains and froze. My heart pounded, my blood raced, I caught my breath, my eyes widened, my hair stood on end, an unseen orchestra played a tremendous chord. Only clichés can describe what no one has ever been able to portray – a vision of God. (BP, 130-1)

▼

It's striking how much of Ken Russell's cinema deals with France and French culture: *The Devils, Always On Sunday, The Debussy Film, Don't Shoot the Composer, Delius: Song of Summer* and *Prisoner of Honor,* are either set in France or are about French art and culture. Meanwhile, French scenes appear in *Savage Messiah, Isadora Duncan,* and *Lisztomania.*[75]

Russia and Russian culture is found in many places in Ken Russell's cinema (as well as pro-Soviet politics): in *The Music Lovers,* obviously, which takes on a Russian musical icon. Also: *Isadora Duncan, Billion Dollar Brain,* the unmade *Nijinsky,* and *Valentino* starred a famous, Russian ballet dancer. Germany and German society and art is another element in Russell's movies, from *Mahler* and *Lisztomania* to *Lotte Lenya Sings Kurt Weill* and *Dance of the Seven Veils.* And of course there are numerous references to German music (Beethoven, Wagner, Strauss) in Russell's cinema.

FILM INFLUENCES.

Ken Russell said in *A British Picture* that he consumed movies by the ton when he was young. Like Ingmar Bergman, Russell had his own film projectors, and played Fritz Lang, Leni Reifenstahl, Harold Lloyd, Charlie Chaplin, Felix the Cat, Mickey Mouse, Snub Pollard, Betty Boop, and, later, Jean Cocteau, René Clair, Jean Vigo and Orson Welles. The visionary epics *Die Niebelungen* (1924) and *Metropolis* (1926) were some of Russell's most beloved early influences. 'I'd seen thousands of films by then but never any that excited me as much as these', Russell recalled in 1973 (Bax, 62). *The Secret of the Loch* was another favourite. At the local flea pit he saw *Flash Gordon*, Felix the Cat, Betty Boop and Old Mother Reilley;

---

[75] But very few of Russell's Francophone flicks were filmed in France.

later, he devoured F.W. Murnau, Jean Vigo, G.W. Pabst, Sergei Eisenstein, Jean Renoir and Jean Cocteau (BP, 16-17). Orson Welles was another inspiration for Russell:

> Orson Welles had that magic as well. I still think *Citizen Kane* is a masterpiece. There's nothing like that ever made in English cinema, not with that style and flair.[76]

There's so much one can say about *Citizen Kane,* of course, but here I'll emphasize one aspect in relation to the cinema of Ken Russell, and that's the feeling of *play,* of experimentation, of trying all sorts of stuff out in a movie. In short, the utter *joy* of making movies. Orson Welles had that, and Russell has it in spades. And it never leaves him (just as it never left Welles: Welles simply *adored* making movies).

The *sheer joy* of making cinema bounces out of *Citizen Kane,* and it does in Ken Russell's finest work. It's the pleasure of putting sounds and music and images together, which's an important aspect of the some of the best movies – you can see it in *An American In Paris* or *Contempt* or *Porco Rosso* or *Once Upon a Time In China.* The filmmakers' enjoyment undoubtedly helps to keep these movies alive in the very crowded world of cinema.

And in Ken Russell's movies and TV shows, you can see that he and the production teams were having a ball. True, there were productions that were fraught with problems, but you don't make as many movies and TV shows as Russell has unless you're crazy about the whole process.

In his films, Ken Russell, like many another filmmaker, would create conscious nods to some of his favourite filmmakers: silent comedy *à la* Harold Lloyd or Charlie Chaplin (in *Tommy*);[77] a slice of epic action from Sergei Eisenstein[78] (in *Billion Dollar Brain*); the Surrealism

---

[76] Ken Russell has cribbed the beginning of *Citizen Kane* a number of times – consciously, of course. At the beginning of *Isadora Duncan*, for instance, or in *The Debussy Film*, or the multiple viewpoint form of *Valentino*.
[77] Ken Russell adores the silent comedy classics, and has references to Charlie Chaplin, Laurel and Hardy, Harold Lloyd, and Buster Keaton in numerous places in his movies.
[78] There's quite a bit of Eisenstein in Russell's œuvre.

and dreamy fantasy of Jeans Cocteau and Vigo; or the deep focus, black-and-white cinematography of Orson Welles and Ingmar Bergman (in *Delius: Song of Summer* and *Dante's Inferno*), plus plenty of Bergman's penchant for angst and intensity.

It's clear that Ken Russell would've flourished in the early days of Hollywood, for instance – working alongside giants like D.W. Griffith or Cecil B. DeMille, or turning out knockabout comedy for Mack Sennett or Charlie Chaplin. Indeed, the melodrama and spectacle of Griffith's cinema has so many affinities with Russell's – such as *Intolerance*, with its grandiose sets, its extravagant costumes, its parallel stories, its incredible climaxes, its eye-popping action, and the screen teeming with details and life.

In fact, silent comedy is an *enormous* influence on Ken Russell's cinema, and scenes filmed in a silent comedy manner can be found everywhere in his work. Silent comedy is one of Russell's default modes of film-making; it's something he can do as naturally as anything else. A *major* fan, a *passionate* fan of all of silent cinema – there are references to it in every single one of Russell's movies and TV shows.

Ken Russell would've been quite at home in the Germany of the 1920s, too, in amongst great productions such as *Nosferatu, Metropolis* or *Die Niebelungen.* The silent cinema era features prominently in *Mahler, Tommy, Lisztomania, Isadora Duncan, Dante's Inferno, The Dance of the Seven Veils, The Boy Friend,* and the whole of *Valentino.*

When considering Ken Russell's influences from the history of cinema, it's striking just how many were French and German: Fritz Lang, F.W. Murnau, René Clair, G.W. Pabst, Jean Renoir, Leni Reifenstahl, Jean-Luc Godard and two Jeans (Vigo and Cocteau). So as well as consuming the usual North American and British movies (Disney, Chaplin, Lloyd, *Betty Boop, Fritz the Cat,* etc), Russell was very into European cinema.

SYMBOLS AND MOTIFS

Among the numerous recurring symbols or motifs that Ken Russell employs are circles, the sun, mountains, mirrors, fire, water (lakes, rivers, waterfalls), the colour red, symmetry, trains, and crosses (and anything Catholic or Christian). Russell loves circular motifs, and they appear throughout his work; there are circular windows, circular staircases, circular mirrors, close-ups of mouths and eyes; and course buildings and rooms.

Linked to circles is Ken Russell's use of the spinning camera – when a scene gets really intense, the camera rotates wildly (and there are many upside-down shots too). There are circular dances (like around the Maypole penis in *Lisztomania*); carousels; and spinning pianos (also in *Lisztomania*, and in *The Music Lovers*).

Mountains and spectacular landscapes such as lakes and rivers and the ocean are in Ken Russell's cinema embodiments of romantic, pantheistic, lyrical, life-affirming feelings. Russell becomes a late addition to the roster of Romantic poets: Gerald Crich under the Matterhorn; Tommy standing in the sun; Ursula and Skrebensky running around naked on the hills; Edward Elgar on the Malvern Hills; Grandier communing by the lake in *The Devils*; and Henri Gaudier at the Isle of Portland in *Savage Messiah*.

Often there's a character standing with their arms outstretched, embracing the natural world and fusing with it, in *Women In Love, Tommy, Savage Messiah, Delius: Song of Summer, The Devils, Dante's Inferno,* etc. As Ken Russell describes Tommy's act at the end of *Tommy* in the shooting script: it is 'an affirmation of Man's eternal divinity. Tommy raises his arms as if to embrace the life giving sun' (the image was put on Russell's coffin at his funeral). D.H. Lawrence was well-known for his extensive use of sun symbolism.

Fire would typically connote chaos and destruction (as in *Mahler, The Devils* and *The Music Lovers*): no one can forget the startling image of the burning fields in *The Music*

Lovers, when Peter Tchaikovsky returns to his country estate to find himself locked out by Madame von Meck (after Count Chiluvsky has told von Meck that Tchaikovsky is gay). In D.H. Lawrence's art, however fire was most often linked to erotic desire (and of course, there's a fire roaring in the famous nude wrestling scene in *Women In Love*).

Symmetry is a favourite visual motif: so often, Ken Russell and his cinematographers will place a character or subject of a scene dead centre. And Russell likes a frontal, *tableau* approach too, as part of his stylization of cinema (like Sergei Paradjanov or Pier Paolo Pasolini). That is, very often scenes will be staged with the characters, props and scenery arranged along lines at right angles to the direction of the camera. However, although the *tableau* approach can produce rather static cinema, Russell's films contain so much dynamism in other areas they are seldom static.

Although he began by making black-and-white movies (as so many have done), and some of his finest pieces, such as *Delius: Song of Summer* and *The Debussy Film*, are in black-and-white, Ken Russell is certainly a remarkable director of *colour* movies. From his first major colour movie – *Billion Dollar Brain* – onwards, Russell has devoted plenty of energy to colour. His techniques include highlighting a particular colour (with red as a favourite, as with Jean-Luc Godard in the Sixties), and also by selective colour, draining all of the colours out of a scene except for one (such as the '1812 Overture' fantasy in *The Music Lovers,* where the scene's reduced to the grey of Peter Tchaikovsky's statue).[79]

DEATH.

Examining the narratives of many of Ken Russell's movies, and the paths they pursue, reveals unusual results. Take the topic of death, for example. In the action-adventure movies and formula dramas, such as *Billion*

---
[79] Yet the five masterpieces Ken Russell made for television in the late 1960s – *Delius: Song of Summer, The Dance of the Seven Veils, Dante's Inferno, Isadora Duncan* and *The Debussy Film* – are all in black-and-white. And that's partly a cost issue, because the BBC wanted to keep costs low. Thankfully, they were filmed on 35mm film stock, because 16mm from that era looks horrible).

Dollar Brain and *Dogboys*, one expects the bad guys to die. But many characters die in Russell's other movies, underlining the themes of tragedy, toxic personalities and self-destruction.

At the end of *Women in Love*, Gerald Crich stalks off into the snowy mountains to die. Peter Tchaikovsky dies at the end of *The Music Lovers* (and his mother at the beginning). So does Gustav Mahler, and Henri Gaudier, and Rudolph Valentino, and Frederick Delius, and Franz Liszt. Tommy's parents are killed in front of him. Urbain Grandier in *The Devils* has the lengthiest and most gruesome demise, in a movie literally littered with corpses. 'The emphasis on death and violence in my films could be a reaction against death being hushed up', Russell mused in 1973 (Bax, 200).

Clearly, for his artist characters, Ken Russell uses death as the means of closing the piece dramatically *and* thematically. And these deaths are not tacked on to the piece, to give it some serious import, as lesser filmmakers do, they are signalled throughout the piece (with their death drives, their suicidal tendencies, their corrosive personalities which affect everyone around them).

We're not talking in terms of some viewers in the audience knowing that Gustav Mahler or Henri Gaudier-Brzeska died before their time. We're talking about *movie* logic. And by that same dramatic logic, other characters should really die – for instance, after that feverish night in 1987's *Gothic*, one of those crazy writers and poets should die (Lord Byron definitely, and perhaps Percy Bysshe Shelley, too). That would ram home the cost of creativity in the Russellian manner (of course, *Gothic does* end with a corpse – the dead baby, with its Frankensteinian features).

KEN RUSSELL'S INFLUENCE

You don't think of Ken Russell as an influential filmmaker, like, say, Orson Welles or D.W. Griffith, Stanley Kubrick or Jean-Luc Godard, filmmakers who have certainly influenced many, many film folk. But Russell has definitely had an impact on cinema, and not only in Blighty. Anyhoo, a filmmaker with such a strong style is bound to influence somebody. *Women In Love* has certainly influenced pretty much all adaptions of D.H. Lawrence's work.

For instance, when he was shooting what is perhaps the greatest war movie, *Apocalypse Now* (1979), Francis Coppola said he was directing it like a Ken Russell movie, operatic, with coloured flares. And Coppola again took up the Ken Russell approach when he adapted *Dracula* for the screen in 1992 (as critics such as Ken Gelder have pointed out in *New Vampire Cinema*).

You can detect Ken Russell's impact in the films of Oliver Stone (*The Doors*), Baz Luhrmann (*Romeo + Juliet, Moulin Rouge*), Rob Marshall (*Chicago*), Peter Jackson (*The Lord of the Rings*), Derek Jarman (*The Tempest, Caravaggio*), Peter Greenaway, Franc Roddam (*Quadrophenia*), Milos Forman (*Amadeus*), Alan Parker (*Pink Floyd: The Wall, Evita*), Bob Fosse (*All That Jazz*) and Michelangelo Antonioni (*Blow Up*).

The 1963 documentary *Watch the Birdie*, about the photographer David Hurn, apparently influenced Italian director Michelangelo Antonioni when he came to direct *Blow Up* in Londinium (according to Ken Russell [G, 44]). Antonioni used it for research into Swinging London.

Rainer Werner Fassbinder was also influenced by Ken Russell, according to Joseph Lanza (who discerns Russell's impact on *Berlin Alexanderplatz*; it's easy to spot the affinities between Fassbinder and Russell!). 2001's *Moulin Rouge* is a Ken Russell movie in all but name (but not as good), as are *Amadeus* and *Shine*.

Sometimes filmmakers – and film critics – have used Ken Russell as an example of the kind of filmmaking they *don't* want to produce or to see more of. The socialist-realist school, those filmmakers who derive from the British 'kitchen sink', the 'Angry Young Men' and the documentary tradition, sometimes use Russell as the sort of filmmaking they want to avoid (even though Russell has of course produced many documentaries, and he also emerged from the documentary tradition in Britain of the early 1960s which also helped to form prominent filmmakers such as Ken Loach, Mike Leigh, Lindsay Anderson and Karel Reisz).

There's no doubt that in the realm of acting and performance, Ken Russell has had an influence. Russell has coaxed out some marvellous and memorable performances from his casts. For someone who says he doesn't really know how to direct actors, the performances mentioned below (there are many more) are proof that Russell must've been doing something right: Oliver Reed and Vanessa Redgrave in *The Devils,* Reed and Judith Paris in *Dante's Inferno*, Alan Bates, Glenda Jackson and Reed in *Women in Love*, Max Adrian in *Delius*, Richard Chamberlain and Jackson in *The Music Lovers*, Ann-Margaret in *Tommy,* Robert Powell in *Mahler,* Roger Daltrey in *Lisztomania* and *Tommy*, Christopher Gable in *Dance of the Seven Veils* and Amanda Donohue in *The Lair of the White Worm.*

CLASSICAL MUSIC

> The combination of pictures and music has always been my favourite form of expression – surmounting all language barriers.
>
> Ken Russell (BP, 209)

Music ♪, for Ken Russell, is perhaps

the most incredible event in human history.[80]

I love that remark!

Ken Russell has never lost that sense of awe of music, and the ecstatic pleasure it gives. I totally agree with him:

I could not live without music.

Many times Ken Russell has employed music on set to get his actors (and crew) into a mood: for the 'rape of Christ' scene in *The Devils*, Russell

> found the most barbaric bit of *The Rite of Spring*, the music to which I had danced naked myself in my parents' house, and played it flat out. Without it the nuns were simply unable to cope: they were totally inhibited. There's a liberating force in music which, even if they don't appreciate the music as such, people can't help responding to, being primitive creatures at heart. If you let it take you over, as Glenda did, you can do anything you like. (Bax, 188-9)

The number of classical composers that Ken Russell made films about is very impressive: Peter Tchaikovsky, Gustav Mahler, Richard Wagner, Franz Liszt, Sergei Prokofiev, Claude Debussy, Frederick Delius, Richard Strauss, Edward Elgar (twice), Ralph Vaughan Williams, Sir Arnold Bax, Anton Bruckner, Béla Bartók, Boshuslav Martinu, and Gustav Holst. Extraordinarily, although most of those studies of classic composers were made for television, the first four were feature films (Wagner and Liszt appeared in *Lisztomania*).

And he staged operas by Igor Stravinsky (*The Rake's Progress*, 1982), Giacomo Puccini (*Madame Butterfly*,

---

[80] L. Langley, 1971.

1983 and *La Bohéme*, 1984), Gioacchino Rossini (*The Italian Woman In Algiers*, 1984), Bernd-Alois Zimmermann (*Die Soldaten*, 1984), Charles Gounod (*Faust*, 1985), Arrigo Boito (*Méphistophélès*, 1989),[81] Gilbert & Sullivan (*Princess Ida*, 1992) and Richard Strauss (*Salomé*, 1993).[82] This's one reason why there were fewer movies in Russell's later years – he was working in live opera.

Ken Russell directed operas, but he could've had a career directing stage musicals for Broadway and the West End. His flair for combining images, sets, costumes, colours, lighting, movement, dance and dialogue with music is simply extraordinary (and *timing*, too: Russell has a showman's sense of timing, rhythm and pace, of knowing just when to slow a movie down, and when to ramp up the energy. He is also a master of the sudden reveal and the surprising jolt, the equal of Alfred Hitchcock or D.W. Griffith).

Then there was a documentary called *Classic Widows* (1995) about the wives of William Walton, Benjamin Frankel, Humphrey Searle and Bernard Stevens, a revisit to Edward Elgar on TV in 2002, a documentary about folk songs (*In Search of the English Folk Song*, 1998),[83] and a guide to British music (1988).

And more recently, in the 2000s, Ken Russell embarked upon some fictionalized accounts of classical composers: essentially, they are novelizations of his movies (such as Frederick Delius, Ludwig van Beethoven, Johannes Brahms and Edward Elgar), focussing (inevitably) on their erotic relationships, in book form (and also as e-books).

Over the years, Ken Russell worked with many composers and conductors who were important figures in the British (and international) classical music scene: Peter Maxwell Davies, Richard Rodney Bennett, André Previn

---

[81] This was filmed by Valiant SRL.
[82] Ken Russell's approach to opera was to deliver a new interpretation – rather than a traditional take (BP, 227), and that sometimes led to controversy. In his autobiography, he waxes lyrical about particular singers.
[83] Ken Russell's exploration of the British folk song included performances by a roll call of many big names of the time, including: Waterson Carthy, Eliza Carthy, June Tabor, Osibisa, the Albion Band, the Percy Grainger Chamber Orchestra, Donovan, and Fairport Convention.

and Carl Davis. Russell also collaborated with some of the big names in British pop music: the Who, Elton John, Eric Clapton (*Tommy*), Rick Wakeman (*Lisztomania* and *Crimes of Passion*), and Thomas Dolby (*Gothic*).

However, *very* few biographies of classical music composers have taken an irreverent approach, like Ken Russell's. The opposite is the norm: total awe at the creative process (though the messy private lives are explored in some biopics). Russell's *ir*reverence is still unusual: that sort of attack on a Great Artist is still seen as disrespectful.

When he takes on a classical composer, it is the *music* that is primary for Ken Russell, not only the biography of the composer. *The music*.[84] This cannot be over-stated enough, but it's one of the main reasons for the misunderstandings that Russell's films lead to. He is *not* producing a 'realistic' film or even a standard documentary piece about an artist. He is looking at their *art*, and is regarding music (perhaps incorrectly) as expressing something of the inner life of the subject. As he explains about his approach to the 1974 movie *Mahler*: he 'searched for the soul of the man in his music' (BP, 141). That sums it up neatly: films such as *Mahler, The Music Lovers, Lisztomania, Delius: Song of Summer* and *The Debussy Film* are searches for the soul of the man in his music.

Ken Russell also clearly *understands* music in depth – very few film directors possess that level of understanding and knowledge (many, many famous film directors knew absolutely nothing about music, and weren't able to communicate with their composers beyond simple suggestions. Many of the celebrated directors today can't get beyond statements such as: 'I like the music'). Even when he is being outrageous and conjuring out-size imagery and scenes, you can still tell that Russell understands the music in his movies in an incredibly detailed

---

[84] The title itself – *The Music Lovers* – is clearly deeply personal for Ken Russell.

manner.[85]

Ken Russell's classical music movies and TV shows also depict plenty of musicians at work: composers are seen composing, writing on manuscripts, playing at the piano, conducting, performing live, singing, etc. The trappings of classical music are everywhere, too: musical manuscript paper, the conductor's baton, the metronome, the brass band, the violin, the piano (the props guys must've humped 100s of pianos on and off sets for Russell's movies).

Ken Russell remarked that raising finance for films about classical music composers was difficult. I should say nearly impossible. Many of Russell's films were about artists, and very few biopics about artists cross over into the mainstream and become big hits. You need big stars and a fantastic script and a really sexy subject for your biopic. Films about movie stars or rock stars, well, that's different (*The Doors, Ray, Rock Star, Almost Famous, Dreamgirls*).

MORE ABOUT MUSIC

One of Ken Russell's great passions is classical music. His memoirs abound with references to Tchaikovsky, Mahler, Strauss, Elgar, Liszt, Prokofiev, Beethoven and Bach. 'My imagery comes from listening to music,' Russell asserted (BP, 156). He is a 'slave of music', as Percy Bysshe Shelley put it.

'I was mad on music, and would rush out like a starving man and get all the records I could afford,' Ken Russell recalled of his youth. 'I couldn't get enough of it' (Bax, 82-83). Well, we know that!: music saturates Russell's entire work, in movies, television, books, newspaper articles, and photography. For Russell, music was like oxygen (Bax, 102).

The affinities between cinema and music are count-

---

[85] However, Russell wasn't a musician. But being so knowledgeable about music no doubt made it so much easier for his composers to talk with him about film scoring.

less, and filmmakers have been exploiting them since the birth of cinema. The notion of all the arts moving towards the condition of one art (or as Walter Pater famously put it, towards music), developed in the age of Romanticism. German poet Novalis spoke of 'painting, plastic art are therefore nothing but figurative music. Painting, plastic art – objective music. Music – subjective music or painting'.

Huw Wheldon and *Monitor* was instrumental in getting Ken Russell's ideas for biopics on great composers made – building on the *Monitor* TV programmes, Russell continued with feature films on musicians. Russell noted that there have very few films on composers, apart from his own *The Music Lovers* and Tony Palmer's *Testimony* (presumably he means *his* sort of films about composers). 'What I've always been after is the spirit of the composer as manifest in his music' (1993, 75).

BIOPICS.

Many of Ken Russell's films are drawn from biographies of real people – most obviously, classical composers. Some of those biopics are based on books, and some on extensive research. For the rest of his output, Russell has used, like almost all filmmakers, books and plays: literary works such as *The Rainbow, Women In Love, Lady Chatterley's Lover, Billion Dollar Brain, Altered States, The Fall of the House of Usher, The Lair of the White Worm, The Devils of Loudun,* or plays such as *The Boy Friend, The Devils, Salome's Last Dance* and *Whore*.

So most of Ken Russell's films are not original screenplays in the sense of original stories featuring characters that haven't been seen before. There is plenty of research in a Ken Russell movie. Like Francis Coppola and Stanley Kubrick, Russell enjoys that part of the preparation for a project. But that doesn't mean that the research will end up on screen undiluted by Russell's vision and style.

Before he begins a biopic, Ken Russell said he immersed himself in the

> iconography of the period, the photography, the painting, the literature. I absorb it like a piece of blotting paper and

then I just go and do the film. (In F. Robbins, 1973)

Ken Russell's first biopic was of a classical music composer, naturally – Sergei Prokofiev (*Portrait of a Soviet Composer*, 1961). Many of Russell's programmes for television were about music: *The Miner's Picnic* (brass bands), *Portrait of a Soviet Composer* (Sergei Prokofiev), *Variations On a Mechanical Theme* (mechanical instruments), *Guitar Craze, Lotte Lenya Sings Kurt Weill, Elgar, Bartók, The Debussy Film, Don't Shoot the Composer* (Georges Delerue), *The Dance of the Seven Veils* (Richard Strauss) and *Delius: Song of Summer.*

Two of Ken Russell's early TV films were about dance: *Marie Rambert* (1959) was about the Ballet Rambert company, and *The Light Fantastic* (1960) was about dancing in England. And *Isadora Duncan* was of course about one of Russell's favourite artists (Duncan also influenced Gudrun's dancing style in *Women In Love*, and 'Gosh' Smith-Boyle in *Savage Messiah*).

Then there were shows on painters (*Pop Goes the Easel, McBryde and Colquhoun*, the Pre-Raphaelite Museum in Battersea, Dante Gabriel Rossetti, Henri Rousseau), poets (John Betjeman, and, later, William Wordsworth and Samuel Taylor Coleridge), and architecture (*Antonio Gaudi*).

Ken Russell said he was trying to do what music composers do – to express something inexpressible, to reach an area of divine mystery.[86] You could put it another way: Russell's movies tend towards the condition of music. Or that he is trying to explore the same realms as music.

Life is a mystery for Ken Russell – and one reason why artists were important was because 'artists somehow make mysteries concrete, make them more tangible. They interpret the ineffable for the rest of us' (RC, 246).

For Richard Eder (1976), Ken Russell's biopics are really about Russell himself: they reveal more about the director than they do about Mahler or Tchaikovsky or Liszt.

---
[86] J. Walker, "Ken Russell's New Enigma", *The Observer*, Sept 8, 1974.

> As far as the audience is concerned, it is almost as if Tchaikovsky, Liszt and Mahler had taken turns making films about Mr Russell.

You may not notice a significant omission from many of Ken Russell's films and biographies about classical music composers, and this is the standard *contextualization* of documentaries and biographies. In Russell's TV shows and films about composers (and artists), there is no introductory segment outlining the politics and key events of the period, no images of kings and queens and politicians and big events such as wars or coups or revolutions or assassinations or whatever. There are few dates, too, saying what year it was that, say, Frederick Delius contracted syphilis (it was 1922), or what year Franz Liszt first met Richard Wagner (it was in 1849), or when Gustav Mahler composed his *Ninth Symphony* (it was in 1908-09).

All of that is simply left aside in Ken Russell's TV shows and movies – all of that pedagogical stuff which public service broadcasters such as the BBC and PBS put into their documentaries. Russell's films and television programmes don't lecture their audience, don't assume the role of a teacher or a nanny. (If you want that info, you can look it up in your own time – the movie or TV show won't do it for you).

Instead, the shows go straight for explorations of the artist themselves and their work. And they also assume that their viewers are fairly intelligent, and already know quite a bit about European history from 1800 to the present.

DANCE.

Another Ken Russell passion was dance (at one time he had trained in ballet). He performed with the British Dance Theatre and the London Theatre Ballet, including going on tours, and also with the Norwegian Ballet (including a visit to Oslo). Russell has written of his times with touring dance companies in his autobiographies.

There was an enormous amount of dancing in *The*

Boy Friend; Glenda Jackson cavorted in front of the cattle in *Women in Love* (plus Hermione's dance, and the dance in Switzerland); Rudolf Nureyev, probably the world's foremost ballet dancer of the period, starred in *Valentino*; characters in *The Music Lovers*, and *Mahler,* and *Savage Messiah*, and *The Debussy Film*, and many others move choreographically; dance runs throughout *Isadora Duncan* and *The Dance of the Seven Veils*, movies which're wholly dance-oriented. If there's a chance to squeeze in a dance number into a film, Russell will do it. In fact, it'd be quicker to cite movies and TV shows directed by Russell which *don't* contain any dancing. (And there's plenty of ballet dancing, as well as more popular dancing in Russell's movies; films featuring ballet are a sub-genre of the dance genre. Some are records of performances, like *Swan Lake, A Midsummer Night's Dream* and *The Nutcracker Suite*, or ballet companies such as the Bolshoi Ballet. Russell contributed with ballet documentaries; and one of his key performers, Christopher Gable, was with the Royal Ballet).

'When you're dancing, you're really alive'.

So says Isadora Duncan in Ken Russell's and Sewell Stokes' 1966 BBC movie *Isadora Duncan*. It's certainly one of Russell's credos. No other British filmmaker, and probably no other filmmaker in the history of cinema, even including great dance directors such as Bob Fosse, Gene Kelly or Vincente Minnelli, has included so much dancing in their works. (Fosse, for instance, directed far fewer movies than Russell, and although Minnelli made more musicals than Russell (including some of the classics, Russell includes choreography even in straight melodramas. If Russell had directed a biopic of Vincent van Gogh, he would've been dancing thru the wheatfields).

In other movies, Ken Russell often favours physical acting, rather than verbal dexterity. Russell advocated a cinema of visual spectacle, not people sitting around talking. Like Michael Powell, Russell had admired Vaslav Nijinsky (he had planned a film on the Russian dancer, while Pressburger and Powell's *The Red Shoes* had a

Sergei Diaghilev figure). Dancers such as Nijinsky and Isadora Duncan were touchstones for Russell, even tho' they died before his time. One can imagine that if a time machine were available, Russell would certainly have gone to see them dance, as well as met heroes such as Ludwig van Beethoven and Peter Tchaikovsky (and wherever Russell is now, maybe he's met some of his heroes!).

RELIGION

One aspect of Ken Russell's cinema is so potent and pervasive it's impossible to miss, but it's not uppermost in many appraisals of his output by critics and viewers: *religion*.

What are the major themes in Ken Russell's cinema?

Art and artists, yes. Classical music, yes. 19th and 20th century culture, yes. Sex and love and relationships, yes. Nature and pantheism, yes. Death, suicide, loss, yes. And a stylistic approach which's typically parodic or camp as well as reverential – an approach that simultaneously sends up and celebrates its subject matter, yes.

But there is one theme that often pushes aside all of those themes: religion.

Religion is a major component of the following pieces: *The Dance of the Seven Veils* (Richard Strauss's Catholicism), *Mahler* (Gustav Mahler's conversion to Catholicism), *Lisztomania* (in which the superstar composer lives in Rome (in/ near the Vatican), and hobnobs with the Pope, and Nazism as a new religion), the operas *Faust* and *Méphistophélès* (bargains with the Devil), *Salomé* (Richard Strauss's opera, and Oscar Wilde's play), *Tommy* (a rock messiah with a cult of followers), *Altered States* (religious guilt and drug-taking as self-transcendence), *The Lair of the White Worm* (all about an ancient snake cult), *Crimes of Passion* (featuring a manic priest), and of course *The Devils*. There are many other examples.

No other major British filmmaker in the history of British cinema has put religion to the forefront in so many films and TV shows. It's a concern so fundamental to Ken Russell's cinema, it places him in the same company as Ingmar Bergman, Pier Paolo Pasolini, Andrei Tarkovsky and Carl-Theodor Dreyer.[87]

And *no* other filmmaker in recent times has staged so many crucifixions. Not Martin Scorsese, not Piero Paolo Pasolini, not Abel Ferrara, not Paul Verhoeven, not even the many directors of made-for-TV religious specials and mini-series.[88]

Ken Russell converted to Catholicism around the time he was making his first film, *Peepshow,* in 1956. Catholicism fed most of Russell's subsequent movies, and his movies wouldn't be the same without his conversion:

> All my films have been Catholic films, films about love, faith, sin, guilt, forgiveness, redemption. Films that could only have been made by a Catholic.

What are the views expressed about religion in Ken Russell's cinema? They are very easy to see:

> organized religion has its uses, can be æsthetically pretty, but is all too often corrupt and dangerous.

> individual spiritual feeling and transcendence can occur within organized religions, but often flourishes best outside of them.

> the means to self-transcendence and spirituality are many: in Russell's cinema, they might include:

(1) art,
(2) sex and love,
(3) drugs,
(4) music,
(5) nature mysticism.

---

[87] Needless to say, Ken Russell did not like *The Passion of the Christ*; he felt that Mel Gibson and co. had misinterpreted the *Bible*.
[88] Had Ken Russell been born thirty years earlier, and had be gone to Hollywood, he might have been one of the great filmmakers of religious epics in the Cecil B. De Mille and William Wyler manner in the 1950s and 1960s.

MADNESS.

There are more disturbing images of madness in Ken Russell's films than in the work of many a filmmaker. *Women In Love* features a significant amount of insanity and suicide – which are from the 1920 novel. Nina Milyukova at the end of *The Music Lovers,* for instance, or the nuns in *The Devils* and the artist in *Delius: Song of Summer.* And not only insanity, but also hysteria. Richard Wagner at the end of *Lisztomania,* for instance, or the poets in *Gothic.* So many images, one wonders if there is some biographical reason for it. While the costs of being an artist for some dramatists might be death, in Russell's cinema it can lead to madness (a living death).

And in drama and cinema, the living death of madness can be much more disturbing than death itself. While death might give a character's story a tragic or noble or melancholy ending, insanity, like a severely disabling illness, is much more of a punishment (it sure ain't spiritual transcendence or an upward move into martyrdom). At the end of a Hollywood movie a character might end up heroically sacrificing themselves and dying, and saving the world in the process. But to have that same heroic figure becoming insane is very different.

And suicide is a recurring theme, too: characters take their life, or try to, in *Women In Love, The Music Lovers, The Debussy Film, Dante's Inferno, Isadora Duncan,* and *The Devils.* And often those suicides are linked to the central characters, to the artists: they can't take anymore, so they find a way out.

MAKE YOUR OWN KEN RUSSELL MOVIE.

A do-it-yourself kit for a Ken Russell movie would require the following items:

- a piano
- candles
- smoke and fire
- 19th century costumes

- spangly modern costumes
- S/M gear
- Nazi uniforms
- nun costumes
- a horse (and maybe a carriage)
- crucifixes
- swastikas
- a whip
- a conductor's baton
- swords
- a banana,[89] bottle or other phallic totem
- a brass band
- masks & feathers
- a train
- a mirror
- a theatre
- a church
- an asylum
- a lake
- mountains
- a forest
- champagne
- a CD player or i-Pod plus giant speakers & amp (for music playback)

---

[89] Bananas! In a Jean-Luc Godard movie, when actors are at a loss of what to do in a scene, they light a cigarette (again and again in French movies!). In a Ken Russell movie, when an actor asked, 'what shall I do here, Ken?', the maestro probably replied, 'well, I dunno, how about eating a banana?' And if the actor retorted, 'I did that in the last movie, Ken!', the exasperated director might have replied, 'phooey, love, no one will notice! Terry! Where's my champagne?!'

One of the most celebrated of Ken Russell's BBC works,
the Elgar documentary from the early 1960s

Billion Dollar Brain, the 1967 entry in the Harry Palmer series

Dante's Inferno (1968)

The Music Lovers (1970)

VANESSA REDGRAVE

OLIVER REED

The Devils

HELL HOLDS
NO SURPRISES
FOR THEM...

UNRATED

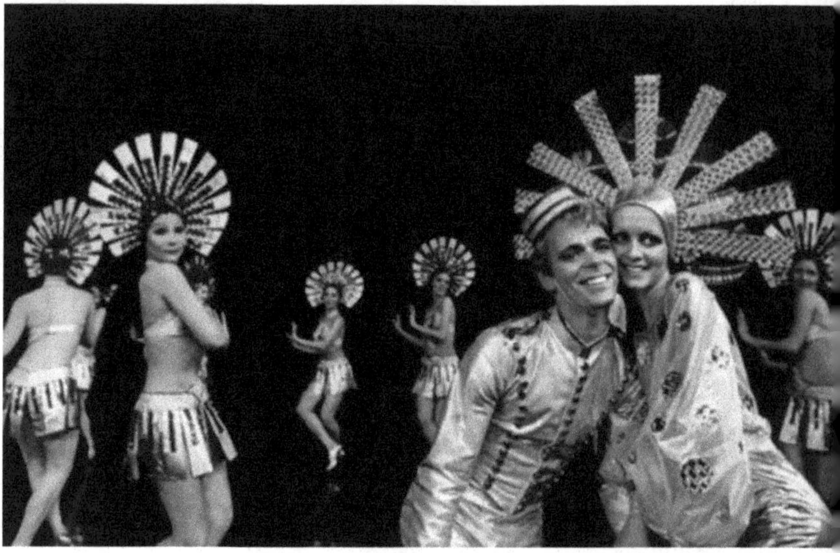

EMI
EMI - MGM Presents
A Ken Russell Production
THE BOY FRIEND
STARRING:
Twiggy

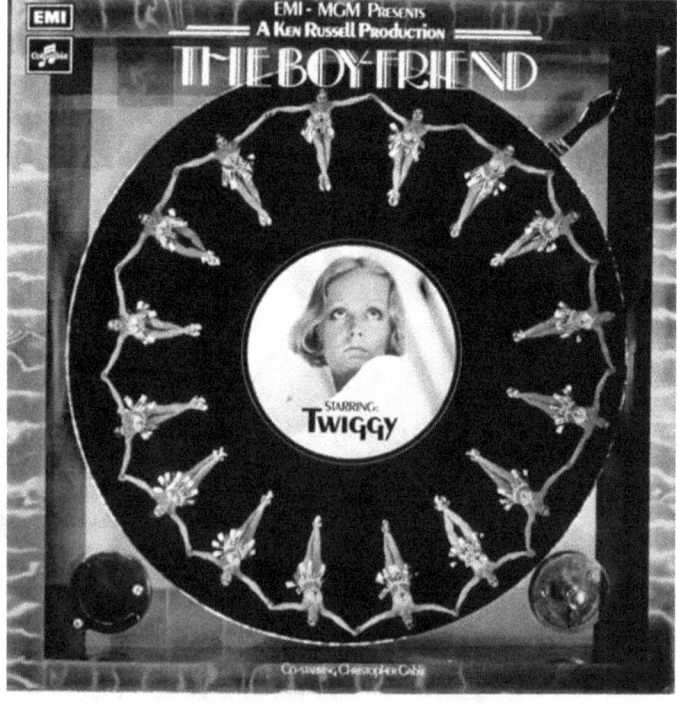

Mahler (1974)

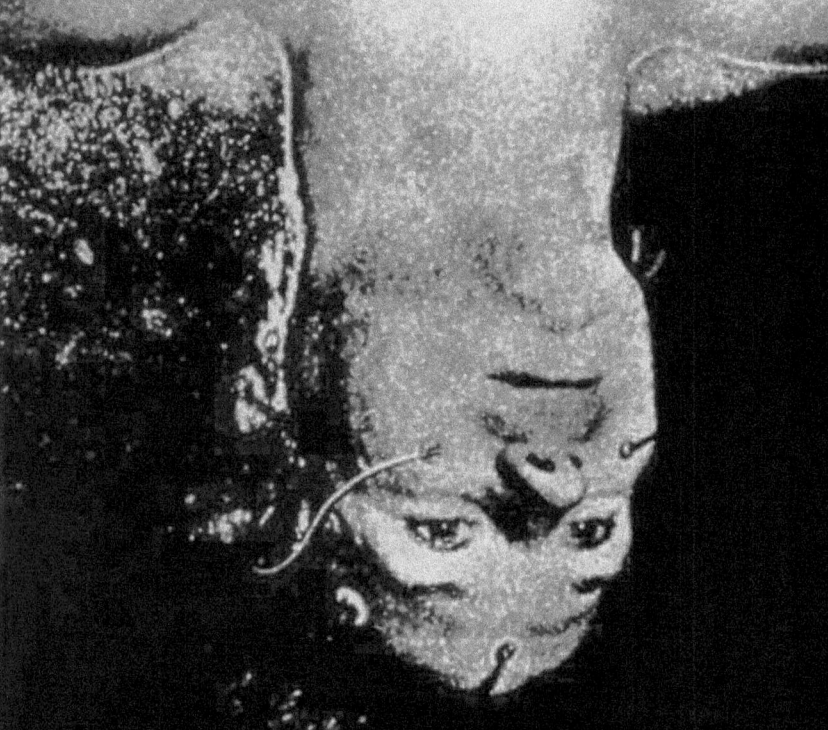

1984's Crimes of Passion

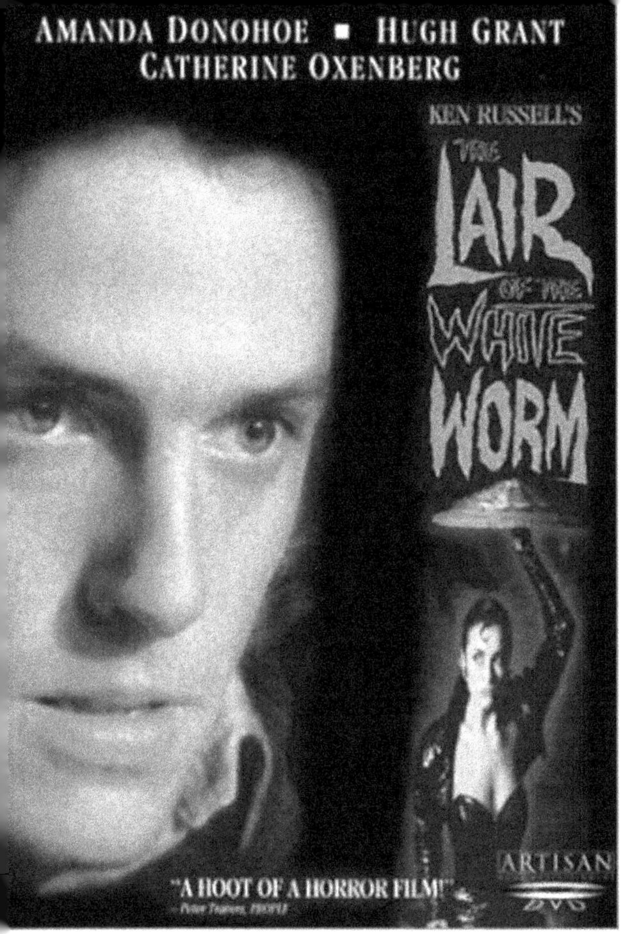
AMANDA DONOHOE ■ HUGH GRANT
CATHERINE OXENBERG
KEN RUSSELL'S
THE LAIR OF THE WHITE WORM
ARTISAN
DVD
"A HOOT OF A HORROR FILM!"

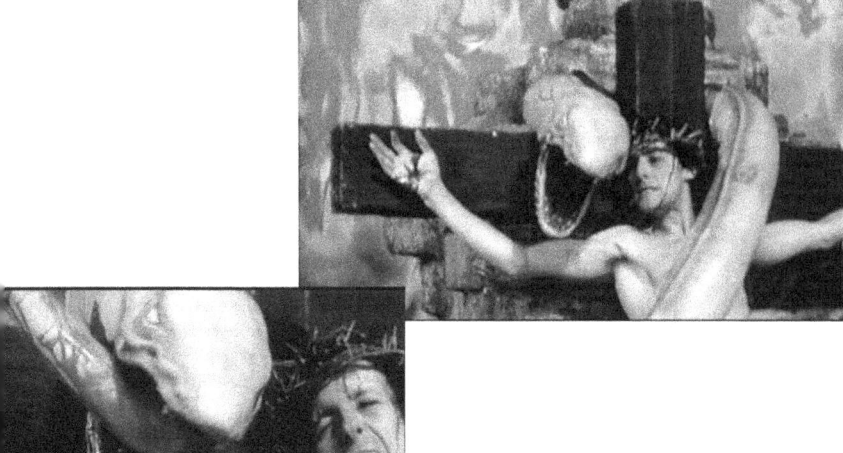

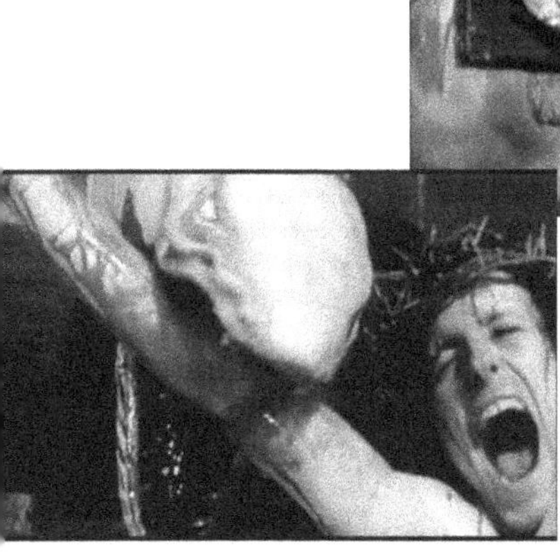

Two movies from the 1990s directed by Ken Russell

APPENDICES

THE RAINBOW

I find *The Rainbow* (1989) difficult to write about, partly because it's my favourite D.H. Lawrence novel and a book I know very well (and have written about in other studies). So I'm precious about it, partly because I know the star, Sammi Davis, really well, partly because I know that D.H. Lawrence's fiction is bloody difficult to adapt, and partly because I love Ken Russell's work, and know that it's a film he's proud of,[1] but I think it is really not very good at all.

The Rainbow's script,[2] by Ken and Viv Russell, was shopped around the studios, according to Russell: EMI, Paramount, Fox, Metro, and Goldcrest, and they all declined (BP, 141). It eventually found a home at Vestron.[3]

The initial budget estimate – £2.5 million ($4m) – was too much for Vestron, and the company wanted half a million to be cut (BP, 275). The production trimmed some of the bigger scenes (including a village crowd scene, a dream sequence, and two night shoots out of doors were combined into one interior scene (the scene where Ursula Brangwen and Skrebensky make love by moonlight). The production was shifted to near London (at Pinewood Studios) instead of the Lake District (though some of it was filmed in Cumbria).[4] The shooting schedule was 51 days (the schedule, and the budget, were much more than many of Russell's earlier works, but that still didn't make it a better movie than, say, *Dante's Inferno* or *Delius*).

Many in the cast and crew on *The Rainbow* were Ken Russell regulars: Judith Paris, Imogen Claire, Glenda Jackson, Dan Ireland, Ronaldo Vasconcellos, Billy Williams, Peter Davies, Luciana Arrighi,[5] Christopher Gable, Dudley Sutton, Ken Colley, etc. (Many had also worked on *Women In Love*).

---

[1] *The Rainbow* was 'a British Picture I could really be proud of' (BP, 274).
[2] The novel was published on Sept 30, 1915.
[3] Ken Russell said he waited 8 years before he was able to make *The Rainbow* (RC, 247).
[4] The novel of *The Rainbow* was set mainly in Cossall in the Midlands, which Lawrence called Cossethay.
[5] Luciana Arrighi designed *Women In Love* and the TV films of the Sixties.

THE CAST.

For Vestron, one of the problems of *The Rainbow* was the lack of star names. David Hemmings played the uncle (after Elton John dropped out, and others such as Alan Bates and Ollie Reed had been tried but said no). By then Hemmings was more an ageing character actor than the famous star of *Blow-Up* and *Alfred the Great*. Christopher Gable was cast as the father (after Jeremy Irons and Charles Dance had declined). Amanda Donohue played Winifred Inger (Theresa Russell, Kelly McGillis and Mariel Hemingway turned the part down because it was too small), but Donohue wasn't then known internationally (*LA Law* was some years off; Donohue had been the amazing villain in *The Lair of the White Worm*).6 Glenda Jackson was a name, but only had a small part, as the mother (Vestron were happy with Jackson; Julie Christie was considered). Paul McGann as Anton Skrebensky was known for his TV roles, such as *The Monocled Mutineer*, and the cult film *Withnail and I*.

As to the casting, well, there are certainly problems there. *The Rainbow* is nowhere near cast on-the-nail, like some of Ken Russell's other movies. No one could dispute that Christopher Gable, Judith Paris, Ken Colley and the rest of the team in *Delius: Song of Summer* weren't fabulous, or that Roger Daltrey, Fiona Lewis and Paul Nicholas weren't spot-on in *Lisztomania*.

However, as I keep harping on and on, casting a D.H. Lawrence film or TV adaption is *very* tricky. Because Lawrence's texts require a talent for delivering arch, heightened dialogue, fit into a historical setting, bags of charisma, enormous acting skills, a lot of physical acting, and nudity. In a way, the *look* of an actor is the least of considerations in a Lawrence piece (though in much of movie casting, it's the *primary* consideration).

Or, to put it another way: you could meet and audition a hundred actors over the course of a few days (as I have done), and find only one or maybe two people who could be one of your leads. And that would be lucky.

SAMMI DAVIS.

The biggest part, and the most problematic to cast, was Ursula Brangwen. When Sammi Davis (b. June 21, 1964) was chosen, she had appeared in a few British movies (such as *Hope and Glory* and *Mona Lisa*) and TV literary adaptions (such as the Thomas Hardy story *A Day At the Fair*), but certainly wasn't a 'star name' (but there were few actresses who were right for the part).

Sammi Davis and I dated for a while. In fact, we came

---
6 Vestron wanted more of a name.

from the same town (Kidderminster in the English Midlands), and I'd cast her in her first film – and *my* first film. It was a romantic drama called *Soosie and Lune* which we made in 1981-82.

When we were living in London, we'd meet up a lot and talk about movies – Sam (I always call her Sam) was just starting to get some good roles, in films like *A Prayer For the Dying* and *Hope and Glory*. We'd sit in the Godfather café on Tottenham Court Road (and many other places), drinking endless cups of coffee and smoking endless cigarettes, and always talk talk talking.

I remember Sam saying how she went to see a fringe theatre production of *The Rainbow* with Ken Russell. We bitched about a rival production of *The Rainbow* (starring Imogen Stubbs, it was a BBC TV series), which couldn't possibly be a patch on Ken's film. I also recall Sam saying how tough the nude scenes had been – not the love scenes, but running around the hills of Northumberland naked.

Ken Russell was full of praise for actress Sammi Davis in his autobiography *A British Picture*, enduring many wounds:

> Despite her wounds and battle fatigue, she continued to soldier on and was a wonderful example to the men. She braved rapids, swam rivers, survived a stampede of wild horses and ran naked to a dangerous mountain peak; she destroyed a field of lettuce single-handed, was sexually assaulted by a soldier, chased by a miner, endured torrential rain and being screwed against a tree in the spray of a raging waterfall... (1989, 291)

Ken Russell described the scene where Anton Skrebensky fucks Ursula Brangwen against a tree beside the deafening waterfall thus:

> All thoughts of directorial subtleties are drowned out but Sammi, with the camera playing on her face, which is visible over Anton's shoulder, wants to know how to grade her orgasm. So I tell her to go for it in four stages and we turn over with someone holding the loud hailer to my lips:
> "One" – she grinds away. I'm operating the camera and she's acting really turned on. "Two" – her face begins to glow. "Three" – she's beginning to smile... "Four" – ecstasy. Perfection in each of the seven takes. If only it were always that easy, I thought, especially against a tree with 25 people looking on. (ibid.)

Sammi Davis told me that the most challenging aspects of *The Rainbow* was the nudity:

The most difficult scenes to deal with during my time on a Ken Russell set, were the numerous nude scenes in *The Rainbow*, I was young and being naked in a movie is a huge step to take when you are new to the business. I had to run naked up hills, stand on a platform to have my portrait painted and my bum slashed with red paint, jump naked into a freezing lake, and be tied (for safety reasons) to a tree for a sex scene. Ken made no big deal about any of it, never made me feel on show or out of context in any way. I had to portray having an orgasm up against the tree. I asked Ken how to do that; he said he'd count out loud to ten as I built up intensity, ten was the moment, and in that way it was easy (and has been ever since!).[7]

THEMES.

Ken Russell and Vivian Jolly weren't much interested in D.H. Lawrence's politics or religious arguments in *The Rainbow*, and cut out most of his metaphysical discourses. Similarly, the 1988 Vestron movie did not address issues of class, gender and labour (the recurrent Lawrencean discussion of work was only covered in the school sequence). It also meant that whole slews of chapters and dialogue were dropped, because *The Rainbow* is very much a *spiritual* and *philosophical* book, in which Lawrence is exploring what it means to be alive, to be human, to connect with other people.

Maybe it's partly because in *The Rainbow* that irony or satire which goes along simultaneously with straight drama in Ken Russell's cinema was somewhat lacking. A Ken Russell Movie will typically send up the characters and situations and the drama even as it presents them as 'real' or straight. There is always at least two levels to the experience. Russell's films like to have it both ways: they like to present stories and dramas, but also to send them up, or add camp or theatrical layers, or whatever.

THE OPENING SCENE.

But from the beginning of *The Rainbow*, which depicts the five year-old Ursula Brangwen running happily through the fields near her home in pursuit of a rainbow in the sky ('I want that,' she tells her father), the approach the movie takes seems uncharacteristically straight. Worse, it appears really schmaltzy, in the treacly, Hollywood manner (I love treacle and schmaltz, but in this case, it's not good treacle or good schmaltz). The sunshine, the smiling child, the summery setting and the clearly fake rainbow – we might be in *Wizard of Oz* or *Alice's Adventures In Wonderland* territory. But we ain't, because this is not a send-up, this is *straight*.

It really *is* meant to be *poetic*, it's meant to be a cinematic

---

7 S. Davis, letter to the author, 2007.

representation or equivalent for D.H. Lawrence's prose. And it *doesn't work*. It doesn't work *from the opening scene*, which is *not good* for a movie. But the beginnings of, say, *Mahler* or *Lisztomania* are spot-on, because they announce the kind of movie that's coming up – and not only the subject of the film, but the *approach* the film will take. And if we're meant to take the opening of this adaption of *The Rainbow* literally... oh dear, oh dear, oh dear.

Because that opening is misjudged, and awkward, and all wrong. Your heart sinks. This is *The Rainbow* we're talking about! One of the great, great novels in English literature. It's *THE RAINBOW*. I repeat: it's *The Rainbow*!!

You just can't start an adaption of *The Rainbow* with that silly scene of little moppet Ursula running through the sunny fields trying to catch a rainbow!!!

OK, let's forget about the novel and D.H. Lawrence. Let's look at that scene just as a *movie* scene. Folks, it *still* doesn't work or convince or send out encouraging signals for the rest of the movie!

If it was a Disney movie about a family from Philadelphia who're going on vacation somewhere pretty and outdoorsy like the Pacific North-West, fine. But not for a drama directed by Ken Russell! And not for *The Rainbow*!

There is *some* Ken Russell humour in the 1989 film of *The Rainbow*, however: a scene where a nude Anton Skrebensky pulls the cork out of a champagne bottle held between his legs (if it was real champers, I bet Russell led the team in partaking of the champagne afterwards); Miss Harby caricatured as a witch on a blackboard; the painter MacAllister quipping that he's not painting Ursula's face (the paintbrush is on her ass, in close-up); in the church, Skrebensky says he'll buy Ursula a lolly; and some quips in the dialogue about marriage. (But the script is too reverential of the novel, which's uncharacteristic of Russell).

The interlude with the painter MacAllister (Dudley Sutton) is a curious addition to the 1915 novel. Distinctly Oscar Wildean, an artist and model scenario, it features MacAllister painting Ursula Brangwen on a plinth in the nude (naturally), but becomes more suggestive when MacAllister hints at the great British pastime of corporal punishment – a little flagellation and classic Russellian kinkiness (again, this is more like *The Romance of Lust* or *The Secret Diaries of Walter*!). But our Urtler's not having any of this, and leaves in a huff.

THE LOOK AND STYLE.

I don't believe the *mise-en-scène* of *The Rainbow* film at all: it is just too summery, too sunny, too cute, too clean, too plastic. It's one aspect of filmmaking that Ken Russell and his many crews are so adept at: delivering lived-in settings on relatively low budgets. And if a low budget hampers the production a little, Russell and the teams can usually make up for that with *tour-de-force* filmmaking.

That does not occur in The Rainbow adaption. the filmmakers' approach needs to be way more moody, brooding, stylized. In short: *cinematic*. Too much of the 1989 *Rainbow* is like filmed theatre. For once, the *tableaux* approach doesn't work, doesn't produce the drama or tension or psychological illumination that the piece requires.

As to the score for *The Rainbow*, Carl Davis (b. 1936) composed a kind of pastiche of Ralph Vaughan Williams, Edward Elgar and William Walton. For a time, Davis seemed to be the composer of the moment in the 1980s,[8] but the score for *The Rainbow* appears a little undistinguished (bet you can't hum any of the cues from it, including the big, orchestral cue that accompanies Ursula Brangwen's climactic rebirth and rush towards the rainbow at the end). Certainly, *The Rainbow* doesn't count among the finest scores to a Ken Russell movie.

WHAT IS *THE RAINBOW* ABOUT?

Question: *What is The Rainbow the novel about?*

That has to be decided very early on in a film or TV or radio or dramatic adaption. Is it a coming-of-age story? Is it a *Bildungsroman*? Is it about a person finding their place in the world? Is is a spiritual quest, a journey in which they discover themselves? Is it a love story? It could be all of the above and many more.

Certainly, *The Rainbow* is *not* an ordinary novel. There are none of the elements that movie-makers looks for: there is no villain, no grand narrative, no suspense, no jeopardy, no big set-pieces (except the flood), no comic sidekicks, no cliff-hangers, no chases or climactic scenes, etc.

And the heroine of *The Rainbow* is impossible to play, and impossible to cast. Who is Ursula Brangwen? Clearly, she is no ordinary heroine of literature. She is not a conventional character in any accepted sense.

So what is the novel *The Rainbow* about? Once you've decided that, many of your decisions in the scripting and production will be easier. But in the 1989 version of *The Rainbow* directed by Ken Russell, and co-written by Russell and Vivian Jolly, it clearly *hasn't* been decided what the novel is about, and what the movie is about.

Compare the film of *The Rainbow* with, say, *Tommy* or *The Music Lovers* or *Delius: Song of Summer* or *The Devils*.

---

[8] Carl Davis's credits in the Eighties include *The French Lieutenant's Woman, Oppenheimer, Scandal, King David, Macbeth* and *The Pickwick Papers*.

Well, you can see Ken Russell and the teams honing in on the subject of those movies like a cruise missile. 'Know what you want' is one of Russell's mantras for good filmmaking. He repeats it many times in his advice to young filmmakers. But in *The Rainbow* it's obvious that Russell and the team had not quite decided what they wanted or what their film is going to be about.

URSULA BRANGWEN AND INFINITE DESIRE.

Ursula Brangwen is a rebel, an outsider, an eternally-dissatisfied soul. She doesn't fit in *anywhere*. In short, she's a punk rocker: she doesn't know what she wants and doesn't know how to get it. She a hippy, a drop-out, a bohemian, decades before her time.

And Ursula is so clearly a poet or a writer or some kind of artist. But she is *not* an artist[9] in the 1915 novel. You can see how much easier it would have been for Ken Russell if Ursula had been a painter or sculptor or musician or poet. Then there would have been ways and means of exploring her character and her dilemma.

The key scene in *The Rainbow* is where Ursula Brangwen is prowling in the surf in moonlight on the South Coast like a wolf after making love with Anton Skrebensky. It's one of the greatest moments in English literature:

> She stood on the edge of the water, at the edge of the solid, flashing body of the sea, and the wave rushed over her feet.
> "I want to go," she cried, in a strong, dominant voice. "I want to go."
> He saw the moonlight on her face, so she was like metal, he heard her ringing, metallic voice, like the voice of a harpy to him.
> She prowled, ranging on the edge of the water like a possessed creature, and he followed her. He saw the froth of the wave followed by the hard, bright water swirl over her feet and her ankles, she swung out her arms, to balance, he expected every moment to see her walk into the sea, dressed as she was, and be carried swimming out.
> But she turned, she walked to him.
> "I want go," she cried again, in the high, hard voice, like the scream of gulls.
> "Where?" he asked.
> "I don't know." (531)

That's as profound as you can get, as an expression of total desire and not knowing what the hell to do with all that feeling: *I want to go... Where? I don't know*. That says it all.

The restless, dissatisfied but eternally yearning elements of

---
[9] Unless she is the artist (architect) of her own life.

that scene are simply exquisitely expressed. And that Ursula Brangwen is prowling through the surf by moonlight makes it all the more powerful.

If I was filming *The Rainbow*, it would be a scene I'd want to get absolutely right. It's the money scene, it's the scene you make the whole of the rest of the movie for. Needless to say, the 1989 version of *The Rainbow* doesn't come within a million miles of that scene or the many others like it in the novel.

But, in fairness, it should be stated that the scene is virtually unfilmable. Despite the magnificent visuals, it is an *internal scene*, a psychological scene.[10]

▼

The first time Anton Skrebensky and Ursula Brangwen make love is upstairs at Uncle Tom's wedding. Reduced from an outdoor nighttime scene for budgetary reasons (it should be in amongst wild nature), it's a deeply disappointing interpretation of D.H. Lawrence's fiction. I could go on and anlayze the scenes in the 1989 picture and the novel, but there's no need to here: you can go back to the novel, and find out in a few seconds that what's on screen is a million miles from Lawrence's 1915 novel.

In the chapter "First Love", there are so many things going in the lovemaking scene in the novel – some subtle, some cruel, some tender, but all intense – that are lost in the movie, which depicts Ursula's first experience of fucking more like the violent deflowering of a virgin out of Victorian porn (nothing wrong with 19th century porn, but this is D.H. Lawrence, supposedly high art and a little more subtle. Maybe Ken Russell and co. should've filmed *Fanny Hill* or *The Romance of Lust* instead).[11]

In the 1989 movie, Anton Skrebensky rams Ursula Brangwen and fucks her until he comes – but she, understandably, wants a little more (and the scene in the novel *isn't* about *his* freakin' orgasm!). How many times have we seen that in movies? The scene plays more like a rape, and is far from what D.H. Lawrence depicts in his novel. (The film introduces the full moon, always such a powerful motif in Lorenzo's writing, but in the movie it's only vaguely suggestive of something other or mysterious, and the flash cuts to the moon, accompanied by a percussive music cue, also don't really evoke what's going on in the 1915 novel. There was apparently more to this scene but according to Joseph Lanza it was deleted by the producers [PF, 286]).

---

10 I had a go at using that scene in my theatre production of *The Horse-Dealer's Daughter* in 2006, switching it to a cemetery, where the heroine has come to visit her mother's grave.
11 He tried to make an adaption of *Moll Flanders*.

LESBIANISM.

Ursula Brangwen's relationship with Winifred Inger was played as a full-on lesbian affair in the 1980s movie. In the 1910s novel, the author had to be more restrained. It's plainly there, the fascination of the younger woman for the older teacher (and also vice versa). But the 1989 adaption was much more explicit – at least in terms of depicting full nudity, images of the women kissing and caressing, massaging each other in front of the fireplace, and dashing about the countryside naked.

For a mainstream movie, this kind of lesbian imagery and relationship is still very rare (many production companies, film studios and TV broadcasters as well as actors wouldn't go anywhere near this sort of material).[12]

Once again, the 1989 Vestron picture doesn't capture the sense or subtlety or poetry of D.H. Lawrence's writing about Ursula Brangwen's love affair with Winifred Inger in *The Rainbow*. The imagery is halfway there – the underwater shots of the women swimming naked in a pool, for instance, or lounging around nude in front of the fire. But Lawrence's prose needs more than that.

SCHOOL.

In one section *The Rainbow* comes vividly alive, and that is the sequence dealing with Ursula Brangwen's experience as a new school teacher. Ken Russell and the team mount a memorable evocation of the horrific psychological and emotional as well as physical abuse in the educational system. On the movie-movie level, it is pure Charles Dickens – it's Russell & co. doing their version of *Oliver Twist* (though without the Gothic, Expressionist *mise-en-scène* of the classic Dickensian adaptions of the 1940s and 1950s).

But you can clearly see the filmmakers going to town on the pettiness, the meanness, the surliness, the stupidity and the intolerance in being at school. It's everyone's nightmare of school days.

In the school sequence in *The Rainbow*, Ursula Brangwen becomes part of the capitalist machine, just another cog in the social system. And when she is pushed to the limit, and finally explodes and thrashes the schoolboy Williams with a cane, the cost to her soul as well as to poor Williams is plain to see. 'She was as if violated to death', as Bertie Lawrence put it in *The Rainbow* (449), and 'she had paid a great price out of her own soul' (455). (There's a whole scene of fall-out from the beating, when William's mother comes to the school to complain,

---

12 There was also a lesbian relationship in *The Boy Friend*, between the characters played by Antonia Ellis and Georgina Hale, but it was cut – it was one sub-plot too many (Bax, 214).

saying that her boy has a weak heart and is delicate).[13]

As well as the mindless routine and dull-as-shit conditions of school life, the 1989 film of *The Rainbow* is particularly strong on the power games played out by the teachers – particularly between Ursula and Miss Harby (the always-wonderful Judith Paris), and Ursula and Mr Harby, the headmaster (Jim Carter). Ken Colley's Mr Brunt acts as a kind of hapless, world-weary go-between.

Ken Russell's films have always been highly adept at depicting power games, whether sexual, social or artistic – think of Franz von Liszt and Richard Wagner in *Lisztomania* or Peter Tchaikovsky and Count Chiluvsky in *The Music Lovers*. In *The Rainbow*, Russell and Vivian Jolly add a layer of sexual violence between Ursula Brangwen and the headmaster – the movie has Mr Harby ogling Ursula, and later cornering her in a corridor, and making a pass at her (after he's gone, Ursula cowers down on the floor, weeping. D.H. Lawrence's Ursula wouldn't do that).

▼

There is an important theme to *The Rainbow* which doesn't really come out in the 1989 movie – the ugliness and dreariness of modern life, the violence and inhumanity of the mines and mining, and the brutality lying underneath relationships. Yes, there are scenes of Ursula Brangwen berating her Uncle Tom for his exploitation of the working people (in scenes which include scale models of mines in Tom's living room – a budget cut solution (and a weedy one) to filming outdoors), and a scene where miners detonate the countryside when Ursula and Winifred are out walking the fells, and have their pleasant ramble interrupted with loud explosions – but they don't really get across the many facets to D.H. Lawrence's deconstruction of work and living in the modern era.

ADAPTING *THE RAINBOW*.

A big problem with *The Rainbow* and D.H. Lawrence's fiction in general is that so much of the novel takes place inside the characters: inside, they are experiencing all sorts of feelings and conflicts. At times, Ursula Brangwen is a volcano of emotions and opinions and ideas. It's expressing that in cinematic language that's the challenge.

Here's a simple test for you, dear reader: pick up a copy of *The Rainbow* or *Women In Love* or *The Plumed Serpent* and choose any page and ask yourself: how am I going to dramatize or visualize these words on celluloid or video?

Here's another test for you: try taking just one scene from

---

[13] Sammi Davis said she went too far in that scene, and was full of remorse when she accidentally hit the boy on the wrist (J. Caryn, *New York Times*, May 5, 1989).

a D.H. Lawrence book and have a go at turning it into a script that can be filmed.

Not easy. Oh no, not easy at all.

It's funking difficult.

For instance, how would you adapt the following couple of extracts?

> But hard and fierce she had fastened upon him, cold as the moon and burning as a fierce salt. Till gradually his warm, soft iron yielded, yielded, and she was there fierce, corrosive, seething with his destruction, seething like some cruel corrosive salt around the last substance of his being, destroying him, destroying him in the kiss. And her soul crystallised with triumph, and his soul was dissolved with agony and annihilation. (*The Rainbow*, 368)

That's a lovemaking scene from *The Rainbow*. So, in your script all it says is: 'THEY MAKE LOVE'. How do you shoot it? How do you show his 'warm, soft will yielding, yielding'? Or someone's 'being'? Or maybe you will instruct your actress: 'I want to see your soul crystallizing with triumph, honey'. And she might reply: 'how the $$$$ do I do that, boss?'

Or what about this, from the 1915 novel's ending:

> Gradually she began really to sleep. She slept in the confidence of her new reality. She slept breathing with her soul the new air of a new world. The peace was very deep and enriching. She had her root in new ground, she was gradually absorbed into growth.
>
> When she woke at last it seemed as if a new day had come on the earth. How long, how long had she fought through the dust and obscurity, for this new dawn? (546)

The Rainbow is about *rebirth* in large part – how a person can give birth to themselves, how they can find a new life in amongst the old life, how they can nurse themselves through darkness and emerge, healed. So towards the end of *The Rainbow*, Ursula Brangwen is in a chrysalis state, struggling to ascend from a cocoon.

How does the 1989 movie of *The Rainbow* adapt such prose? It depicts a young woman emerging from an illness, conversing with her father, and finally, after seeing a rainbow from her window, deciding to leave – to literally follow the rainbow. In the novel, Bertie Lawrence piles on religious and spiritual imagery and motifs, making Ursula Brangwen's convalescence and healing a religious rebirth, as well as (or much more than) a physical one.

The 1989 filmic adaption only suggests such spiritual themes. In cinematic terms, Ursula Brangwen running out of doors towards the giant rainbow hanging above the sunny fields is only part of the thematic, psychological and emotional impact of the novel's ending.

So the close of *The Rainbow* is disappointing – but that's partly because a film of this kind is very difficult to end satisfactorily. It's *not* an ordinary narrative, after all: no heroes, no villains, no guns, no car chases, no simple goals to achieve.

What is *The Rainbow* about? we have to ask yet again.

As to the *action* climax of *The Rainbow*, which derives in part from Lorenzo's Midlands novel, that isn't wholly convincing or successful either. Ursula, poor dear, has been menaced by men throughout this movie – from the headmaster Mr Hanby trying it on at school to the faceless workmen who seem to threaten her in the finale.

▼

For Pauline Kael, *The Rainbow* was spoilt by Ken Russell's 'staggeringly superficial' treatment of the novel; lacklustre and misguided acting; and a misinterpretation of the central role, played by Sammi Davis, whose Ursula Brangwen Kael called 'a snippy, closed-off brat', 'blank-faced and lightweight', 'an impossibly petulant twerp' (1992, 139-40). Well, Kael had it in for Russell throughout her career, of course, but *The Rainbow* is certainly very wide of the mark in relation to the novel, is miscast, is structurally awkward, has the wrong texture, design and look, is indifferently acted, and, worst of all, doesn't satisfy as a movie on its own (if it were a great movie, many of its flaws could be forgiven or ignored).

LADY CHATTERLEY

INTRO: IT DOESN'T WORK.
I can sum up my view of *Lady Chatterley* (directed by Ken Russell for the British Broadcasting Corporation and London Film Productions in 1993) in one, simple phrase:
It doesn't work.
Now, you know by now that I am a MAJOR FAN of the films of Ken Russell, and have regarded him as the greatest living British director ever since – well, Michael Powell, I guess (and even when he's dead, Russell is still the greatest living filmmaker!). Russell is a fantastically amazing film magician, one of the greats without a doubt. He directed *Dante's Inferno*. He directed *The Music Lovers*. He directed *Delius: Song of Summer*. He directed *The Devils*. He directed *Tommy*.

But there are times when, for all sorts of reasons (but very often the script and the concept), it just doesn't work. And *Lady Chatterley* is one of those times.

What a pity.

I know, I know: because the ingredients sound very promising: Ken Russell *plus* D.H. Lawrence *plus* Lady *Chatterley's Lover*! How could it fail? But it did. And I *really* wanted this piece to work. Unfortunately, not every outing can be *The Devils* or *Tommy*.

Why doesn't *Lady Chatterley* work?

Chiefly for the same reason that *The Rainbow* didn't work: *the script.* Lady *Chatterley* has a script credit from Michael Haggiag and Ken Russell. And it's because the fiction of D.H. Lawrence is a heap big challenge to adapt for the screen: in short, it demands heightened, abstract, alternative or visionary interpretations.

Women In Love is a slightly different case: not only was that movie only part of the novel (as with *The Rainbow*), it worked as a movie in its own terms. But when you compare the 1969 picture with the 1920 novel, oh no, *Women In Love* is not particularly successful at all.

In short – and this is so cruel to say – I don't think any of Ken Russell's adaptions of D.H. Lawrence's novels are successful as adaptions for the screen. He and his production teams have taken on the Three Big Novels by the Midlands Maestro, but if you know (and love) the novels, they are very disappointing.

But if you judge *Women In Love, The Rainbow* and *Lady Chatterley* as pieces of cinema or television, you also have to admit that, of the three, only *Women In Love* is truly successful.

The chief flaw in the 1993 BBC *Lady Chatterley* is the script. And it so often is when we're talking about lit'ry adaptions. In short, the script does *not* capture the essence of the three *Lady C* novels – *The First Lady Chatterley, John Thomas and Lady Jane* and *Lady Chatterley's Lover* – the atmosphere of the novels, the themes of the novels or even some of the major imagery of the novels. And, disregarding the source material, it does not work on its own, as a TV series.

Ah but, wait – at least Ken Russell and the production team will pick up some of the great imagery in the novels, one might imagine, and transfer them into spellbinding cinema (or rather, spellbinding television). But they *don't* in *Lady Chatterley*. They just don't.

If you go back to the 1920s books, you find Lorenzo waxing lyrical, as only he can, about trees and woods and pheasants and daffodils and living things. But the 1990s TV series simply doesn't deliver that.

Too much of the 1993 *Lady Chatterley* TV series is talky, talky, talky, and waaaay too static. It's far too much like run-of-the-mill TV drama and not enough like a Ken Russell piece. With Russell, you expect something special, something out-there.

Oh, the BBC TV series does deliver some typical Russelliana: in the first episode, for instance, there's a lengthy, erotic dream sequence in which Connie Chatterley rides a black stallion (the black stallion of the senses, from Socrates, signposted when Clifford reads aloud to Constance), along a summery, garden path lined with red flowers and draped with topless soldiers. They're all young and sexy with khaki pants and bare chests.[14] The fantasy closes with Constance being unable to rescue Clifford, who's drowning in a pool.

This's one of the places where *Lady Chatterley* becomes cinematic – and very much in the Ken Russell manner. In another scene, Connie answers her husband's ringing of the bell from his bed by appearing naked in his room with a veil over her face (she'd mentioned earlier that it would be nice to see people's bodies, not only their faces). The frustration that Clifford feels bursts into rage.[15]

Lady Chatterley is certainly good at hammering home the point that Constance Chatterley must be sexually frustrated because she hasn't got a husband who can satisfy her. The

---

[14] Joseph Lanza identifies the young guys here as a nod to Derek Jarman's movies (307), and I think he may be right.
[15] But, jeez, hasn't he got hands and a tongue?!

script ensures that *everyone* from here to Timbuktu understands that plot point, even though Connie denies it all the time.[16]

▼

Ken Russell's and Michael Haggiag's *Lady Chatterley* was a co-production between London Films, BBC Films and Global Arts. It was shot on 35mm film and broadcast in four 50-minute episodes, which enabled Russell to make a better job of the three novels, he claimed, than he did with *Women In Love*.

Michael Haggiag should take much of the credit for *Lady Chatterley* – he was not only the co-writer, but also the producer. Johan Eliasch, Robert Haggiag, Tom Donald and Barry Hanson were executive producers. Marina Gefter and Wendy Oberman were associate producers.

Pretty much everybody would agree that a four-part TV series adaption of a long novel can do the source material better justice than a two-hour movie. Well, usually, yes. And if you want to tease out all of the material in D.H. Lawrence's three 1920s versions of *Lady Chatterley*, then, yes, 200 minutes would seem to be better than two hours.

But in the case of 1993's *Lady Chatterley*, I don't agree: I wonder if *Lady Chatterley* might've fared much better as a two-hour movie. Certainly there were scenes in the TV series which would've been dropped instantly for a feature film version (the excursion for a spot of painting, for instance). A two-hour movie would've been much pacier, for a start, and it would probably have stuck firmer to the central spine of the D.H. Lawrence novels. The TV series was too meandering, too diffuse.

▼

Another problem with *Lady Chatterley* is the casting. Now, the three principals – Joely Richardson,[17] Sean Bean and James Wilby – are all fine actors, who have done some great work. But none of them quite suit their characters, or play their characters in a way that fits the material, and the tone. It's not simply that every reader has their impression of each character, and that the actors don't look like that (but it is true that the actors are not as the characters are described in the book: Connie Chatterley is much fleshier and curvier than Richardson, for instance, and Oliver Mellors is much tougher

---

[16] Imaginative viewers might be able to think of erotic experiences Connie and Clifford could enjoy – without the need for a penis or an erection. But in them days, no no no, it had to be the dick and nuttin' else. Or at least, in the world of D.H. Lawrence, it had to be the phallus and nothing else. No clitoris, for instance, in Lorenzo's sexual philosophy: his negative views of clitoral sex, for instance, are well-known.

[17] Ken Russell of course used Joely Richardson's mom, Vanessa Redgrave, in *The Devils*, and her sister, Natasha Richardson, in *Gothic*.

and gruffer than Bean. Of the three, Wilby's interpretation of Clifford Chatterley comes out best, but is still very different from the Clifford in the three *Lady Chatterley* books).

It's more that the actors don't seem to have embodied the characters – the way that, say, Martin Sheen in *Apocalypse Now* (1979) completely embodies Captain Willard, or Orson Welles in *Chimes At Midnight* (1966) wholly embodies Falstaff.

Or maybe it's just that the performances in some of Ken Russell's other movies – *The Devils, The Music Lovers, Mahler, Tommy* – are so much more successful in comparison.

ON SOME OF THE DELETED CHARACTERS.

Towards the end of the four-part *Lady Chatterley*, the momentum stumbles and wavers. In the 1928 novel, the drama becomes increasingly desperate, with the return of the formidable Bertha Coutts, and Oliver Mellors taking up with his wife again. The 1993 adaption did away with Coutts completely, so she is a shadowy presence referred to in dialogue by other characters (though Mellors' mom appears, played by Pat Keen). Dropping Bertha, though, alters the book a good deal: in the 1993 TV adaption, Mellors, poor dear, gets beaten up by Bertha's brother, and goes to work in another colliery. In the novel, Bertha moves back in with Mellors. (Bertha Coutts adds plenty of sexual jealousy between her and Connie Chatterley and dramatic tension between her and Mellors, fr'instance, which the TV adaption would've benefitted from.[18] Coutts would thus provide a decent enough obstacle to the lovers, which would've enhanced the melodrama).

It's curious that, although *Lady Chatterley* was stretched over four 50 minute episodes, quite a few of the secondary characters were eliminated. Not only Bertha Coutts, but also figures such as Michaelis, one of Connie's previous boyfriends,[19] Charlie May, and Arnold Hammond. Tommy Dukes (Ben Aris) makes an appearance, but barely makes an impression (in the novel, Dukes has quite a few key lines of dialogue).[20]

In fact, Tommy Dukes is another of the characters that D.H. Lawrence repeats, because he shares traits with Oliver Mellors: both are military men; both live somewhat apart from other people; both espouse a similar life-philosophy; and both

---

[18] There's also a suggestion in the novel that Bertha Coutts enjoys anal sex.
[19] Donald Forbes (Breffni McKenna) instead stands in for Connie's past suitors, an amalgam of characters such as Michaelis and Charlie May.
[20] "Give me the democracy of touch, the resurrection of the body!" yells Dukes in *Lady Chatterley's Lover* (78). Tommy Dukes also complains about women not being fleshy enough for him: "[f]ellows with swaying waists fucking little jazz girls with small boy buttocks" (42).

exalt the phallus (but what Lawrencean man doesn't?!). Like Mellors, Dukes is clearly partly a Lawrencean mouthpiece; much of what he prates not only prefigures what Mellors says, it is also very familiar, Lawrencean metaphysics. Like Mellors, Dukes is mainly womanless: Dukes admits to the stereotype of the army as a surrogate mother: '"[t]he army leaves me time to think, and saves me from having to face the battle of life"' (33). The narrator emphasizes the connection between Dukes and Mellors for Lady C. during one of the first times Connie meets Mellors (50). The decision to drop or severely limit the character of Dukes in the TV series was probably because of the large amount of repetition: that is, in the novel, Dukes is already spouting much of the Lawrencean philosophy that Mellors later takes up.

ASPECTS OF THE PRODUCTION.

Some of the music (by Michael Garrett) isn't particularly distinctive. For other parts of *Lady Chatterley*, Ken Russell and his team seem to have selected out-of-copyright pieces of (I think British) music (or maybe BBC library pieces),[21] which don't quite fit. There's a curiously floaty feeling to the marriage of music and image in *Lady Chatterley*: on most Russell outings, music is foregrounded to the point where the images are sometimes secondary. And the music is usually integrated with immense skill into the piece. That flair for integration in *Lady Chatterley* founders.

You'll recognize some of the locations in *Lady Chatterley* – some of it was filmed at Wrotham Park and Gaddesden Place, which Ken Russell had used in, among others, *Gothic*.[22] The rest of *Lady Chatterley* was shot in Oxfordshire and the Isle of Wight (as well as on the ferry between Southampton and the Isle of Wight). The interiors were filmed at Pinewood Studios, as with so many of Russell's other works.[23]

Lady Chatterley contained many of Ken Russell's regular players, including Judith Paris and Ben Aris. *Lady Chatterley* was also something of a family affair: Ken Russell's new wife Hetty Baynes played Connie's sister Hilda, and did the choreography, and Xavier Russell (Russell's son) was one of the editors (along with Mick Audsley, Peter Davies and Alan Mackay). Molly Russell and Rupert Russell (Russell's children)

---

[21] The Beeb certainly has one of the largest libraries of music anywhere on Earth.
[22] Wragby in *Lady Chatterley* was probably inspired by the Sitwells' home of Renishaw, with other places drawing on Eastwood, Chesterfield, and Staveley.
[23] The TV series of *Lady Chatterley* opens with a church scene (very Lawrencean – and very Russellian!), in which the lines, 'Ours is essentially a tragic age', etc – the first words of *Lady Chatterley's Lover* – are quoted. It's an amusing spoof on Lawrence the preacher, because the speech is delivered by a priest in a pulpit (and Clifford immediately says 'it's absurd').

also appeared.

Other credits included costumes by Evangeline Harrison, design by James Merifield, music by Jean Claude Petit, the DP was Robin Vidgeon, and the line producer was Ronaldo Vasconcellos.

Ken Russell turned in a fun cameo in *Lady Chatterley*, as Sir Michael Reid, an artist. A jolly figure with a shock of white hair and ruddy face, Russell looked like he was enjoying himself in front of the camera. It's one of the pleasures of the piece, Russell's cameo.

THE LOOK OF *LADY C.*

As to the look, design and style of *Lady Chatterley*, I think each element is very disappointing – certainly when compared to the best of Ken Russell's work. One of the biggest challenges for the art department was to represent the four seasons. And the seasons are *so much* a part of D.H. Lawrence's three *Lady C* novels. I mean, you've just *got* to have Connie Chatterley with the chicks in Spring, or the new life of the trees in Summer.

Because *Lady Chatterley* was filmed from May 11 to July 25, 1992, three of the seasons – Spring, Autumn and Winter – had to be faked. So, as on so many movies, the Winter scenes were shot when it was hot. It's always the way.

But strewing bagfuls of dried leaves around the sets, plus a few shrivelled or browned bushes, just didn't give the right impression or texture of Autumn. Not when the camera is using so wide a lens, and captures the trees in full leaf a few feet above the actors' heads, ruining the illusion.

OK, this sounds like nit-picking. Yeah, *it is*! And on most movies or TV shows, it wouldn't matter a jot. But *Lady Chatterley's Lover* is one novel where, if you're going to try to do a 'faithful' adaption (OK, that's impossible, I know!), or at least an adaption that comes close to the novel (or captures something of the novel – otherwise, why the fuck bother with the novel at all!), you simply gotta have a *really strong* and *really poetic* sense of the seasons, of nature, of living things. This is a novel which's *all about* nature and the seasons. (In short, you need a much bigger budget for the production design, greens dept, and practical effects than you've got here. Or you need a greater amount of attention paid to the atmospheres and textures).

And that's the ironic thing about *Lady Chatterley*, because Ken Russell is one of the few filmmakers working in the commercial world of movies who has an acute sense of the natural world! Look at the way he films the Lake District! But, somehow, that intimate feeling for nature eluded him in 1992-1993. You can see the camera picking up the images, and the sound team have added birdsong or the swooshing of the breeze, but it just doesn't gel.

The alchemy that should take place isn't ignited. The poetry that Ken Russell is famous for – rightly – isn't there on the screen.

If you look back to the films Ken Russell directed such as *The Devils* or *Tommy*, there's a visceral genius to the camerawork. I don't mean only the famous shock effects like the crash zooms or the dynamic, handheld movements, I mean the way that scenes are staged, the way the camera interacts with the performers.

Lady Chatterley is filmed in Ken Russell's later style, with wide angles and often static set-ups, rendering the narrative a series of *tableaux* (Russell is credited as camera operator, using his pseudonym Alf Russell, so he was right there in the thick of things behind the camera, as well as being the director and the co-writer).

The *tableaux* and static approach can work fantastically well – think of the films of Sergei Paradjanov, for example, which took the flattened perspectives of *tableaux* to a level of extraordinary sophistication (it worked for the stage play *Salomé's Last Dance*). But in *Lady Chatterley* it dampens the dynamics of the plot and the themes down to the level of mediocre TV drama. A *tableaux* approach to *Lady C* simply does *not* translate the material into compelling television.

And then you've got the worst kind of cinema or television: *people talking in a room*. Talking heads. Static camera. Like filmed theatre, as Robert Bresson once called it. Or filmed radio (which's what most television is: a camera pointed at someone reading from an autocue. Radio on film).

But when *Lady Chatterley* jettisons the 500-page wedge of paper called the script, and shifts into Ken Russell's favoured images-plus-music approach to cinema, it comes alive. Maybe the whole of *Lady Chatterley* could've been done as a silent movie. I know that Russell might have delivered that brilliantly, but of course the British Brainwashing Corporation and London Films and Global Arts didn't want that. They wanted (and paid for) a TV drama series they could show after the 9 p.m. water-shed (and later sell on video, and to other territories).

The lighting, too (courtesy of DP Robin Vidgeon) often appears either flat or too bright, as if the sets were being lit for video in a TV studio rather than celluloid. Why is that? Why does so much of *Lady Chatterley*, and other later productions directed by Ken Russell, have such flat, all-over lighting? (Especially when you consider just how many of the great Russellian outings have been stellar in terms of lighting).

SEX IN *LADY C.*

OK, so what about the love and sex in 1993's *Lady Chatterley*? That's what *Lady Chatterley's Lover* is all about, isn't it? Plenty of tupping? A really *good* fuck?!

Oh dear. Not good. Not good at all. D.H. Lawrence wanted readers to believe that his story was more than just a Good Fuck – a line that is quoted in the 1993 TV series. Lorenzo wanted a new religion founded on the body, on sensuality, on sex. Unfortunately, the 1993 BBC adaption seemed to reduce the novel again to a 'good fuck' (but the fucking depicted in this version of *Lady Chatterley* doesn't seem particularly good or enjoyable).

The trouble with the 1993 BBC adaption of *Lady Chatterley's Lover* is that the whole enterprise boils down to a young wife being bored and restless and aching for sensuality and companionship and, yes, some sex. For the critics who don't like D.H. Lawrence – and there are plenty of them – *Lady Chatterley's Lover* is a terrible novel because it tries to build a new religion or new spirituality out of sex, and also because it reduces love to sex, and also because it presents a tired and clichéd situation, of a young woman deprived of affection and sex when her husband is wounded in the war (it's the 'bored housewife' scenario of porn).

In other words, for the detractors of D.H. Lawrence's Twenties book, Connie Chatterley is an upper-class woman who fancies a bit of sex and finds it with her gamekeeper. And that's all there is to it. It's Mills & Boon or two-cent romantic fiction. It's *Sleeping Beauty* or *Cinderella* with some rough sex thrown in.

And the 1993 TV series does deliver something of that: it sends up the situation as the same time as wanting to keep it straight. And that is very typical of the cinema of Ken Russell, to simultaneously spoof a topic while also playing it straight (which's partly what irritates some viewers about Russell's movies – they can't take something that's meant to be consumed on two apparently conflicting levels).

But Bertie Lawrence intended *Lady Chatterley's Lover* to be *much* more than that. And that's where the 1993 adaption comes unstuck, and that's where all other adaptions of the novel go to pieces, and it's also where *all* screen adaptions of Lawrence's fiction fall apart.

They can render the melodrama, the conflicts between characters, and even a bit of simulated sex (usually badly), but they can't do the transcendence of sex, the religion of sex, the new spirituality based on touch and the body, which Lorenzo was so passionate about, and which fuelled so much of his art.

And yet, *without* that mysticism of sensuality in a D.H. Lawrence screen adaption, you don't have the full impact of the books. Instead, you have melodrama that looks like any other TV costume drama.

In short: D.H. Lawrence's fiction requires something very special from filmmakers. And no one yet has achieved it. *No one.*

Because what do Russell, Haggiag, Eliasch, Hanson, Gefter, Oberman, Vasconcellos and the rest of the production team give us in the 1993 *Lady Chatterley* adaption? Feebly-staged sex scenes, a real lack of chemistry between the principals (Joely Richardson and Sean Bean), some pontifications upon love and women and men, and so the whole project of Lawrencean sensuality and spirituality falls to bits.

The script of the 1993 *Lady Chatterley* is the main problem, because it simply *does not* render the essence (or even the superficial elements) of D.H. Lawrence's three *Lady C.* novels. Assuredly, at the level of the tro-ings and fro-ings between the country house and the hut in the woods and Oliver Mellors' cottage, at the level of the intrigue and melodrama between the four main characters – Connie, Mellors, Clifford and Mrs Bolton – the 1993 *Lady Chatterley* is solid. The narrative set-up at the Wragby mansion between Connie, Clifford, Bolton and the servants is clearly drawn, and the domestic aspects of life there is convincing (the games of chess, trays of food being brought to Clifford, the meal times, the evening pastimes of Clifford reading aloud and Connie sewing, for instance – all of that is great).[24]

Unfortunately, *Lady Chatterley* is not a Jane Austen or E.M. Forster adaption, where people in pretty frocks sip tea in drawing rooms and discuss the weather with the vicar.

There has to be *more* going on than that. This is *Lady Chatterley's Lover*! This is the great, infamous British novel of spiritual, transformative love-making. Or at the very least, a good fuck! And I do mean a *good fuck.* A *really* good, super-transcendent fuck, where the lovers are coming in mystical bliss.

But aside from the problems with the script, and the casting, you have to acknowledge that the direction must take some of the blame for the disappointment of the 1993 *Lady Chatterley.* Part of the problem here I think is that Ken Russell simply prefers to portray love and sex in unusual or weird or anything-but-straight ways. Oh, Russell can depict regular sex and love when he wants to, but I get the impression that he's bored by that. Rather like Jean-Luc Godard often said that he tried to make a regular film with regular storylines, but he just couldn't, he always found himself disrupting the usual A-B-C logic of traditional narrative.

So, in a film like *Women In Love*, each sexual encounter

---

24 Is this a snapshot of Russell's home life?!

was staged and shot in a manner that departed (slightly) from the norm. Also, it really grates, and was a mistake, I think, to have Oliver Mellors always be so rough with Connie Chatterley in the TV *Lady Chatterley*. I mean, he was really manhandling her harshly, like a piece of meat. Although Mellors is meant to be working-class, and passionate (i.e., the stereotypical 'bit of rough'), he's also meant to be a fabulous lover, and a tender lover. And Sean Bean grabbing Joely Richardson like an ape didn't convince: you don't believe for a second that Bean could make Richardson come and come (as Connie does in the novel).

However, when the sex in *Lady Chatterley* was filmed in a regular way – such as when Connie C. visits Oliver M. at his cottage and she straddles him – that too didn't capture anything like the transformative sex that the books portrayed. Because the night in the cottage is the famous 'night of sensual passion'! That is, the scene of anal sex.

It's the highpoint of the sexual discourse in *Lady Chatterley's Lover*, on pages 257-8, chapter sixteen, when sex is used to burn out and purify the body and the soul. Connie reaches to 'the very heart of the jungle of herself'. The lovers embrace in a sharp, searing sensuality, which is intended to be more than sentimentality, or mere hedonism – and more than a good ass fuck – but a religious, ontological catharsis. After it, Connie is purified, made whole. After this an 'ultimate nakedness', a poetry of absolutes, of extremes, of totality.

D.H. Lawrence tries to describe going over the edge in sensuality, a breaking-through. The sexual scenes have been building up to this point, in which Connie Chatterley, as in some fierce, painful religious ritual, loses herself, and is purified by sheer sensuality.

The narrator of *Lady Chatterley's Lover* says it is a phallic, not sexual, transformation, on the 'night of sensual passion'. It is this for him because life sears through the lovers, not sex in particular (sex is the means of the 'democracy of touch', but the phallus = life). D.H. Lawrence put life above passion, sex, desire, phallic transformation or whatever else he called it. Passion, sex, desire, and so on, are simply terms for the manifestation of the Lawrencean life-force. The power behind the phallus is life itself. The means are masculine – the phallus is used in a mystical fashion. The phallus is a god, associated with Pan at the end of *Lady Chatterley's Lover* (315).[25] It is an ithyphallic, pagan, burning religion Lawrence proposed.

The scene of ass fucking in the novel of *Lady Chatterley's Lover* has given literary critics plenty to drool about. Some critics suggested that it was D.H. Lawrence's fear of women

---

25 Quotes are from *Lady Chatterley's Lover* unless otherwise stated.

that prompted him to employ a scene of anal intercourse.[26] Ridiculous, but typical of the way some critics interpret fiction (i.e., always literally, or, even duller, biographically). In *Lady Chatterley's Lover,* there is an element of sadomasochism in the depiction, with Oliver Mellors the active one, with his phallic thrusting, and Connie Chatterley as the passive recipient (again, a hopelessly reductive view of what sex is and how it is experienced).

The anal intercourse in *Lady C.* also appears 'unfeminine' to some critics, bypassing the vulva, an act that perhaps expresses D.H. Lawrence's latent homosexual desire (as if enjoying anal sex means you're gay! *Arrgh!*).[27] Another suggestion is that the gamekeeper, having 'specific and different phobias about female genitalia' (D. Britton, 51), avoids the pussy.

Some commentators[28] criticized D.H. Lawrence for concealing or misrepresenting the anal sex scene in *Lady Chatterley's Lover.* However, Derek Britton points out (in *Lady Chatterley: The Making of the Novel*) that Lawrence was writing in an age in which an explicit depiction of sodomy would be too controversial (1988, 278).

OK, so the 1993 TV adaption of *Lady Chatterley's Lover* probably wouldn't have got away with depictions of ass fucking. But it didn't even (bother to) suggest that this was what was happening (but D.H. Lawrence too is self-consciously vague – remember that *Lady Chatterley's Lover* was published privately first, because Lawrence knew it wouldn't have been published by an establishment firm).

Ken Russell, Michael Haggiag, Johan Eliasch *et al* also chickened out on the worshipping of the phallus scene, too, where Connie Chatterley kneels in front of Oliver Mellors and coos and caws over his prick. For D.H. Lawrence, the erect phallus was a holy male secret, at the base of secular power. It rises out of gold-red hair, again, the Lawrencean colour of phallic, fiery power:

> The sun through the low window sent in a beam, that lit up his thighs and slim belly and the erect phallos, rising darkish and hot-looking from the little cloud of vivid gold-red hair. She was startled and afraid.
> "How strange!" she said slowly. "How strange he stands there! So big! and so dark and so cock-sure! Is he like that?" (218)

Feminists have rightly sprung upon this scene as an example of D.H. Lawrence's misogyny. He is at least honest,

---

26 W. Ober, 1979, 113.
27 W. Ober, 112; K. Millett, 241; D. Britton, 51.
28 W. Ober, 114, H. Daleski, 308, E. Delavenay, 60.

artistically, in this scene. But it can't work. It is laughable. Meanwhile Ken Russell has sent up the whole, phallic worship thing often in his movies – think of the mighty dong that Franz Liszt wields in *Lisztomania*, for example (there are numerous other examples).

In sum, the 1993 TV adaption of *Lady Chatterley* had to convince that the love-making that Connie Chatterley and Oliver Mellors was something special, something more than just a tup in a hut or a rut in the rain. Because that's what the novel promises – and, for those who love *Lady Chatterley's Lover*, it delivers.

It might be reductive and misogynist of D.H. Lawrence to elevate sex so much in a novel, but that's what he did. *Lady Chatterley's Lover* is a novel about the rebirth of a woman through sex as well as love, and the author admits that sex is primary in this instance. So a film or TV or radio or theatrical adaption has to be true to that.

Thus, in a way, Ken Russell was *not* the most suitable director for this project, because he is known for subverting sex as well as conventional melodrama. Russell would not do a straight interpretation of the novel, but even as 'A Ken Russell Movie' or 'A Ken Russell TV Series', *Lady Chatterley* still doesn't work.

CHEER US UP, SPIKE!

To counter the seriousness of the *Lady Chatterley* enterprise, and to finish up, it's worth lightening up with a little humour – courtesy of the brilliant Spike Milligan (Ken Russell had produced a documentary about Milligan in 1959). Milligan later in life created marvellous spoofs of famous works – *The Bible, Wuthering Heights* and *Lady Chatterley's Lover*:

> After her affair with Paddy, other men meant nothing to her. Tom Loon meaning nothing to her, nor did Dick Squats, Len Lighthower, nor Lord Louis Mountbatten nor Eric Grins, not even Houdini. No, she was married to Clifford, she would stand by him, something he couldn't do for her. She wanted a good deal from life but this poor cuckolded cripple couldn't give it to her, he had tried but it gave him a nose-bleed. She had insured his legs in the event of him walking again. She thought of Paddy and knew that their affair was at an end, she knew he couldn't keep anything up (Eh?). The world was full of possibilities. There was lots of fish in the sea but no chips. The vast masses of fish were mackerel or herring, so reasoned Constance, if you're not mackerel or herring, you're not likely to find good fish in the sea.

The cast of The Rainbow

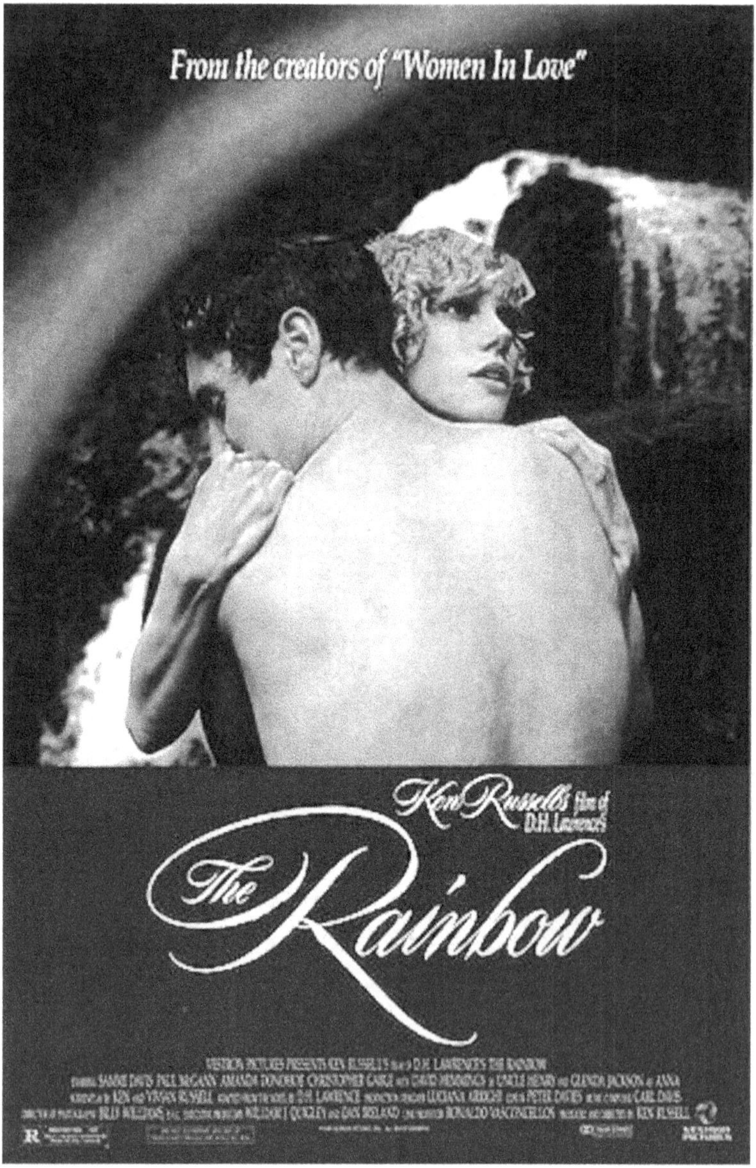
From the creators of "Women In Love"
Ken Russell's film of D.H. Lawrence's
The Rainbow

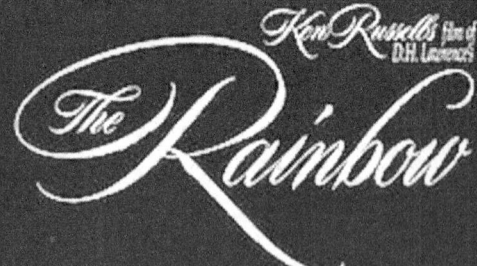

Running around the mountains of the Lake District in Britain
in an erotic dream sequence from a D.H. Lawrence adaption:
it can only be a Ken Russell movie

This page and over:
the adaption of D.H. Lawrence's Lady Chatterley novels

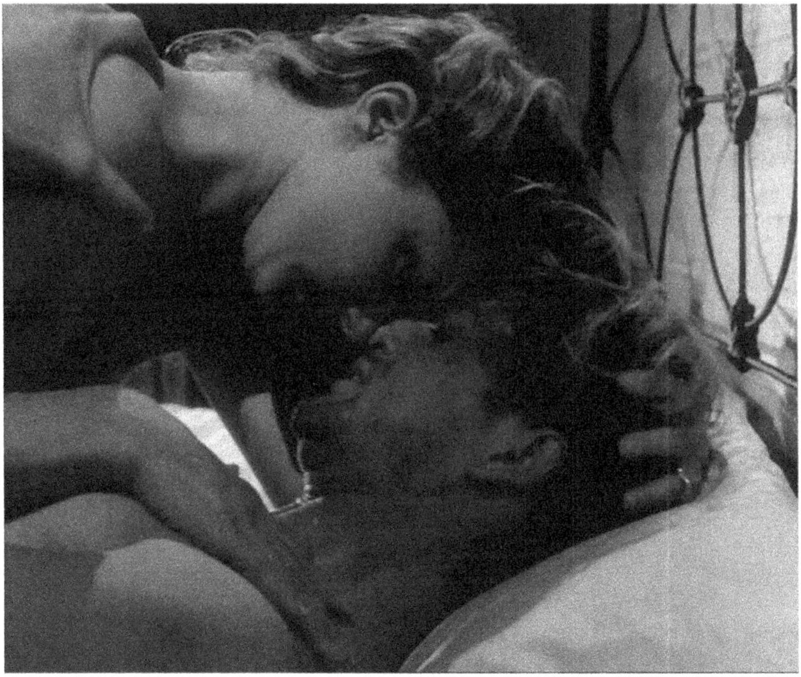

Two other adaptions of Lady C, including a dreadful recent French version.

APPENDICES

VIDEO AND DVD: AVAILABILITY

Here's a reminder about access to Ken Russell's movies and TV work, as listed in the filmography, because it's a fairly fundamental issue: some films are easy to buy or rent on home entertainment formats like video, Blu-ray and DVD, but some are either difficult to track down, or unavailable. Most of Russell's television work of the 1960s, for instance, is not available on DVD or video, and has only the occasional airing on television. And the LWT and *South Bank Show* pieces, which were terrific television, also aren't in print (altho' some *South Bank Shows* have more recently been released on DVD. I would highly recommend the stunning North American release *Ken Russell At the BBC*).

As to showings on television, very occasionally pieces are re-broadcast. But don't expect *Dance of the Seven Veils: A Comic Strip In Seven Episodes On the Life of Richard Strauss, 1864-1949* to be shown after another re-run of *Cheers* or *Friends* or *Letterman* on CBS or ABC or the BBC any time soon.

But some releases feature audio commentaries by Ken Russell, and these are by far and away the most valuable editions of Russell's work on the home entertainment market. I highly recommend the DVDs releases of *Lisztomania* and *Tommy*. *The Devils* came in 2012. *The Music Lovers*, Russell's own favourite movie, has recently been released.

FANS ON KEN RUSSELL

A selection of reviews of *Women In Love* on Amazon.com. (I haven't included film critics on *Women In Love* – no need to dish out more dirt here!).

Can you really do better that Alan Bates AND Oliver Reed? I love everything about this movie. It is filmed so beautifully and Glenda Jackson's performance gives me the chills. Many people know about this film because of its treatment of sexuality, but it is not raunchy or tasteless, it is perfect. This is one of my favorite movies to curl up and watch on a rainy afternoon. I suppose it is dated, but give it a chance and as crazy as it sounds, you too will start to fall in love.

•

Flipping through cable stations late one night, I came across a bearded Alan Bates intellectually and poetically analogizing a fig to "the female part" before a party of mesmerized and embarrassed picnickers. I, too, was mesmerized, especially by the quiet, deep, limpid restraint of the scene, the little subtle expressions on the faces of the main characters revealing their fundamental natures, Bates's clear, precise voice, his deadly serious playfulness, the rich green English countryside, etc. Oliver Reed's reaction to the monologue was especially impressive for its understated humor and intelligence.

•

I think a film can only attempt to show what the book more specifically says so to the mind the book will always be preferred but with a writer like Lawrence film makes perfect sense. In fact Lawrence's flaw is perhaps that he at times uses too many words when an image would suffice. So I love that someone as visually audacious as Ken Russell made this film.

I've seen it many times and always love different things about it. Russell is usually equated with excess but here everything exists in just the right amount, nothing is overdone, he finds just the right way to convey literary content without overly revering it and so framing it too neatly.

•

This is one of my all time favourite movies and after seeing it again on DVD, it still holds up really well. The photography and location shots are lush, beautiful and sensual, with superb acting by the whole cast.

•

There is no need to summarize the story of the two sets of lovers; just see it. The major actors have never been better. They become the complex characters, who while not totally explained are something better: totally present and alive. They pick up a big slice of the private and public aura of the period in their wake. Also, the film has the most incredible punch line at the end which Russell just perfectly transmits.

FILMOGRAPHIES
KEN RUSSELL

Films as director

Peepshow (1956)
Knights on Bikes (1956)
Amelia and the Angel (1957)
Lourdes (1958)
French Dressing (1964)
Billion Dollar Brain (1967)
Women In Love (1969)
The Music Lovers (1970)
The Devils (1971)
The Boy Friend (1971)
Savage Messiah (1972)
Mahler (1974)
Tommy (1975)
Lisztomania (1975)
Valentino (1977)
Altered States (1980)
Crimes of Passion (1984)
Gothic (1986)
Aria (1987) (Segment: Nessun Dorma)
Salomé's Last Dance (1988)
The Lair of the White Worm (1988)
The Rainbow (1989)
Whore (1991)
Tales of Erotica (1996) (Segment: The Insatiable Mrs. Kirsch)
Mindbender (1996)
The Lion's Mouth (2000)
The Fall of the Louse of Usher (2002)
Trapped Ashes (2006) (Segment: The Girl With Golden Breasts)
Hot Pants (2006)

Television work as director

Scottish Painters (1959)
Variations on a Mechanical Theme (1959)
Guitar Craze (1959)
Gordon Jacob (1959)
Poet's London (1959)
Portrait of a Goon (1959)
Journey Into a Lost World (1960)
Marie Rambert Remembers (1960)
Cranko at Work (1960)
The Light Fantastic (1960)
Shelagh Delaney's Salford (1960)
A House in Bayswater (1960)
The Miner's Picnic (1960)
Architecture of Entertainment (1960)
London Moods (1961)
Old Battersea House (1961)
Lotte Lenya Sings Kurt Weill (1961)
Antonio Gaudi (1961)
Pop Goes the Easel (1962)
Preservation Man (1962)
Mr. Chesher's Traction Engines (1962)
Elgar (1962)
Prokofiev: Portrait of a Soviet Composer (1963)
Lonely Shore (1964)
The Dotty World of James Lloyd (1964)
Watch the Birdie (1964)
Bartók (1964)
Diary of a Nobody (1964)
The Debussy Film (1965)
Always On Sunday (1965)
Isadora Duncan, the Biggest Dancer in the World (1966)
Don't Shoot the Composer (1966)
Dante's Inferno (1967)
Song of Summer: Frederick Delius (1968)
A House in Bayswater: Prokofiev (1968)
Dance of the Seven Veils (1970)
Clouds of Glory: William and Dorothy (1978)
Clouds of Glory: The Rime of the Ancient Mariner (1978)
The Planets (1983)
The South Bank Show: Vaughan Williams: A Symphonic Portrait (1984)
Faust (1985)
Ken Russell's ABC of British Music (1988)

A British Picture (1989)
Méphistophélès (1989)
Women and Men: Stories of Seduction (1990) (Segment: Dusk Before Fireworks)
The Strange Affliction of Anton Bruckner (1990)
Road To Mandalay (1991)
Prisoner of Honor (1991)
The Secret Life of Arnold Bax (1992)
Lady Chatterley (1993)
The Mystery of Dr Martinu (1993)
Classic Widows (1995)
Alice in Russialand (1995)
Treasure Island (1995)
In Search of the English Folk Song (1997)
Dogboys (1998)
Brighton Belles (2001)
Elgar: Fantasy of a Composer on a Bicycle (2002)
Revenge of the Elephant Man (2004)
A Kitten For Hitler (2007)
Boudicca Bites Back (2009)

WOMEN IN LOVE (1969)

131 minutes. Released: September, 1969 (G.B). May 25, 1970 (U.S.A.). Colour: Deluxe Laboratory. 35mm (1: 1.85). Rated: 'R'. Budget: $1.25 million ($1.6 million).

CREW

Directed by Ken Russell
Written by Larry Kramer
D.H. Lawrence – novel
Larry Kramer – producer
Martin Rosen – co-producer
Roy Baird – associate producer
Cinematography – Billy Williams
Film Editing – Michael Bradsell
Art Direction – Kenneth Jones
Costume Design – Shirley Russell
Music – Georges Delerue (and conductor)
Jonathan Benson – assistant director
Charles E. Parker – makeup artist
A.G. Scott – hairdresser
Neville C. Thompson – unit manager
Luciana Arrighi – set designer
Harry Cordwell – set dresser
Shura Cohen – wardrobe supervisor
George Ball – property master
Jack Carter – construction manager
Maurice Askew – dubbing mixer
Terry Rawlings – dubbing editor
Brian Simmons – sound recordist
Garth Marshall – boom operator
Lionel Strutt – sound re-recording mixer
Steve Claydon – assistant cameraman
George Cole – electrical supervisor
David Harcourt – camera operator
Paul Borg – electrician
Chris Kelly – assistant editor
Angela Allen – continuity
Harry Benn – production controller

Lee Bolon – location manager
Tom Erhardt – assistant to producers
Terry Gilbert – choreographer
Larry Kramer – presenter
Martin Rosen – presenter

CAST

Alan Bates – Rupert Birkin
Oliver Reed – Gerald Crich
Glenda Jackson – Gudrun Brangwen
Jennie Linden – Ursula Brangwen
Eleanor Bron – Hermione Roddice
Alan Webb – Thomas Crich
Vladek Sheybal – Loerke
Catherine Willmer – Mrs. Crich
Phoebe Nicholls – Winifred Crich
Sharon Gurney – Laura Crich
Christopher Gable – Tibby Lupton
Michael Gough – Mr. Brangwen
Norma Shebbeare – Mrs. Brangwen
Nike Arrighi – Contessa
James Laurenson – Minister
Michael Graham Cox – Palmer
Richard Heffer – Loerke's Friend
Michael Garratt – Maestro
Leslie Anderson – Barber
Christopher Ferguson – Basis Crich
Richard Fitzgerald – Salsie
Barrie Fletcher – Miner
Brian Osborne – Miner
Petra Siniawski – Dancer
Charles Workman – Gittens
Alex Russell

BIBLIOGRAPHY

KEN RUSSELL

" *The Music Lovers*", *Filmfacts*, 14, 1971
"Conversation With Ken Russell", in T. Fox, *Oui*, June, 1973
"Mahler the Man", *Mahler Brochure*, Sackville Publishing, London, 1974
A British Picture: An Autobiography, Heinemann, London, 1989
Altered States, Bantam Books, New York, 1991
Fire Over England: The British Cinema Comes Under Friendly Fire (a.k.a. *The Lion Roars*), Hutchinson, London, 1993
Mike and Gaby's Space Gospel, Little, Brown, 1999
Violation, Author House, 2001
Directing Film, Brassey's, Washington DC, 2001
Elgar: The Erotic Variations and *Delius: A Moment With Venus*, Peter Owen, London, 2007
Beethoven Confidential and *Brahms Gets Laid*, Peter Owen, London, 2007
"Ken Russell, the master director", *The Observer*, Aug 30, 2009

D.H. LAWRENCE

The Letters of D.H. Lawrence, ed. A. Huxley, Heinemann, London, 1934
Selected Essays, Penguin 1950
Phoenix: The Posthumous Papers, ed. Edward Macdonald, Heinemann 1956
Lady Chatterley's Lover, Penguin, London, 1960
Fantasia of the Unconscious and Psychoanalysis of the Unconscious, Heinemann 1961
The Collected Letters of D.H. Lawrence, ed. Harry T.Moore, 2 vols, Heinemann 1962
Selected Literary Criticism, ed. Anthony Beal, Heinemann 1967
Phoenix II: Uncollected, Unpublished and Other Prose Works, eds. Warren Roberts & Harry T.Moore, Heinemann 1968
A Selection from Phoenix, ed. A.A.H. Inglis, Penguin, 1971

The Complete Poems, ed. Vivian de Sola Pinto & Warren Roberts, 2 vols, Heinemann, London 1972
The First Lady Chatterley, Penguin, London, 1973
John Thomas and Lady Jane, Penguin, London, 1973
Collected Short Stories, Heinemann 1974
Apocalypse, ed. Mara Kalnins, Granada 1981
The Rainbow, ed. J. Worthen, Penguin, London, 1981/86
Women In Love, ed. C.L. Ross, Penguin, London, 1982/86
The Complete Short Novels, ed. Keith Sagar & Melissa Partridge, Penguin 1982/87
The Letters of D.H. Lawrence, vol.III, Cambridge University Press 1984
Selected Short Stories, ed. Brian Finney, Penguin 1982/85
Study of Thomas Hardy and Other Essays, ed. Bruce Steele, Cambridge University Press 1985
Poems, ed. Keith Sagar, Penguin 1986
The Letters of D.H. Lawrence, vol. IV, Cambridge University Press 1987
Lady Chatterley's Lover, ed. J. Lyon, Penguin, London, 1990
Lady Chatterley's Lover and *A Propos of Lady Chatterley's Lover*, ed. M. Black, Cambridge University Press, Cambridge, 1993

OTHERS

Richard Aldington: *Portrait of a Genius, But...,* Reader's Union/ Heinemann 1951
Keith Alldritt: *The Visual Imagination of D.H. Lawrence*, Arnold 1977
Y. Allom *et al*, eds. *Contemporary British and Irish Film Directors, A Wallflower Critical Guide,* Wallflower, London, 20001
R. Armes. *A Critical History of British Cinema*, Secker & Warburg, London, 1978
J. Ashby & A. Higson, eds. *British Cinema, Past and Present*, Routledge, London, 2000
T. Atkins, ed. *Ken Russell*, Monarch/ Simon & Schuster, New York, 1976
S. Au. *Ballet and Modern Dance*, Thames & Hudson, London, 2012
M. Auty & N. Roddick, eds. *British Cinema Now*, British Film Institute, London, 1985
Peter Balbert: *D.H. Lawrence and the Psychology of Rhythm: The Meaning of Form in The Rainbow*, Mouton, The Hague 1974
M. Barker, ed. *The Video Nasties: Freedom and Censorship In*

the Media, Pluto Press, London, 1984
—. & J. Petley, eds. *Ill Effects: The Media/ Violence Debate*, Routledge, London, 1997
J. Baxter. *An Appalling Talent: Ken Russell*, M. Joseph, London, 1973
—. "The Television Films", in T. Atkins, 1976
L. Bawden, ed. *The Oxford Companion To Film*, Oxford University Press, Oxford, 1976
M. Beja. *Film and Literature: An Introduction,* Longman, London, 1979
R. Bell-Metereau: *"Altered States", Journal of Popular Film and Television*, 9, 4, 1982
Leo Bersani: *A Future For Astynanax*, Marion Boyars 1978
E. Blom, ed. *The New Everyman Dictionary of Music*, J.M. Dent, London, 1988
C. Bloom, ed. *Gothic Horror*, Macmillan, London, 1998
G. Bluestone. *Novels Into Film*, University of California Press, Berkeley, CA, 1961
D. Bordwell & K. Thompson. *Film Art: An Introduction*, McGraw-Hill Publishing Company, New York, NY, 2001
—. et al. *The Classical Hollywood Cinema: Film Style and Mode of Production To 1960*, Routledge, London, 1985
—. *Narration In the Fiction Film*, Routledge, London, 1988
—. *The Way Hollywood Tells It*, University of California Press, Berkeley, CA, 2006
F. Botting. *Making Monstrous: Frankenstein, Criticism, Theory*, Manchester University Press, Manchester, 1991
—. *Gothic*, Routledge, London, 1996
C. Bowen & B. von Meck. *Beloved Friend*, Random House, New York, 1937
J. Brady. *The Craft of the Screenwriter*, Touchstone, New York, 1982
M. Bragg. *The Seventh Seal*, BFI Classics, British Film Institute, London, 1993
A. Britton *et al. American Nightmare: Essays On the Horror Film*, Toronto, 1979
D. Britton. *Lady Chatterley: The Making of the Novel*, Unwin Hyman, London, 1988
H. Brodzky. *Henri Gaudier-Brzeska*, Faber, London, 1933
J. Brosnan. *Primal Screen: A History of Science Fiction Film*, Orbit, London, 1991
Keith Brown, ed. *Rethinking Lawrence*, Open University Press, Milton Keynes 1990
P. Buckley. "Savage Saviour", *Films and Filming*, Oct, 1972
S. Bukatman. *Terminal Identity: The Virtual Subject In Postmodern Science Fiction*, Duke University Press, Durham, NC, 1993

G. Burt. *The Art of Film Music*, Northeastern University Press, 1994

I. Butler. *Religion In the Cinema*, A.S. Barnes, New York, NY, 1969

Ross Care, *Film Quarterly*, Spring, 1978

K. Carroll. "The Dark Brilliance of Ken Russell", *Sunday News*, March 30, 1975

D. Cavallaro. *The Gothic Vision*, Continuum, New York, NY, 2002

Maurice Charney: *Sexual Fiction*, Methuen 1981

I. Christie. *Arrows of Desire: The Films of Michael Powell and Emeric Pressburger*, Faber, London, 1994

Colin Clarke: *River of Dissolution: D.H. Lawrence and English Romanticism*, Routledge and Kegan Paul 1969

—. ed: *D.H. Lawrence: 'The Rainbow' and 'Women In Love': A Casebook*, Macmillan 1969

M. Cloonan. *Banned! Censorship In Popular Music In Britain, 1967-92*, Arena, Aldershot, 1996

D.A. Cook. *A History of Narrative Film*, W.W. Norton, New York, NY, 1981, 1990, 1996

P. Cook & M. Bernink, eds. *The Cinema Book*, 2nd ed., British Film Institute, London, 1999

J. Crist, ed. *Take 22: Moviemakers On Moviemaking*, Continuum, New York, NY, 1991

R. Crouse. *Raising Hell*, ECW Press, 2012

J. Curran & V. Porter, eds. *British Cinema History*, Weidenfeld & Nicolson, London, 1983

H.M. Daleski. *The Forked Flame: A Study of D.H. Lawrence*, London, 1968

W. Darby & J. Du Bois. *American Film Music*, McFarland, Jefferson, NC, 1990

E. De Grazia & R.K. Newman. *Banned Films: Movies, Censors and the First Amendment*, Bowker, New York, NY, 1982

Paul Delany: *D.H. Lawrence's Nightmare: The Writer and His Circle in the Years of the Great War*, Basic, New York 1978

E. Delavenay. *D.H. Lawrence: The Man and His Work: The Formative Years, 1885-1919*, tr. K.M. Delavenay, Southern Illinois University Press, Carbondale, 1972

M. Dempsey: "The World of Ken Russell", *Film Quarterly*, 25, 3, 1972

—. "Ken Russell Again", *Film Quarterly*, 31, 2, 1977-78

L. Denham. *The Films of Peter Greenaway*, Minerva Press, London, 1993

Maria DiBattista: "*Women In Love*: D.H. Lawrence's Judgment Book", in P. Balbert, 1985, 67-90

Carol Dix: *D.H. Lawrence and Women*, Macmillan 1990

W.W. Dixon, ed. *Re-viewing British Cinema*, State University of

New York Press, Albany, NY, 1994

K.J. Donnelly, ed. *Film Music*, Edinburgh University Press, Edinburgh, 2001

O. Doughty. *Dante Gabriel Rossetti*, Yale University Press, New Haven, 1949

R.D. Draper: *D.H. Lawrence*, Routledge & Kegan Paul 1969

S.C. Dubin. *Arresting Images: Impolitic Art and Uncivil Actions*, Routledge, London, 1992

R. Durgnat. *A Mirror For England: British Movies From Austerity To Affluence*, Faber, London, 1970

J. Eberts. *My Indecision Is Final: The Rise and Fall of Goldcrest Films*, Faber, London, 1990

H.S. Ede. *Savage Messiah*, 1931

R. Eder. "The Screen: Ken Russell's *Mahler*", *New York Times*, Apl 5, 1976

Duane Edwards: *The Rainbow: A Search for New Life*, Twayne/ G.K. Hall, Boston 1990

J. Eszterhas. *The Devil's Guide To Hollywood*, Duckworth, London, 2006

S. Farber, "Russellmania", *Film Comment*, 11, 6, Nov, 1975

E. Fenby. *Delius As I Knew Him*, Icon Books, London, 1966

J. Finler. *The Movie Director's Story*, Octopus Books, London, 1985

A. Finney. *The Egos Have Landed: The Rise and Fall of Palace Pictures*, Heinemann, London, 1996

J. Fisher. "Three Masterpieces of Sexuality", in T. Atkins, 1976

Kevin M. Flanagan, ed. *Ken Russell: Re-Viewing England's Last Mannerist*, Scarecrow Press, 2009

G. Flatley. "I'm Surprised My Films Shock People", *New York Times*, Oct, 1972

G.E. Forshey. *American Religious and Biblical Spectaculars*, Praeger, Westport, CT, 1992

T. Fox. "Conversation With Ken Russell", *Oui*, June, 1973

K. French, ed. *Screen Violence*, Bloomsbury, London, 1996

L. Friedman, ed. *Fires Were Started: British Cinema and Thatcherism*, UCL Press, London, 1993

H. Gal, ed. *The Musician's World*, Thames & Hudson, London, 1965

K. Gelder. *Reading the Vampire*, Routledge, London, 1994

—. *New Vampire Cinema*, BFI/ Palgrave Macmillan, London, 2012

J. Gelmis. *The Film Director as Superstar*, Penguin, London, 1974

R. Gentry: "Ken Russell", *Post Script*, 2, 3, 1983

L. Gianetti. *Understanding Movies*, Prentice-Hall, NJ, 1982

R. Giddings *et al*. *Screening the Novel: The Theory and Practice of Literary Dramatisation*, Macmillan, London, 1990

—. & E. Sheen, eds. *The Classic Novel From Page To Screen,* Manchester University Press, Manchester, 2000

D. Gifford. *The British Film Catalogue, 1895-1985,* David & Charles, London, 1986

H. Mark Glancy. *When Hollywood Loved Britain,* Manchester University Press, Manchester, 1999

J. Gomez. *Ken Russell,* Muller, 1976

—. "Russell's Methods of Adaption", in T. Atkins, 1976

—. "Russell's Images of Lawrence's Vision", in M. Klein, 1981

Eugene Goodheart: *Desire and Its Discontents,* Columbia University Press, New York 1991

C. Goodwin. *Evil Spirits,* Virgin Books, 2001

B.K. Grant, ed. *Planks of Reason: Essays on the Horror Film,* Scarecrow Press, Metuchen, NJ, 1984

—. ed. *The Dread of Difference: Gender and the Horror Film,* University of Texas Press, Austin, TX, 1996

S. Grantley & A. Parker. *The Who By Numbers,* Helter Skelter, London, 2010

J. Green. *The Encyclopedia of Censorship,* Facts on File, New York, NY, 1990

L. Greiff. *D.H. Lawrence: 50 Years On Film,* Southern Illinois University Press, Carbondale, IL, 2001

Elizabeth Grosz. *Sexual Subversions,* Allen & Unwin, London, 1989

—. "Lesbian Fetishism?", *differences,* 3, 2, 1991

—. *Volatile Bodies,* Indiana University Press, Bloomington, IN, 1994

—. *Space, Time and Perversion,* Routledge, London, 1995

J. Hacker & D. Price, eds. *Take 10: Contemporary British Film Directors,* Oxford University Press, Oxford, 1991

L. Halliwell. *Halliwell's Filmgoer's Companion,* 7th edition, Granada, London, 1980

—. *Halliwell's Film and Video Guide,* 15th ed, ed. J. Walker, HarperCollins, 2000

K. Hanke. Ken *Russell's Films,* Scarecrow Press, New Jersey, 1984

P. Hardy, ed. *The Aurum Encyclopedia of Science Fiction,* Aurum, London, 1991

S. Harper. *Picturing the Past: The Rise and Fall of the British Costume Film,* British Film Institute, London, 1994

C. Heylin. *All the Madmen,* Constable, London, 2012

Christopher Heywood, ed: *D.H. Lawrence: New Studies,* Macmillan 1987

G. Hickenlooper. *Reel Conversations: Candid Interviews With Film's Foremost Directors and Critics,* Citadel, New York, NY, 1991

A. Higson. *Waving the Flag: Constructing a National Cinema In*

Britain, Oxford University Press, Oxford, 1995
—. *English Heritage, English Cinema: Costume Drama Since 1980*, Oxford University Press, Oxford, 2003
J. Hill *et al*, eds. *Border Crossing*, British Film Institute, London, 1994
—. *British Cinema In the 1980s*, Oxford University Press, Oxford, 1999
J. Hillier. *The New Hollywood*, Studio Vista, London, 1992
Philip Hobsbaum: *A Reader's Guide to D.H. Lawrence*, Thames and Hudson 1981
D. Holbrook. *The Quest For Love*, Methuen, London, 1964
—. *Where D.H. Lawrence Was Wrong About Woman*, Bucknell University Press, 1992
Graham Hough: *The Dark Sun: A Study of D.H. Lawrence*, Duckworth 1970
L. Hunt. *British Low Culture: From Safari Suits To Sexploitation*, Routledge, London, 1998
I.Q. Hunter. *British Science Fiction Cinema*, Routledge, London, 1999
A. Huxley. *The Devils of Loudun*, Chatto & Windus, London, 1970
G.M. Hyde: *D.H. Lawrence*, Macmillan 1990
I. Inglis, ed. *Popular Music and Film*, Wallflower Press, London, 2003
G. Jackson. *Esquire*, May, 1972
D. Jarman. *Dancing Ledge*, Quartet, London, 1984
D. Jones, ed. *Meaty Beaty Big & Bouncy! Classic Rock & Pop Writing From Elvis To Oasis*, Hodder & Stoughton, London, 1996
P. Kael, *Kiss Kiss Bang Bang*, Bantam, New York, NY, 1969
—. "Hyperbole and Narcissus", *The New Yorker*, Nov 18, 1972
—. *Taking It All In*, Marion Boyars, 1986
—. *State of the Art*, Marion Boyars, London, 1987
—. *Movie Love*, Marion Boyars, London, 1992
K. Kalinak. *Settling the Score: Music and the Classical Hollywood Film*, University of Wisconsin Press, Madison, WI, 1992
F. Karlin. *Listening To Movies*, Schirmer, New York, NY, 1994
B.F. Kawin. *How Movies Work*, Macmillan, New York, NY, 1987
Nigel Kelsey: *D.H. Lawrence: Sexual Crisis*, Macmillan 1991
P. Keough, ed. *Flesh and Blood: The National Society of Film Critics on Sex, Violence, and Censorship*, Mercury House, San Francisco, CA, 1995
M. Kermode. "Raising Hell", *Sight & Sound*, 2002
—. *Hatchet Job*, Picador, 2013

Mark Kinkead-Weekes, ed: *Twentieth-Century Interpretations of The Rainbow,* Prentice-Hall, New Jersey 1971

C. Kipps. *Out of Focus: Power, Prejudice: David Puttnam In Hollywood,* Century Hutchinson, London, 1989

M. Klein & G. Parker, eds. *The English Novel and the Movies,* F. Ungar, New York, NY, 1981

P. Kolker. *The Altering Eye: Contemporary International Cinema,* Oxford University Press, New York, NY, 1983

—. *A Cinema of Loneliness: Penn, Stone, Kubrick, Scorsese, Spielberg, Altman,* Oxford University Press, New York, NY, 2000

J. Kristeva. *Powers of Horror: An Essay on Abjection,* tr. Leon S. Roudiez, Columbia University Press, New York, 1982

—. *Tales of Love,* tr. Leon S. Roudiez, Columbia University Press, New York 1987

—. *Black Sun: Depression and Melancholy,* tr. L.S. Roudiez, Columbia University Press, New York, 1989

—. "A Question of Subjectivity: an interview" [with Susan Sellers], *Women's Review,* 12, 1986, in Philip Rice & Patricia Waugh, eds. *Modern Literary Theory: A Reader,* Arnold, 1992

L. Langley, "Ken Russell", *Show*, Oct, 1971.

J. Lanza. *Fragile Geometry: The Films, Philosophy and Misadventures of Nicolas Roeg,* PAJ, New York, NY, 1989

—. *Phallic Frenzy: Ken Russell and His Films,* Aurum Pres, London, 2008

P. Leprohan. *The Italian Cinema,* tr. R. Greaves & O. Stallybrass, Secker & Warburg, London, 1972

F.R. Leavis: *D.H. Lawrence: Novelist,* Penguin 1964

J. Lewis. *The Road To Romance and Ruin: Teen Films and Youth Culture,* Routledge, London, 1992

—. *Hollywood v. Hard Core: How the Struggle Over Censorship Created the Modern Film Industry,* New York University Press, New York, NY, 2000

C. Lyons. *The New Censors,* Temple University Press, Philadelphia, PA, 1997

T.D. Matthews. *Censored,* Chatto & Windus, London, 1994

R. Manvell. *New Cinema In Britain,* Dutton, New York, NY, 1968

G. Mast *et al,* eds. *Film Theory and Criticism: Introductory Readings,* Oxford University Press, New York, NY, 1992a

—. & B. Kawin, *A Short History of the Movies,* Macmillan, New York, NY, 1992b

J.R. May & M. Bird, eds. *Religion In Film,* University of Tennessee Press, Knoxville, 1982

—. *New Image of Religious Film,* Sheed & Ward, London, 1996

Sheila Macleod: *Lawrence's Men and Women*, Heinemann 1985

S.Y. McDougal. *Made Into Movies: From Literature To Film*, Holt, Rinehart and Winston, New York, NY, 1985

Neil McEwan: *D.H. Lawrence: Selected Short Stories*, Longman 1991

B. McFarlane, ed. *An Autobiography of British Cinema*, Methuen, London, 1997

Jeffrey Meyers, ed: *The Legacy of D.H. Lawrence: New Essays*, Macmillan 1987

—. ed: *D.H. Lawrence and Tradition*, Athlone Press 1985

P. Mezan. "Relax, It's Only a Ken Russell Movie", *Esquire*, May, 1973

M. Miles. *Seeing and Believing: Religion and Values In the Movies*, Beacon, Boston, MA, 1996

F. Miller. *Censored Hollywood: Sex, Sin and Violence On Screen*, Turner Publishing, Atlanta, 1994

H. Miller. *The World of Lawrence: A Passionate Appreciation*, ed. Evelyn J. Hinz & John J. Teunissen, Calder, 1985

K. Millett. *Sexual Politics*, Doubleday, Garden City, 1970

Harry T.Moore: *The Intelligent Heart: The Story of D.H. Lawrence*, Penguin 1960

—. *The Priest of Love: A Life of D.H. Lawrence*, Penguin 1976

—. & Warren Roberts: *D.H. Lawrence*, Thames and Hudson 1966/88

G. Mulholland. *Popcorn: Fifty Years of Rock 'n' Roll Movies*, Orion Books, London, 2011

R. Murphy. *Realism and Tinsel: British Cinema and Society, 1939-48*, London, 1989

—. *Sixties British Cinema*, British Film Institute, London, 1992

—. ed. *British Cinema of the 90s*, British Film Institute, London, 2000

—. ed. *The British Cinema Book*, Palgrave/ Macmillan, London, 2nd edition, 2009

R. Murray. *Images In the Dark: An Encyclopedia of Gay and Lesbian Film and Video*, Titan Books, London, 1998

S. Neale & M. Smith, eds. *Contemporary Hollywood Cinema*, Routledge, London, 1998

Edward Nehls, ed: *D.H. Lawrence: A Composite Biography*, 3 vols, University of Wisconsin Press, Madison 1958

K. Newman. *Nightmare Movies*, Harmony, New York, NY, 1988

—. *Millennium Movies*, Titan Books, London, 1999

—. ed. *Science Fiction/ Horror: A Sight & Sound Reader*, British Film Institute, London, 2002

Carol Nixon: *Lawrence's Leadership Politics and the Turn Against Women*, University of California Press, Berkeley

1986

G. Nowell-Smith, ed. *The Oxford History of World Cinema*, Oxford University Press, Oxford, 1996

W. Ober. *Boswell's Clap and Other Essays*, Southern Ilinois University Press, IL, 1979

Daniel O'Hara: "The Power of Nothing in *Women In Love, Bucknell Review: A Scholarly Journal of Letters, Arts and Science,* ed. Harry R. Garvin, 28, 1983, and in P. Widdowson, 146-159

M. O'Pray, ed. *The British Avant Garde Film, 1926-1995*, University of Luton Press/ John Libbey, London, 1996

J. Orr. *Contemporary Cinema*, Edinburgh University Press, Edinburgh, 1998

C. Paglia. *Sexual Personae: Art and Decadence From Nefertiti To Emily Dickinson*, Penguin, London, 1992

J. Park. *Learning To Dream: The New British Cinema*, Faber, London, 1984

—. *British Cinema*, B.T. Batsford, London, 1990

D. Parkinson. *The Rough Guide To Film Musicals*, Penguin, London, 2007

D. Peary, ed. *Omni's Screen Flights, Screen Fantasies,* Doubleday, New York, NY, 1984

C. Penley, ed. *Feminism and Film Theory*, Routledge, London, 1988

—. et al, eds. *Close Encounters: Film, Feminism and Science Fiction*, University of Minnesota Press, Minneapolis, 1991

G. Perry. *Life of Python*, Pavilion, London, 1983

—. *The Great British Picture Show*, Pavilion, London, 1985

D. Petrie. *Creativity and Constraint In the British Film Industry*, Macmillan, London, 1991

—. ed. *New Questions of British Cinema*, British Film Institute, London, 1992

—. *Screening Europe: Image and Identity In Contemporary European Cinema*, British Film Institute, London, 1992

—. *The British Cinematographer*, British Film Institute, London, 1996

G. Phelps. *Film Censorship*, Gollancz, London, 1975

G. Philips. "Ken Russell as Adaptor", *Literature/ Film Quarterly*, 5, 1977

—. *Ken Russell*, Twayne, Boston, MA, 1979

F.B. Pinion: *A D.H. Lawrence Companion: Life, Thought and Works*, Macmillan 1978

Tony Pinkey: *D.H. Lawrence,* Harvester Press 1990

D. Pirie. *A Heritage of Horror: The English Gothic Cinema*, Gordon & Fraser, 1973

M. Powell. *A Life In the Movies*, Heinemann, London, 1986/ 1992

—. *Million-Dollar Movie*, Heinemann, London, 1992

R. Prendergast. *Film Music*, W.W. Norton, New York, NY, 1992

Peter Preston & Peter Hoare, eds: *D.H. Lawrence in the Modern World,* Macmillan 1989

S. Prince, ed. *Screening Violence*, Athlone Press, London, 2000

R.E. Pritchard: *D.H. Lawrence: Body of Darkness,* Hutchinson 1971

D. Puttnam. *The Undeclared War: The Struggle For Control of the World's Film Industry*, HarperCollins, London, 1997

M. Pye & Lynda Myles. *The Movie Brats: How the Film Generation Took Over Hollywood*, Faber, London, 1979

J. Pym. *Film On Four*, British Film Institute, London, 1992

D. Quinlan. *The Illustrated Guide To Film Directors*, B.T. Batsford, London, 1983

T. Reeves. *The Worldwide Guide To Movie Locations*, Titan Books, London, 2003

J. Richards, ed. *Films and British National Identity*, Manchester University Press, Manchester, 1997

M. Richardson. *Surrealism and Cinema*, Berg, New York, NY, 2006

F. Robbins, "The Savage Russell", *Gallery*, May, 1973

J. Robertson. *The British Board of Film Censors*, Croom Helm, 1985

—. *The Hidden Cinema*, Routledge, London, 1989

W.H. Rockett. *Devouring Whirlwind: Terror and Transcendence In the Cinema of Cruelty*, Greenwood Press, New York, NY, 1988

J. Romney & A. Wooton, eds. *Celluloid Juke Box*, British Film Institute, London, 1995

Charles L. Ross: *The Composition of "The Rainbow" and "Women In Love": A History*, University Press of Virginia, Charlottesville 1979

—. "The Revisions of the Second Generation in *The Rainbow*", *Review of English Studies*, 27, 1976, 277-95

Keith Sagar: *A D.H. Lawrence Handbook*, Manchester University Press 1982

—. *The Life of D.H. Lawrence: An Illustrated Biography*, Eyre Methuen 1980

—. *Life Into Art*, Viking 1985

—. *The Art of D.H. Lawrence*, Cambridge University Press 1966

V. Sage. *The Gothick Novel: A Casebook*, Macmillan, London, 1990

Gamini Salgado: *A Preface to Lawrence*, Longman 1982

—. and G.R. Das, eds: *The Spirit of D.H. Lawrence: Centenary*

Studies, Macmillan 1988

Scott Sanders: *D. H. Lawrence: The World of the Major Works,* Vision Press 1973

D. Schaefer & L. Salvato, eds. *Masters of Light,* University of California Press, Berkeley, CA, 1984

T. Schatz. *Old Hollywood/ New Hollywood,* UMI Research Press, Ann Arbor, MI, 1983

—. *The Genius of the System: Hollywood Filmmaking In the Studio Era,* Pantheon, New York, NY 1988

R. Sellers. *Oliver Reed,* Constable & Robinson, London, 2013

T. Shaw. *British Cinema and the Cold War,* I.B. Tauris, London, 2001

D. Shipman. *The Story of Cinema,* Hodder & Stoughton, London, 1984

—. *Caught In the Act: Sex and Eroticism In the Movies,* Hamish Hamilton, London, 1986

T. Shone. *Blockbuster: How the Jaws and Jedi Generation Turned Hollywood Into a Boom-Town,* Scribner, London, 2005

L. Sider *et al*, eds. *Soundscapes: The School of Sound Lectures 1998-2001,* Wallflower Press, London, 2003

Carol Siegel: *Lawrence Among the Women: Wavering Boundaries in Women's Literary Tradition,* University Press of Virginia, Charlottesville 1991

Hilary Simpson: *D.H. Lawrence and Feminism,* Croom Helm 1982

N. Sinyard. *Filming Literature: The Art of Screen Adaption,* Croom Helm, Beckenham, Kent, 1986

A. Slide. *'Banned In the USA': British Films In the United States and Their Censorship, 1933-1960,* I.B. Tauris, London, 1998

Anne Smith, ed: *Lawrence and Women,* Vision Press 1978

Frank G. Smith: *D.H. Lawrence: The Rainbow,* Edward Arnold 1971

J. Smith. *Withnail and Us: Cult Films and Film Cults In British Cinema,* Tauris, London, 2010

Mark Spilka, ed: *D.H. Lawrence: A Collection of Critical Essays,* Prentice-Hall, New Jersey 1963

—. *The Love of D.H. Lawrence,* Indiana University Press, Bloomington 1953

J. Squire, ed. *The Movie Business Book,* Fireside, New York, NY, 1992

G. Stewart. *Between Film and Screen: Modernism's Photo Synthesis,* University of Chicago Press, Chicago, IL, 1999

S. Street. *British National Cinema,* Routledge, London, 1997/ 2009

D Strerritt, "Whole Film Is 'One Flash' In His Mind", *Christian*

Science Monitor, June 2, 1975

J. Stringer, ed. *Movie Blockbusters*, Routledge, London, 2003

P. Swann. *The Hollywood Feature Film In Postwar Britain*, Croom Helm, 1987

K. Thompson & D. Bordwell. *Film History: An Introduction*, McGraw-Hill, New York, NY, 1994

—. *Storytelling In the New Hollywood*, Harvard University Press, Cambridge, MA, 1999

D. Thomson. *A Biographical Dictionary of Film*, Deutsch, London, 1995

C. Tohill & P. Tombs. *Immoral Tales: Sex and Horror Cinema In Europe 1956-1984*, Titan Books, London, 1995

P. Townshend. *Who I Am*, HarperCollins, London, 2012

G. Tremlett. *Rock Gold: The Music Millionaires*, Unwin Hyman, London, 1990

J. Trevelyan. *What the Censor Saw*, Michael Joseph, London, 1973

P. Tyler. *Screening the Sexes: Homosexuality In the Movies*, Doubleday, New York, NY, 1973

K. Van Gunden. *Fantasy Films*, McFarland, Jefferson, NC 1989

G. Vincendeau, ed. *Encyclopedia of European Cinema*, British Film Institute, London, 1995

—. ed. *Film/ Literature/ Heritage: A Sight & Sound Reader*, British Film Institute, London, 2001

H. Vogel. *Entertainment Industry Economics*, Cambridge University Press, Cambridge, 1995

R. Wakeman. *Grumpy Old Rock Star*, London, 2008

—. *Further Adventures of a Grumpy Old Rock Star*, Arrow, 2010

A. Walker. *National Heroes: British Cinema In the Seventies and Eighties*, Harrap, London, 1985

—. *Hollywood, England: The British Film Industry In the Sixties*, Harrap, London, 1986

J. Walker. *The Observer*, Sept 8, 1974

J. Walker. *The Once and Future Film: British Cinema In the 1970s and 1980s*, Methuen, London, 1985

—. *Art and Artists on Screen*, Manchester University Press, Manchester, 1993

P. Webb. *The Erotic Arts*, Secker & Warburg, London, 1975

E. Weiss. & J. Belton, eds. *Film Sound: Theory and Practice*, Columbia University Press, New York, NY, 1989

O. Welles. *Orson Welles: Interviews,* ed. M. Estrin, University of Mississippi Press, Jackson, 2002

Peter Widdowson. *Hardy in History: A study in literary sociology,* Routledge, London, 1989

C. Wilson. *Ken Russell*, Intergroup, London, 1974

M. Wolf. *The Entertainment Economy*, Penguin, London, 1999

L. Wood, ed. *British Films, 1971-1981*, British Film Institute, London, 1983

J. Wyatt. *High Concept: Movies and Marketing In Hollywood*, University of Texas Press, Austin, TX, 1994

A. Yule. *Fast Forward: David Puttnam, Columbia Pictures and the Battle For Hollywood*, Delacorte, New York, NY, 1989

A.L. Zambrano: *"Women In Love"*, *Literature/ Film Quarterly*, 1, Jan, 1973

J. Zipes, ed. *The Oxford Companion To Fairy Tales*, Oxford University Press, 2000

—. *The Enchanted Screen: The Unknown History of Fairy-tale Films*, Routledge, New York, NY, 2011

—. *The Irresistible Fairy Tale*, Prince University Press, Princeton, NJ, 2012

WEBSITES

D.H. LAWRENCE

dh-lawrence.org.uk
lawrenceseastwood.co.uk
dhlsna.com
dhlawrencesocietyaustralia.com.au

KEN RUSSELL

Savage Messiah/ Ken Russell:
iainfisher.com/Russell

Jeremy Robinson has written many critical studies, including *Hayao Miyazaki, Walerian Borowczyk, Arthur Rimbaud,* and *The Sacred Cinema of Andrei Tarkovsky,* plus literary monographs on: William Shakespeare; Samuel Beckett; Thomas Hardy; André Gide; Robert Graves; and John Cowper Powys.

It's amazing for me to see my work treated with such passion and respect. There is nothing resembling it in the U.S. in relation to my work.
Andrea Dworkin (on *Andrea Dworkin*)

This model monograph – it is an exemplary job, and I'm very proud that he has accorded me a couple of mentions... The subject matter of his book is beautifully organised and dead on beam.
Lawrence Durrell (on *The Light Eternal: A Study of J.M.W. Turner*)

Jeremy Robinson's poetry is certainly jammed with ideas, and I find it very interesting for that reason. It's certainly a strong imprint of his personality.
Colin Wilson

Sex-Magic-Poetry-Cornwall is a very rich essay... It is a very good piece... vastly stimulating and insightful.
Peter Redgrove

Thomas A. Christie

JOHN HUGHES
& EIGHTIES CINEMA
Teenage Hopes & American Dreams

John Hughes (1950-2009) is one of the best-loved figures in 1980s American filmmaking, and considered by many to be among the finest and most celebrated comedy writers of his generation. His memorable motion pictures are insightful, humanistic, culturally aware, and paint a vibrant picture of the United States in a decade of rapid social and political change.

Bibliography, notes, illustrations   372pp.
ISBN 9781861713896 Pbk   ISBN 9781861713988 Hbk
Also available: *Ferris Bueller's Day Off: Pocket Movie Guide*

Walerian Borowczyk
Cinema of Erotic Dreams

by Jeremy Mark Robinson

Walerian Borowczyk (1923-2006) was a Polish artist, animator and filmmaker who lived in France for much of his life. He is the author of European art cinema masterpieces *Goto: Island of Love*, *Blanche* and *Immoral Tales*, some surreal animated shorts, and controversial films such as *The Beast*. This new book concentrates on Borowczyk's feature films, from *Goto* to *Love Rites*, which contain some of the most extraordinary images and scenes in recent cinema. Erotica for some, porn for others, Borowczyk's films are highly idiosyncratic and unforgettable.

Bibliography, notes, 110 illustrations   252pp.
ISBN 9781861713674 Pbk   ISBN 9781861713124 Hbk
Also available: *Walerian Borowczyk: The Beast: Pocket Movie Guide*

MAURICE SENDAK
& the art of children's book illustration

L.M. Poole

Maurice Sendak is the widely acclaimed American children's book author and illustrator. This critical study focuses on his famous trilogy, *Where the Wild Things Are*, *In the Night Kitchen* and *Outside Over There*, as well as the early works and Sendak's superb depictions of the Grimm Brothers' fairy tales in *The Juniper Tree*. L.M. Poole begins with a chapter on children's book illustration, in particular the treatment of fairy tales. Sendak's work is situated within the history of children's book illustration, and he is compared with many contemporary authors.

Fully illustrated. The book has been revised and updated for this edition.
ISBN 9781861714282 Pbk   ISBN 9781861713469 Hbk

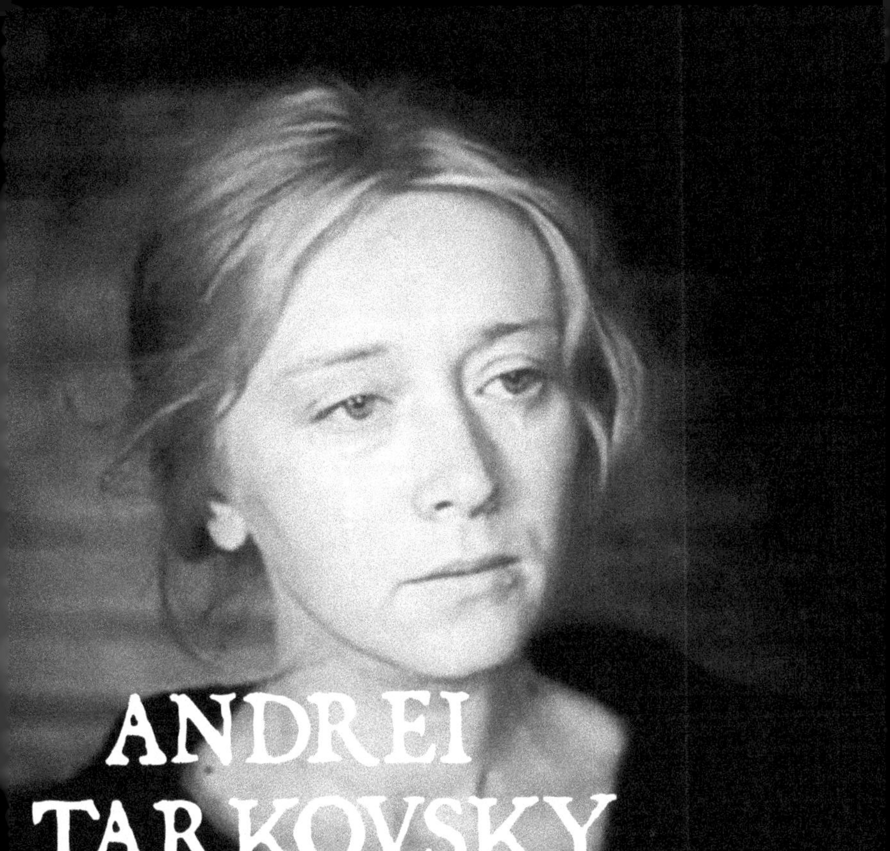

ANDREI TARKOVSKY
JEREMY MARK ROBINSON

POCKET GUIDE

Andrei Tarkovsky is one of the great filmmakers of recent times.

This book covers every aspect of Tarkovsky's artistic career, and all of his output, concentrating on his seven feature films: *Ivan's Childhood, Andrei Roublyov, Solaris, Mirror, Stalker, Nostalghia* and *The Sacrifice*, made between 1962 and 1986.

Part One of this study focusses on the key elements and themes of Andrei Tarkovsky's art: spirituality; childhood; the film image; poetics; painting and the history of art; the family; eroticism; symbolism; as well as technical areas, such as script, camera, sound, music, editing, budget and production.

Part Two explores Tarkovsky's films in detail, with scene-by-scene analyses (in some cases, shot-by-shot). Tarkovsky emerges as a brilliant, difficult, complex and poetic artist.

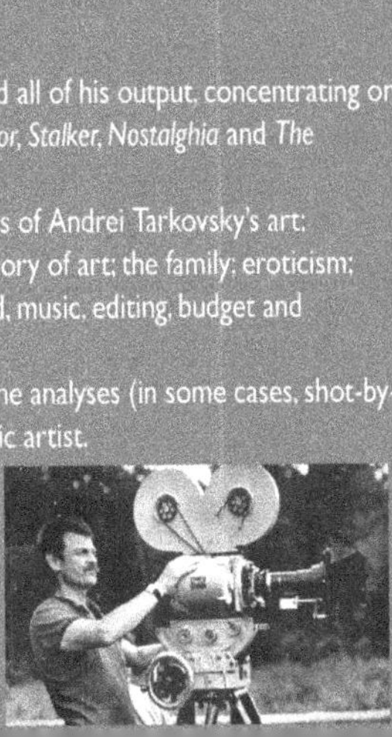

Fully illustrated. This new edition has been revised and updated.
ISBN 19781861713957 Pbk 9781861713834 Hbk

ARTS, PAINTING, SCULPTURE

web: www.crmoon.com • e-mail: cresmopub@yahoo.co.uk

The Art of Andy Goldsworthy
Andy Goldsworthy: Touching Nature
Andy Goldsworthy in Close-Up
Andy Goldsworthy: Pocket Guide
Andy Goldsworthy In America
Land Art: A Complete Guide
The Art of Richard Long
Richard Long: Pocket Guide
Land Art In Great Britain
Land Art in Close-Up
Land Art In the U.S.A.
Land Art: Pocket Guide
Installation Art in Close-Up
Minimal Art and Artists In the 1960s and After
Colourfield Painting
Land Art DVD, TV documentary
Andy Goldsworthy DVD, TV documentary
The Erotic Object: Sexuality in Sculpture From Prehistory to the Present Day
Sex in Art: Pornography and Pleasure in Painting and Sculpture
Postwar Art
Sacred Gardens: The Garden in Myth, Religion and Art
Glorification: Religious Abstraction in Renaissance and 20th Century Art
Early Netherlandish Painting
Jasper Johns
Brice Marden Leonardo da Vinci
Piero della Francesca
Giovanni Bellini
Fra Angelico: Art and Religion in the Renaissance
Mark Rothko: The Art of Transcendence
Frank Stella: American Abstract Artist
Alison Wilding: The Embrace of Sculpture
Vincent van Gogh: Visionary Landscapes
Eric Gill: Nuptials of God
Constantin Brancusi: Sculpting the Essence of Things
Max Beckmann
Gustave Moreau
Caravaggio
Egon Schiele: Sex and Death In Purple Stockings
Delizioso Fotografico Fervore: Works In Process 1
Sacro Cuore: Works In Process 2
The Light Eternal: J.M.W. Turner
The Madonna Glorified: Karen Arthurs

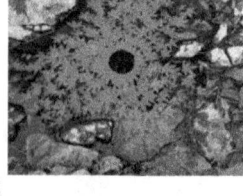

LITERATURE

J.R.R. Tolkien: The Books, The Films, The Whole Cultural Phenomenon
J.R.R. Tolkien: Pocket Guide
Beauties, Beasts and Enchantment: Classic French Fairy Tales
Tolkien's Heroic Quest
Brothers Grimm: German Popular Stories
Sexing Hardy: Thomas Hardy and Feminism
Thomas Hardy's *Tess of the d'Urbervilles*
Thomas Hardy's *Jude the Obscure*
Thomas Hardy: The Tragic Novels
Love and Tragedy: Thomas Hardy
The Poetry of Landscape in Hardy
Wessex Revisited: Thomas Hardy and John Cowper Powys
Wolfgang Iser: Essays and Interviews
Petrarch, Dante and the Troubadours
Maurice Sendak and the Art of Children's Book Illustration
Andrea Dworkin
Cixous, Irigaray, Kristeva: The *Jouissance* of French Feminism
Julia Kristeva: Art, Love, Melancholy, Philosophy, Semiotics and Psychoanalysis
Hélene Cixous I Love You: The *Jouissance* of Writing
Luce Irigaray: Lips, Kissing, and the Politics of Sexual Difference
Peter Redgrove: Here Comes the Flood
Peter Redgrove: Sex-Magic-Poetry-Cornwall
Lawrence Durrell: Between Love and Death, East and West
Love, Culture & Poetry: Lawrence Durrell
Cavafy: Anatomy of a Soul
German Romantic Poetry: Goethe, Novalis, Heine, Hölderlin
Novalis: *Hymns To the Night*
Feminism and Shakespeare
Shakespeare: *The Sonnets*
Shakespeare: Love, Poetry & Magic
The Passion of D.H. Lawrence
D.H. Lawrence: Symbolic Landscapes
D.H. Lawrence: Infinite Sensual Violence
The Ecstasies of John Cowper Powys
Sensualism and Mythology: The Wessex Novels of John Cowper Powys
Amorous Life: John Cowper Powys (H.W. Fawkner)
Postmodern Powys: New Essays on John Cowper Powys (Joe Boulter)
Rethinking Powys: Critical Essays on John Cowper Powys
Paul Bowles & Bernardo Bertolucci
Rainer Maria Rilke
Joseph Conrad: *Heart of Darkness*
In the Dim Void: Samuel Beckett
Samuel Beckett Goes into the Silence
André Gide: Fiction and Fervour
Jackie Collins and the Blockbuster Novel
Blinded By Her Light: The Love-Poetry of Robert Graves

POETRY

Ursula Le Guin: *Walking In Cornwall*
Peter Redgrove: Here Comes The Flood
Peter Redgrove: Sex-Magic-Poetry-Cornwall
Dante: Selections From the *Vita Nuova*
Petrarch, Dante and the Troubadours
William Shakespeare: *The Sonnets*
William Shakespeare: Complete Poems
Blinded By Her Light: The Love-Poetry of Robert Graves
Emily Dickinson: Selected Poems
Emily Brontë: Poems
Thomas Hardy: Selected Poems
Percy Bysshe Shelley: Poems
John Keats: Selected Poems
John Keats: Poems of 1820
D.H. Lawrence: Selected Poems
Edmund Spenser: Poems
Edmund Spenser: *Amoretti*
John Donne: Poems
Henry Vaughan: Poems
Sir Thomas Wyatt: Poems
Robert Herrick: Selected Poems
Rilke: Space, Essence and Angels in the Poetry of Rainer Maria Rilke
Rainer Maria Rilke: Selected Poems
Friedrich Hölderlin: Selected Poems
Arseny Tarkovsky: Selected Poems
Paul Verlaine: Selected Poems
Novalis: *Hymns To the Night*
Arthur Rimbaud: Selected Poems
Arthur Rimbaud: *A Season in Hell*
Arthur Rimbaud and the Magic of Poetry
D.J. Enright: By-Blows
Jeremy Reed: *Brigitte's Blue Heart*
Jeremy Reed: *Claudia Schiffer's Red Shoes*
Gorgeous Little Orpheus
Radiance: New Poems
Crescent Moon Book of Nature Poetry
Crescent Moon Book of Love Poetry
Crescent Moon Book of Mystical Poetry
Crescent Moon Book of Elizabethan Love Poetry
Crescent Moon Book of Metaphysical Poetry
Crescent Moon Book of Romantic Poetry
Pagan America: New American Poetry

MEDIA, CINEMA, FEMINISM and CULTURAL STUDIES

J.R.R. Tolkien: The Books, The Films, The Whole Cultural Phenomenon
J.R.R. Tolkien: Pocket Guide
The *Lord of the Rings* Movies: Pocket Guide
The Ghost Dance: The Origins of Religion
The Cinema of Hayao Miyazaki
Hayao Miyazaki: *Princess Mononoke*: Pocket Movie Guide
Hayao Miyazaki: *Spirited Away*: Pocket Movie Guide
The Peyote Cult
HomeGround: The Kate Bush Anthology
Tim Burton : Hallowe'en For Hollywood
Ken Russell
Cixous, Irigaray, Kristeva: The *Jouissance* of French Feminism
Julia Kristeva: Art, Love, Melancholy, Philosophy, Semiotics and Psychoanalysis
Luce Irigaray: Lips, Kissing, and the Politics of Sexual Difference
Hélene Cixous I Love You: The *Jouissance* of Writing
Andrea Dworkin
'Cosmo Woman': The World of Women's Magazines
Women in Pop Music
Discovering the Goddess (Geoffrey Ashe)
The Poetry of Cinema
The Sacred Cinema of Andrei Tarkovsky
Andrei Tarkovsky: Pocket Guide
Andrei Tarkovsky: *Mirror*: Pocket Movie Guide
Walerian Borowczyk: Cinema of Erotic Dreams
Jean-Luc Godard: The Passion of Cinema
Jean-Luc Godard: Pocket Guide
John Hughes and Eighties Cinema
Ferris Buller's Day Off: Pocket Movie Guide
The Cinema of Richard Linklater
Liv Tyler: Star In Ascendance
Blade Runner and the Films of Philip K. Dick
Paul Bowles and Bernardo Bertolucci
Media Hell: Radio, TV and the Press
Detonation Britain: Nuclear War in the UK
Feminism and Shakespeare
Wild Zones: Pornography, Art and Feminism
Sex in Art: Pornography and Pleasure in Painting and Sculpture
Sexing Hardy: Thomas Hardy and Feminism

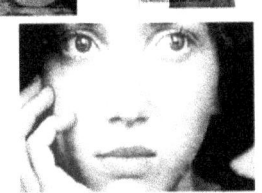

The Light Eternal *is a model monograph, an exemplary job. The subject matter of the book is beautifully organised and dead on beam.* (Lawrence Durrell)
It is amazing for me to see my work treated with such passion and respect. (Andrea Dworkin)
Sex-Magic-Poetry-Cornwall *is a very rich essay... It is like a brightly-lighted box.* (Peter Redgrove)

CRESCENT MOON PUBLISHING P.O. Box 1312, Maidstone, Kent, ME14 5XU, Great Britain
0044-1622-729593 cresmopub@yahoo.co.uk www.crmoon.com